AT MILLENNIUM'S END

AT
MILLENNIUM'S
END

new essays on the work of
kurt vonnegut

edited by
KEVIN ALEXANDER BOON

with a foreword by
KURT VONNEGUT

STATE UNIVERSITY OF NEW YORK PRESS

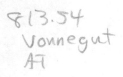

Cover art by Kurt Vonnegut. "Self-Portrait #1, black and white silkscreen."
© Kurt Vonnegut 2000, All Rights Reserved.

Inside art by Kurt Vonnegut.
© Kurt Vonnegut 2001, All Rights Reserved.

Thanks to Kurt Vonnegut and Joe Petro III at www.vonnegut.com

Published by
STATE UNIVERSITY OF NEW YORK PRESS
ALBANY

© 2001 State University of New York

For information, address
State University of New York Press,
90 State Street, Suite 700, Albany, NY 12207

Production, Marilyn P. Semerad
Marketing, Fran Keneston

Library of Congress Cataloging-in-Publication Data

At millennium's end : new essays on the work of Kurt Vonnegut / edited by Kevin
Alexander Boon.
    p. cm.
  Includes bibliographical references and index.
  ISBN 0-7914-4929-7 (acid-free paper) — ISBN 0-7914-4930-0 (pbk. : acid-free paper)
    1. Vonnegut, Kurt—Criticism and interpretation. 2. Science fiction, American—History
and criticism. I. Boon, Kevin A.

PS3572.O5 Z535 2001
813'.54—dc21

00-045054

10   9   8   7   6   5   4   3   2   1

CONTENTS

FOREWORD

I sometimes say in lectures that I suffer from "survivor's syndrome," but not because of the Battle of the Bulge or the firebombing of Dresden in World War II, man-made calamities during or after which I saw more corpses than you can shake a stick at. A young woman complained to me after my lecture about that war, evidently feeling incomplete, that she had never seen a dead person. I made a joke. I said to her, "Be patient."

I do feel lousy, however, about the many passionate and gifted artists I know or knew, writers, painters and composers, dancers and comedians, actors and actresses, singers and cartoonists, who died or are dying in obscurity, more often than not in poverty. To quote the humorist Kin Hubbard: "It's no disgrace to be poor, but it might as well be." Audiences failed these friends and acquaintances of mine. Audiences were too barbarous and inattentive to realize how good they were and to reward them with sustained applause and a living wage.

I am reminded of a cartoon of long ago which depicted war as a rouged, warty old whore. She says to a youth about seventeen years old, "Hello, Sonny. I knew your Dad." She could represent the arts instead of war, and the cartoon would make just as much sense to a lot of people. The creation of works of art that a sizeable audience may appreciate and even pay for isn't all that different from an attack by either side in World War I, in which thousands of brave, good-hearted young people left their trenches at dawn, and practically everybody wound up draped over barbwire, or drowning face down in water at the bottom of a shellhole.

Again: I suffer from "survivor's syndrome."

Anyone who survives a human wave attack against such daunting odds, whether in war or the arts, does so because of dumb luck. Agility and courage and character, or whatever, have nothing to do with how it all turns out. Gifted artists have to be what they are, have to do what they do the way they do it. Whether they earn a living and fame thereby is a matter of happening by chance upon breaks in the barbwire, unswept by machinegun fire.

So to speak.

Mark Twain, a better writer and human being than I am, marveled, when an old man like me, at the durability of his works' popularity. He thought this might be due to his willingness to moralize. It was lucky for him that moralizing paid off so handsomely. In any case, Mark Twain was simply born to moralize.

I think I was, too. When I look back at my incredibly lucky career as a writer, it seems that there was never time to think. It was as though I were skiing down a steep and hazardous mountain slope. When I look back at the marks my skis made in the snow on the way down, I only now realize that I wrote again and again about people who behaved decently in an indecent society.

I received a letter from a sappy woman a while back. She knew I was sappy, too, which is to say a New Deal Democrat. She was pregnant. She wanted to know if it was a bad thing to bring an innocent little baby into a world as awful as this one is. I replied that what made living almost worthwhile for me were the saints I met. They could be anywhere. They were people who behaved decently in an indecent society.

Perhaps, you, dear reader, are or will become a saint for her child to meet. I thank you for your attention.

KURT VONNEGUT (JR.)
NOVEMBER 11, 1998

WHAT TO DO WHEN
A POOL-PAH IS YOUR
ZAH-MAH-KI-BO

Kevin Alexander Boon

This collection of essays began around the time Vonnegut's final novel, *Time-quake*, was going to press. It represents the first look back at Vonnegut's recently completed canon. In these pages, eleven human beings gather with Vonnegut, like friends around a fire at the end of a long day, to discuss his work. Several of the writers count themselves among Vonnegut's circle of friends; some have dedicated a large percentage of their careers to the examination of his works; a few are probably members of Vonnegut's "*karass*;" but all are Vonnegut scholars compelled to assemble here by a deep appreciation for the man and his writing.

Fifty years into the twenty-first century, when future scholars look back at Vonnegut's work, they may not label him the voice of the postnuclear twentieth century, but they will certainly recognize him as its conscience. For nearly five decades his novels, essays, and short stories have all attempted to talk some sense into people who are willing to balance the world on the precipice of utter annihilation, willing to imprison other human beings in concentration camps and ghettos, and worst of all, willing to entrust "power to people" who are "sickies" (*Fates Worse Than Death* 135). Vonnegut's message is simple: don't wage war, and treat each other with "a little more common decency" (*Slapstick* 3).

You get the sense, perusing the body of his work, that through the decades Vonnegut's respect for the individual has increased as his approval of humanity as a whole has declined. Taken individually, human beings are, for Vonnegut, quirky and fascinating universes, and Vonnegut's novels are full of these charming examples of human complexity. Topping the list is Kilgore Trout, Vonnegut's alter ego, who is followed by a collection of some of literature's most endearing characters: Billy Pilgrim, Eliot Rosewater, Rabo Karabekian, Circe Berman, Malachi Constant, Bokonon, Rudy Waltz, Howard Campbell, Walter F. Starbuck, Wilbur Swain, Eugene Debs Hartke, Leon Trout, and dozens of others. However, human beings taken as a whole are often portrayed in Vonnegut's works as ignorant, myopic warmongers who form corrupt governments, greedy corporations, amoral scientific-research organizations, and soulless militaries. The moral at the heart of this dichotomy is inscribed on Kilgore Trout's gravestone: "We are healthy only to the extent that our ideas are humane" (*Breakfast of Champions* 16). This is the message Vonnegut sends into the next millennium.

Vonnegut is a postmodern Mark Twain, whose own personality permeates everything he writes. Whether we are reading about Martian invasions, the firebombing of Dresden, time-tripping, or the de-evolution of the human race, we never lose touch with the character behind the characters—the reassuring, avuncular voice of the author. Continuing a trend in American literature that began with Benjamin Franklin, Vonnegut's style is ripe with irony and full of aphoristic wit. The maxims in Franklin's *Poor Richard's Almanac*—sayings such as "Lost time is never found," "Whatever's begun in anger, ends in shame," and "There are no ugly loves, and there are no handsome prisons"—are now inextricable from American mythology. Like Franklin, Vonnegut fills his writing with pithy witticisms—clever sayings and mottoes for the modern age, such as: "Before you kill somebody, make absolutely sure he isn't well connected" (*Slaughterhouse-Five* 109); "The main business of humanity is to do a good job of being human beings, not to serve as appendages to machines, institutions, and systems" (*Player Piano* 287); "Poverty is a relatively mild disease . . . but uselessness will kill strong and weak souls alike" (*God Bless You, Mr. Rosewater* 210–11); and my personal favorite, "No damn cat, and no damn cradle" (*Cat's Cradle* 114). These Vonnegutisms have also infiltrated American discourse, indicative of Vonnegut's role as a key spokesman for the twentieth century and as a principle figure in the history of American literature.

Unlike the lure of many of his contemporaries, Vonnegut's appeal dissolves elitist intellectual boundaries. Vonnegut has the relatively unique ability to attract diverse groups of readers. Since the critical success of *Slaughterhouse-Five*, scholars and teachers have been increasingly drawn to his work, but so have lay readers, office managers, and computer programmers. His writing is regularly assigned at universities, where it is studied along with the works of Thomas Pynchon, Don DeLillo, and Vladimir Nabokov, but his novels are also taught in high schools, purchased by hoi polloi, and read along with the novels of Piers Anthony and Terry Pratchett. It is not so much that Vonnegut's writing crosses the line between popular fiction and literature, as it makes us stand back, scratch our heads, and wonder what made us think there was a line there in the first place.

My goal in putting together this book was to cover most of Vonnegut's writing up to the end of the millennium. This coverage begins with Jerome Klinkowitz's "Vonnegut the Essayist," a discussion of Vonnegut's three essay collections. Klinkowitz elaborates on Vonnegut's journalistic background and his career-long commitment to the genre. He traces Vonnegut's work as an essayist from Vonnegut's days as an editor on student daily newspapers in high school to the syncretism of essay and novel found in Vonnegut's last book.

Jeff Karon, in "Science and Sensibility in the Short Fiction of Kurt Vonnegut," closely examines the role of science in Vonnegut's often ignored, early science-fiction short stories, offering us valuable insight into how these early works interrelate with Vonnegut's other writing, and bringing to light the extremely useful notion of "ironic science" as literary device in Vonnegut's "science" fiction. Loree Rackstraw's "Quantum Leaps in the Vonnegut Mindfield" provides another view of Vonnegut's work and science, exploring important parallels between quantum mechanics and myth.

Lawrence Broer's "Vonnegut's Goodbye" analyzes the nexus between Vonnegut and Ernest Hemingway and sheds light on Vonnegut's career-long debate with masculinity. In "You Cannot Win, You Cannot Break Even, You Cannot Get Out of the Game," Donald Morse argues that Vonnegut's novels dismiss the notion of progress, and therefore redirect "humans . . . to look again at themselves and their planet." In a similar vein, Hartley Spatt's "Kurt Vonnegut: Ludic Luddite" elaborates Vonnegut's reprobation of technology and explores his long-standing role as the twentieth century's most well-known Luddite.

Looking to the heart of Vonnegut's work, Todd F. Davis's "Apocalyptic Grumbling" helps us to define Vonnegut's "postmodern humanism," and Bill Gholson's "Narrative, Self, and Morality in the Writing of Kurt Vonnegut" explores morality in the novels. David Andrews provides us with the first close examination of Vonnegut's aesthetics, and the final chapter in the book, "Vonnegut Films," critiques film adaptations of Vonnegut's writing. In it David Pringle takes on *Mother Night*, and I look at *Slaughterhouse-Five*, *Slapstick*, and the made-for-TV adaptations.

The title of this book, *At Millennium's End*, is based on a coincidence. As it happened, Kurt Vonnegut's career as a novelist and the millenium came to an end around the same time. Vonnegut reached what he called the "coda on my career" just as time's odometer was getting ready to roll over to 2000. That is, just as the *Christian* odometer was getting ready to roll over to 2000. The Jewish odometer was getting ready to roll over to 5761, and the Islamic odometer was getting ready to roll over to 1421—both very untidy numbers and not nearly as portentous. But the Christian calendar was the one that stimulated end-of-the-millennium mania, despite the fact that the year 2000 marked a point in humanity's timeline 1,999 years from a clerical error. What happened was this: Around the middle of the sixth century AD (before there technically was a sixth century AD) Dionysius Exiquus set up a system for numbering years based on when Jesus was supposedly born. The church later learned that Jesus had most likely been born three years earlier than Dionysius's estimate, but by then everyone was used to the system. Thus, the year 2000 has all the metaphysical and historical significance of an automobile odometer. Ironically, the publication of Vonnegut's last novel in 1997 coincides more accurately with the end of the second millennium after the birth of Jesus than the Christian calendar does. As Vonnegut might say, make of that what you will.

Despite its superstitious foundation, the coinstantaneous occurance of these two events makes an amusing footnote to the career of a writer who spent his life warning human beings of the future science prefigures, and of the price humanity might pay for its blind loyalty to technology. Vonnegut said of this project: "It all seems very spooky to me—my being seventy-five, this being 1998, and all those people writing essays about my oeuvre." Perhaps it is spooky for Vonnegut, but for those of us who have appreciated his writing for half a century, the fact that Vonnegut's canon reached its denouement as the millennium drew to a close and the human race slipped into the twenty-first century seems like poetic irony.

CHAPTER ONE

VONNEGUT THE ESSAYIST

Jerome Klinkowitz

The key to understanding Kurt Vonnegut's seemingly unconventional work has always been to address that work's accessibility. When considering the literary role a novelist who has broken so many rules plays in the present world, one is well advised to consider the kind of writing training he had and the type of work he does on an almost daily basis. In each case we are obligated to look at Vonnegut's essays—essays that are just as unconventional as his novels, and whose violations of tradition are directed to the same purpose as his fiction: the desire to speak directly and convincingly to his audience. Reading anything Kurt Vonnegut has written is to engage in a remarkably personal dialogue with the man himself, and it is in his nonfiction prose that this manner is most apparent.

For a novelist whose books challenge the most established practices of traditional fiction, it should be remembered that Vonnegut was not taught to write like most belletristic authors. He wasn't an English major, for example. His high school courses were taken to prepare him for study in the sciences as pursued at Cornell University, where his father (an architect) and older brother (with a doctorate in atmospheric physics from the Massachusetts Institute of Technology) had determined he would have a "useful" rather than "ornamental" education—the Great Depression had soured his once-accomplished family on the arts. Vonnegut chose to major in chemistry and biology, with an eye toward becoming a biochemist. When World War II took him out of college and into the Army, he trained as a mechanical engineer, spending time at

Carnegie Tech. After the war and graduate study in anthropology at the University of Chicago, Vonnegut was able to return to what had been his first love: writing. But not writing novels or short stories. In both high school and college, Vonnegut had been an editor of the student daily newspaper, learning journalism from the ground up with hands-on experience that could not be duplicated by any purely academic program. And so his qualifications for employment as a writer took him to the General Electric Research Laboratory in Schenectady, New York, where with his brother's help he became one of the lab's publicists.

Hence by 1949 he had published more words than Norman Mailer, Saul Bellow, Grace Paley, or any other fiction writer his age. But none of it was in fiction. Instead, he had become a master of writing on deadline about assigned topics, all of them of great immediate interest and scheduled to run with very short lead time. Though daily journalism and flack work are not regarded as eminent professions, the subject matter these writers address is immensely serious and attended to with concern by readers. In the way that his father and brother had intended, Kurt Vonnegut was doing something useful, not ornamental. There was nothing ornamental about the great technological innovations General Electric was introducing into American life. The company's motto, "Progress Is Our Most Important Product," would help set the tone for the coming decade's lifestyle and the values behind it. In Schenectady Vonnegut lived within a stimulating environment; both work and social circles included the foremost scientists of his day, and the company's policy of letting them work unfettered on their own projects made for an ideal atmosphere. What Vonnegut wrote about as a publicist was of interest to himself and to his readers. Years later he might regret the confinement of a nine-to-five office job and resent its managerial pressures, but the substance of what he was doing has never been disavowed. In similar manner Vonnegut has spoken of what a serious accomplishment student journalism was, especially at Cornell, where the paper was an independent corporation, student-owned, and not subject to faculty or administrative control. Forty years later, as a world-famous novelist, he returned to address the newspaper's annual banquet. As collected in his volume *Palm Sunday*, Vonnegut's comments attest to the power and maturity of such work:

> I was happiest here when I was all alone–and it was very late at night, and I was walking up the hill after having put the *Sun* to bed.
>
> All the other university people, teachers and students alike, were asleep. They had been playing games all day long with what was known about real life. They had been repeating famous arguments and experiments, and asking one another the sorts of hard questions real life would be asking by and by.
>
> We on the *Sun* were already in the midst of life. By God, if we weren't! We had just designed and written and caused to be manufactured yet another morning newspaper for a highly intelligent

American community of respectable size—yes, and not during the
Harding administration, either, but during 1940, '41, and '42, with
the Great Depression ending, and with World War Two well begun.

I am an agnostic as some of you may have gleaned from
my writings. But I have to tell you that, as I trudged up the hill
so late at night and all alone, I knew that God Almighty approved
of me. (66–67)

Hence, seriousness in communicating with a responsive body of readers
was from the very first a key element in Vonnegut's writing. Throughout his
career that would remain the standard: getting something that mattered across.
This called for two abilities, having something to say and an engaging way of
saying it. When his son Mark wrote a book about his recovery from schizophrenia (*The Eden Express*), Vonnegut suggested the young man had managed
to make a success of the project because he had something to say, and probably would write another book only if he had something else to say. As for
reaching readers, Vonnegut had made that the essence of every lesson he taught
during his 1965–67 residency at the University of Iowa Writers Workshop. To
students in his fiction seminars he'd repeat that anything they'd write did not
automatically merit an eager readership. In reaching out toward a public, they
were not being coddled by family and friends. There had to be something evident in their work, from the very first lines, that would convince readers that
here was somebody to be liked and trusted and worth the investment of reading time. At the beginning of each class, from the semester's start to its finish,
Vonnegut would write the same admonition on the blackboard: "Face the
audience of strangers." It was not a lesson he himself had learned in any English course or perfected in the pursuit of great literature. But it was to be an
essential technique in his writing.

On February 11, 1950, Vonnegut's first professionally published short
story appeared in *Collier's*. His G. E. coworker Ollie Lyon recalls that Vonnegut
and his friends had a party to celebrate the occasion; everyone in the group was
happy that the first of them was breaking out into the world of success beyond
the office routine. Vonnegut used the occasion to write his father. He told him
of the sale and his plans to keep submitting stories, saving the income until he'd
have the equivalent of a year's salary put aside—at which point he promised to
quit his office job and never take another, dedicating himself to living as a creative writer.

"Report on the Barnhouse Effect," "Thanasphere," "Epicac," "All the
King's Horses," "Mnenomics," "The Euphio Question"—these half dozen stories, published within Kurt Vonnegut's first sixteen months at the trade, got him
out of General Electric and into what he considered the more artistic environs
of Provincetown, Massachusetts. Soon his short stories were appearing in the
age's best venue for such work, *The Saturday Evening Post*, and his dystopian
novel *Player Piano*, in which progress was anything but a benign product, was

ready to make any return to the G. E. fold an impossibility. For the next decade *Player Piano* would be the author's only hardcover novel; short stories were his bread and butter; forty-four of them published in good-paying markets such as *Collier's*, the *Post*, *Redbook*, *Cosmopolitan*, and *Ladies Home Journal*. *The Sirens of Titan* and *Mother Night* were paperback originals written only because an outline had been sold, a way to make money when the family weeklies reduced their story acquisitions (before going out of business entirely). *Cat's Cradle* and *God Bless You, Mr. Rosewater* only appeared as hardcovers because Kurt's paperback editor had changed jobs and taken his authors with him. Neither novel sold well. Indeed, it would not be until *Slaughterhouse-Five* that Vonnegut would have any commercial success as a novelist. But *Slaughterhouse-Five* was by no means Kurt Vonnegut's beginning, for by that time he had already kept his pledge and was supporting himself by writing short stories and idiosyncratically creative essays. Both genres would influence his novels to come.

Those forty-four stories have much in common with the daily journalism and publicity work their author had been pursuing beforehand. For the magazines he published in, particularly *Collier's* and *The Saturday Evening Post*, he was writing with short lead time. Not only were his topics popular, but they had to have the currency typical of a weekly magazine. Though fictive, pieces such as "Report on the Barnhouse Effect" and "All the King's Horses" featured persons, places, things, and issues common to the day's news stories. Any *Collier's* or *Post* in which Vonnegut's short stories appeared would include advertisements and real-life features complementary with issues the fictionist was addressing, issues such as the ethics of new products developed by scientific research or the psychological terror of a new ideological enemy being fought in the Korean War. Even more familiar issues were found in stories such as "The Foster Portfolio" and "More Stately Mansions," in which wealth and its pretensions were gently mocked in a way that reaffirmed a middle-class readership's values. "Face the audience of strangers," the author would later tell his writing students; here he was doing it on a regular basis and succeeding as someone found to be comfortable, trustworthy, entertaining, and instructive. Having moved early on from arty Provincetown to middle-class West Barnstable, on the domestic (as opposed to resort) side of Cape Cod, Vonnegut had established himself as a tradesperson in the manufacture and installation of short stories; no wonder that his most frequent narrator for these stories would be a salesman, peddling anything from insurance to storm windows as a way of getting a foot in the door and letting the author's art happen.

With the exception of two atypical later stories written for special venues ("Welcome to the Monkey House" for *Playboy* and "The Big Space Fuck" for a Harlan Ellison anthology), Kurt Vonnegut's career as a short fictionist came to an end in 1963. Yet it is incorrect to assume that with his story markets gone the author turned at once to the novel for financial support. True, *Cat's Cradle* and *Rosewater* appeared in 1963 and 1965 respectively, but their royalties (on sales of just a few thousand copies each) would not have supported a starving artist, let alone a family man with six kids to feed, clothe, shelter, and educate. Nor did the lectureship he took at the University of Iowa's Writers Workshop help appreciably. Because the University of Chicago had rejected his M.A. thesis and he had left Cornell without a B.A., Vonnegut qualified for a salary at the bottom rung, less than $7,000 annually. Compare that to the half-again or twice as much he earned during good years a decade earlier with *The Saturday Evening Post*. The economic truth is that beginning in 1964 the author's most consistent source of income was from essay writing. He began with travel essays for a handsome new glossy called *Venture*, continued with major book reviews for *Life* and *The New York Times Book Review*, and reached his full development with feature personal essays for such well-paying and culturally important magazines as *Esquire*, *Horizon*, *Harper's*, and *McCall's*. Undertaken before the success of *Slaughterhouse-Five*, but then propelled by that novel's cultural notoriety, Vonnegut's essays became an important mode of artistic expression and helped shape the revolutionary formats of his novels.

A look at Kurt Vonnegut's last major short story and first significant essay shows how his fiction and nonfiction share similar writing strategies. "The Hyannis Port Story" had been purchased by *The Saturday Evening Post* and was scheduled to run late in 1963. It was already set in galleys at the time of President John F. Kennedy's assassination. Because Vonnegut's short story spoofed the Kennedy mystique, it suffered the fate of much humor of its type popular up to this time and was cancelled. It did not see print until *Welcome to the Monkey House*, where it appeared with a selection of other Vonnegut stories and two nonfiction pieces: a hilarious review of *The Random House Dictionary* (published in *The New York Times Book Review* for October 30, 1966, the piece brought Vonnegut to Seymour Lawrence's attention and led to the contract for *Slaughterhouse-Five*) and "Where I Live," the author's first feature essay, published in *Venture's* October 1964 issue as "You've Never Been to Barnstable?" Both the Kennedy and Barnstable pieces are set on Cape Cod and are told from the perspective of local, unassuming familiarity rather than glamour or fame. Each teaches the same lesson about how simple homely values win out over self-seriousness and pretensions. Most emphatically, both pieces use a key technique just then becoming popular as The New Journalism, in which writers made sense of a situation by placing themselves at its center and describing their own experience. Using techniques from fiction to enhance journalism became a staple in the works of Tom Wolfe, Joan Didion, Dan Wakefield, Gay Talese, and many others beginning in the middle 1960s. With "Where I Live" Vonnegut joined the first wave of New Journalism, drawing on a method he had perfected in dozens of short stories for the family weeklies.

"The Hyannis Port Story" could almost be an essay, given its famous real-life subject and its strong dose of current-day politics. In time, footnotes may be needed to tell readers of the nuances involved with Adlai Stevenson's ambassadorship to the United Nations, Walter Reuther's presidency of the United Auto Workers, the late Senator Robert Taft's reputation among Republican

Party stalwarts, the nature of Dwight D. Eisenhower's nomination to run for president (instead of Taft), Kennedy's nomination as a Democrat (instead of Stevenson), Attorney General Robert Kennedy's position with the big unions, historian Arthur Schlesinger Jr.'s service as a presidential advisor, and several other minutiae, not to mention the overriding themes of Barry Goldwater's coming challenge in the 1964 election, the Cold War battles with Soviet premier Nikita Khrushchev, and the celebrity of the entire (and extensive) Kennedy family during these years. These persons and subjects fill the story, which is propelled by a debate between Republican and Democrat, conservative and liberal, old wealth and new money, old age and youth, and inherited versus earned income. All of these are dealt with from the unique perspective of a storm-window tradesman who has come down from North Crawford, New Hampshire, to install a set of storms and screens on the Hyannis Port mansion next to President Kennedy's.

As an innovative storyteller, Vonnegut cleverly lets the essay aspects of his subject emerge by themselves. The narrator keeps his options open for more important things. The storm-window sale has been made at a local Lions Club meeting where the anticipated Kennedy-Goldwater presidential race is being debated. No hotter political topic in 1963 could be imagined, yet Vonnegut's spokesman shrugs it off (quite wisely for a tradesperson) by saying, "I hadn't made up my mind one way or the other" (133). The evening's speaker has, and as a Goldwater supporter is heatedly debated by a local Democrat. When the narrator gets into an argument later on with this same activist over a leaky bathtub enclosure, the speaker's father mistakes it for Goldwater support and awards a lavish contract on the spot. Thus is Vonnegut's narrator brought down to Hyannis, where in search of the job location he finds himself driving past "the *Presidential Motor Inn*, the *First Family Waffle Shop*, the *PT-109 Cocktail Lounge*, and a miniature golf course called the *New Frontier*" (136). Stopping for lunch, he finds the waffle shop's menu similarly rife with commercialization of the president's family. "All the different kinds of waffles were named after Kennedys and their friends and relatives," he notes. "A waffle with strawberries and cream was a *Jackie*. A waffle with a scoop of ice cream was a *Caroline*. They even had a waffle named *Arthur Schlesinger, Jr.*" Not to be mortified by a cutesy menu, he orders "a thing called a *Teddy*," mercifully undescribed, "and a cup of *Joe*," the patriarch's name letting the narrator speak like the worker he is.

"A man who sells storm windows can never really be sure about what class he belongs to, especially if he installs the windows, too" (137)—this reminder, voiced at the climax of the story's first rising action, is an important credo to both the narrator and Vonnegut himself. It is part of the author's "face the audience of strangers" imperative, a key device by which he makes himself likeable, trustworthy, and above all someone with whom his *Saturday Evening Post* readers can identify. Much as they might wish, they surely can't identify with John F. Kennedy; he's the one to be treated like an idol. Nor can they identify with the lofty world of international politics swirling around Hyannis

Port. Hence, when the narrator gets stuck in a traffic jam with Adlai Stevenson, he passes time by asking the ambassador how things are going at the United Nations. He is told things are going about as well as could be hoped for, and lets the matter go as easily as any back-fence chat with a neighbor over pleasant nothings. Thus readers are brought into the whole heady situation with Vonnegut's narrator as their spokesperson. This plain, simple, and unassuming posture turns out to be the only way of surviving the maelstrom intact, for at the maelstrom's center, facing the Kennedy home, is something more ridiculous than any of the town's commercialization: a giant floodlit billboard-sized portrait of Republican presidential candidate Barry Goldwater, an outrage to President Kennedy constructed by his neighbor who has ordered the storms and screens.

"The Hyannis Port Story" pauses at this point, much like its narrator, to take stock of the situation. The narrator's customer, Commodore Rumfoord, is in every respect the antithesis of President Kennedy. The last thing the simple, honest narrator wants to do is get involved in their squabble. So he carries on as what he is: a plain hard worker, trying to ignore the battiness around him. It is his good example that resolves the plot complications and lets the story end on a happy note. Deflated by the news that his son may be about to marry a Kennedy, the commodore is revived by his wife's encouragement to take back control of his life and do some meaningful work, with the tradesman's steady presence an implied example. Chastened, Rumfoord decides to leave his Goldwater sign unlit, only to be roused to action by his neighbor, President Kennedy, who ends the story by asking that the absurd display be activated for two reasons: so that the president can show it off to a visitor, Khrushchev's son-in-law, and so that its beacon can help the president find his way home.

Thus Vonnegut's roller coaster ride of absurdities is brought to an end on a happily harmless note. The obnoxious Goldwater sign has not insulted the president at all, and the two men are able to act toward each other as neighbors instead of ideologists—just as the narrator had chatted with Ambassador Stevenson. "The Hyannis Port Story" takes celebrity and reduces it to familiarity at the same time it transforms aggression into aid and angry confusion into friendly understanding. As a piece of writing, it has not only the subject matter of an essay but the rhetoric as well. Yet the method of telling is immensely personal.

"Where I Live" (as Vonnegut's title is restored for *Welcome to the Monkey House*) is explicitly an essay, written for *Venture* as a view of this less-visited side of Cape Cod and starting off the author's collection of short stories as an introduction to his life and times. Its beginning, however, might as well be a short story, for Vonnegut's method is decidedly anecdotal—not exactly "once upon a time," but close. The story opens with the news that "Not very long ago, an encyclopedia salesman stopped by America's oldest library building, which is the lovely Sturgis Library in Barnstable Village, on Cape Cod's north shore" (1). The story's point is how astonished the salesman was that this eminent collection's newest resource was a 1938 *Britannica*, nearly thirty years out of date. The opening introduces the essay's theme, that the place where its author lives is not only quaintly superannuated but also dedicated quite consciously to remaining that way. As a matter of fact, the Barnstable library's newest encyclopedia *was* a '38 model, something a catalog check would confirm. But in terms of the methods of fiction, it is possible the salesman's visit was invented, just like the storm-window salesman's visit to Hyannis Port across the Cape. Confirming this suspicion is Vonnegut's choice to stay with the device, having the man prowl around Barnstable for a bit (and be amazed at even more intentionally backward idiosyncrasies, by which time he finds himself "strangling on apathy, an affliction epidemic among casual visitors to Barnstable Village" (2).

This is a strange way to begin a travel essay, indicating that the destination has nothing whatsoever to interest tourists, but it will become a factor in many of Kurt Vonnegut's essays: deliberately breaking conventional rules. Consequently, the salesman heads for a nearby tourist haven, letting the narrative continue in a way reminiscent of "The Hyannis Port Story":

> He took the customary cure, which was to jump into his car and roar off toward the cocktail lounges, motor courts, bowling alleys, gift shoppes, and pizzerias of Hyannis, the commercial heart of Cape Cod. He there worked off all his frustrations on a miniature golf course called Playland. At that time, that particular course had a pathetic, maddening feature typical of the random butchery of the Cape's south shore. The course was built on the lawn of what had once been an American Legion Post—and, right in the middle of the cunning little bridges and granulated cork fairways was a Sherman tank, set there in simpler and less enterprising days as a memorial to the veterans of World War Two.
>
> The memorial has since been moved, but it is still on the south side, where it is bound to be engulfed by indignities again.
>
> The dignity of the tank would be a lot safer in Barnstable Village, but the village would never accept it. It has a policy of never accepting anything. As a happy consequence, it changes about as fast as the rules of chess. (2–3)

Here, by a very round-about way (another Vonnegut technique for both fiction and essays), the author gets to the point he wants to make: that Barnstable is indeed worth a visit, because it is so uniquely insulated from casual tourism, and therefore shows itself as a pristine example of how commercialism can be avoided in favor of maintaining a place where real people just simply live.

One of those people is Kurt Vonnegut himself. Although readers can easily surmise the type of guy he is by considering the values and manners of expressing them in this volume's twenty-three short stories (several of which are narrated by the same village tradesperson as "The Hyannis Port Story," where North Crawford stands in for West Barnstable), they can find factual evidence in this collection's other piece of nonfiction prose, the author's review of *The Random House Dictionary*. Over the course of his three subsequent collections of essay materials, Vonnegut included very few book reviews, although reviewing has been an important part of his work and constituted most of his livelihood in the mid-1960s. This very assignment speaks for the financial straits he was in: who else would accept the daunting task of reviewing a dictionary? His brilliance is that he takes the job and completes it in an informative, interesting, and entertaining way. He is not a lexicographer, so he can find just one such issue to consider: does the new dictionary contain dirty words? Nor is he a linguist, and so the best he can make of their debates is that "Prescriptive, as nearly as . . . [he] could tell, was like an honest cop, and descriptive was like a boozed-up war buddy from Mobile, Ala." (108). Much of what Vonnegut has to say is culled from dinner conversations with two of his own present buddies, novelist Richard Yates and critic Robert Scholes. This deliberate informality provides an unexpected benefit when at the review's conclusion the author has some fun at the expense of the dictionary's publisher, Random House president Bennett Cerf. Cerf had once employed (and apparently put through the wringer) a young vice-president named Seymour Lawrence. The reference to his old boss caught Lawrence's eye, and a reading of Vonnegut's review made him think that anyone who could make such a dull review assignment so funny to read must have great talents as a novelist. Within three years Vonnegut had his first bestseller published by Lawrence, together with his five previously neglected novels brought back into print.

As a famous novelist in the 1970s, 1980s, and 1990s, Vonnegut no longer had to write essays and reviews to support himself. But as a public spokesperson, he was in great demand, and remained committed to the great social issues of his day. Hence he continued writing nonfiction prose, and by 1974 had determined that it (and not his two dozen short stories that hadn't been republished) would provide the contents of future collections. The first, *Wampeters, Foma, and Granfalloons* shows how selective the author is. He discarded thirteen book reviews (in favor of saving just three) while passing over just one essay, the very early and atypically fabulative "Der Arme Dolmetscher," published in the *Atlantic Monthly* for July of 1955, but advertised as forthcoming in that journal as early as 1953. The canonical lesson is clear: although book reviewing was mostly work, essay writing was a practice of literary art, art that Kurt Vonnegut was happy to see preserved alongside his now-famous novels. The reviews themselves, both collected and not, often rely on autobiography, as the author relates the book at hand to his childhood in Indiana or early days with General Electric. In terms of reviewer objectivity, this practice can be considered as breaking the rules. But it is in the essays that Vonnegut shatters conventions by taking every opportunity to do something wrong. In "Science Fiction," a *New York Times Book Review* essay arguing against his own inclusion in the subgenre, it is a case of using rhetorical fallacies, in this case the excluded middle —saying that when SF advocates try to include writers such as Leo Tolstoi and Franz

Kafka in their clan it is as ridiculous as Vonnegut claiming that everyone of note belonged to his own fraternity, Delta Upsilon, whether he knew it or not, and then remarking how "Kafka would have been a desperately unhappy D. U." (4).

In "Yes, We Have No Nirvanas," an *Esquire* essay treating the Maharishi and transcendental meditation, Vonnegut breaks the rule of his own agnosticism by citing Christ's better religious example, and in "Excelsior! We're Going to the Moon! Excelsior!" (a *New York Times Magazine* feature growing out of a CBS Television News assignment) he mocks the seriousness of the Apollo space program by first comparing it to childlike endeavors and then by responding like an overexuberant drunk. Asked to speak to the American Physical Society, he argues not for science but for humanism; seeking an example of a human-ist, he picks not a great artist or philosopher but his sheep dog Sandy, who likes people. Even for one of the book reviews he includes, "Oversexed in Indi-anapolis" (covering Dan Wakefield's novel *Going All the Way* for *Life* magazine), he begins by breaking three cardinal rules of the trade: he reviews the book of a friend, he admits that friendship in the first line, and he adds that even if he didn't think the book was good he'd say that it was.

Other pieces expand this habit of contrariness with convention into a vision. "Brief Encounters on the Inland Waterway" deglamorizes the Kennedys and demystifies yacht ownership; "There's a Maniac Loose Out There" makes the depersonalization of mass murder suddenly quite personal; the awesome doings of the Vietnam era's secretary of defense are related to the doings of high school friends, while "Torture and Blubber" compares military weaponry to juvenile fantasies.

Throughout, timing is of the essence, with short paragraphs and single-word sentences set in a rhythm much like that in *Cat's Cradle*. Deft little orig-inalities of statement are crafted, such as this warning to fellow Indianapolis native Dan Wakefield that his sexually frank novel means that he can never go home again: "From now on, he will have to watch the 500–mile Speedway race on television" (118). Similar lines from other writers are equally treasured, such as when during the 1972 Republican National Convention (which Vonnegut is covering for *Harper's* magazine) columnist Art Buchwald comes up with an idea for the Party's two billion dollar campaign surplus: a plan "to buy some-thing nice for the American people," namely "a free week's bombing of Viet-nam" (188). The purpose of such timing is to disarm expectations, not just for the fun of it, but to let some new, otherwise rejectable wisdom fill the gap. Such is the technique Vonnegut uses in his graduation address to the students of Ben-nington College, who instead of being told to go out and change the world are encouraged to lay back and take it easy for a while, that there's nothing they alone can do to improve things or stop the war in Vietnam—the only person to ever stop a tank single-handed was John Wayne, and he was in another tank. Nor should they cry voluptuous tears over the world's suffering, for "To weep is to make the less of grief" (162). Above all, these bright graduates should not put too much trust in knowledge, for knowledge (especially as perfected by the

military) establishes how contemptible human life is; far better to be superstitious and have faith that life might matter.

Wampeters, Foma, and Granfalloons is a culling, as Vonnegut explains in its
preface, a selection of materials from a much larger variety of work reaching
back to before he had become famous. With the Delacore Press / Seymour
Lawrence publication *Palm Sunday* in 1981, the author has his first opportunity
to weave a volume more in the manner of whole cloth, incorporating the
recent nonfiction prose that he'd written from a widely acknowledged point of
view and in appreciation that these pieces would stand next to his novels as
another Vonnegut book. The key difference between *Wampeters* and *Palm Sunday* is indicated by their subtitles: "opinions" versus "an autobiographical collage." Most of the former essays were written before their author was famous;
they were, in other words, assignments, and though they were interesting
enough to elicit his opinions and sufficiently important to appear in leading
magazines, their collective impression could only be called various—from the
Maharishi and the space program to Madame Blavatsky and Biafra it would be
hard to establish a pattern other than concerns of the day, and therefore concerns of a working journalist. In *Palm Sunday* all that changes. As the best-selling author of *Slaughterhouse-Five* and several other number-one-listed novels,
Vonnegut could choose his own occasions to write. The title itself refers to his
new fancy of giving sermons from the pulpits of renowned churches, such as
New York's Cathedral of St. John the Divine. Most important, the materials
were bridged by fresh commentary linking them together by means of transi-
tions, prefaces, and afterwords for each piece, producing the "autobiographical
collage" as promised by the subtitle.

There is still a variousness of sorts to *Palm Sunday*, but it is a variousness
relating to the author himself. The volume is divided into nineteen titled sections—some of them containing several essays, others just two or one, and in
the case of section ten, "Embarrassment," no essay at all, just an autobiographical note on how the author proved an embarrassment to his Indianapolis relatives. In all cases the new interweaving material is substantial in itself and
important to *Palm Sunday*'s integrity as a book and not just a collection. This
ongoing commentary combines with individual essays to produce a theme and
a rhetoric for advancing it. This theme is the power of writing, and the rhetoric
involves Vonnegut's autobiographical experiences in living by the word. As any
reader of his novels would know, here was a man who treasured vernacular
speech and used it quite effectively to both instruct and entertain. *Palm Sunday*
puts that practice on record, explains how it came about, and indicates how the
author has perfected it as his most successful manner. He explains how jokes
work. He considers how libraries are important for preserving and making
available personal visions expressed in a way that readers can share and recreate. He honors the First Amendment as the protector in principle of such
expression. He examines how other writers have chosen such forms, from Swift
and Céline to the vernacular mastery of Mark Twain. In the sermon that gives

his book its title, Vonnegut retranslates Jesus' words into a more common idiom so his thoughts can be better understood. How such writing works in practice is the subject of the advice he gives in an advertisement for a paper company, a matter having something to say and the ability to say it honestly and convincingly, lessons the author himself learned first hand as a student journalist. "Find a subject you care about and which you in your heart feel others should care about," he advises writing students. "It is this genuine caring, and not your games with language, which will be the most compelling and seductive element in your style" (77). As for the voice to express it, "I myself find that I trust my own writing most, and others seem to trust it most, too, when I sound like a person from Indianapolis, which is what I am" (79).

As the nonfiction prose written during the period of Kurt Vonnegut's greatest fame and busiest professional involvement, *Palm Sunday* is an active and even combative book. In it he takes on censoring school boards to defend the First Amendment and a selfish restaurant customer to speak for the waitress he has had unfairly fired. He mounts the pulpit to sermonize, and speaks consolingly at the funeral of an old friend's wife. He studies his ancestors to learn where he has come from, and talks about his children as examples of where the family genius is now leading, all of it undertaken with great seriousness. He is candid about his bad old ways of expression, having too much to drink and spending late evenings writing letters and making phone calls to old enemies, real or presumed. Now, when moved by righteous ire, he has pulpits and editorial pages open to his thoughts, and his happy resolve is to use those forums properly and effectively. *Palm Sunday* is the work of an essentially committed writer, and it is the manner of his commitment that gives it its form.

Kurt Vonnegut's novels during the decades of *Wampeters* and *Palm Sunday* parallel his evolving manner as an essayist. The author's tendency to introduce autobiographical elements into his fiction coincides with the self-apparent personal qualities in the essays and book reviews he began writing during this same period. The method reaches full expression with the revolutionary nature of *Slaughterhouse-Five*, where chapters 1 and 10 describe the author's crafting of the novel that will itself include three mentions of Vonnegut as a character within the wartime action. Readers can see it coming in the highly autobiographical introduction added to Harper & Row's 1966 hardcover edition of *Mother Night* and *Welcome to the Monkey House*'s preface, each of which relates Kurt Vonnegut directly and extensively to the fictive writing that follows. These elements were developed between 1966 and 1968, just as the most characteristic essays of *Wampeters* were taking shape. In both fiction and nonfiction, the author was not only drawing on his autobiography but using elements of his life to alter each genre's form, suspending the novel's customary suspension of disbelief in favor of self-evident and actively present authorship at the same time the customary objectivity of journalism gave way to an honest appraisal of the self's role in this business. Vonnegut's fiction of the later 1960s, then, with its nondescript protagonists, reflects his essays of the period, which take an appealingly aw-shucks posture toward topics otherwise supposed to be impressive (the Mararishi, the moon launch). When during the 1970s (and now famous himself) his novels are narrated by loftier personages (a U.S. president, a high-level Nixon administration official), Vonnegut's committed manner and more serious topicality coincide with similar qualities of his '70s nonfiction adding up to *Palm Sunday*.

In the 1980s Kurt Vonnegut's writing takes another turn, once again paralleled by fiction and nonfiction. Although usually set in the future, these novels have a retrospective quality to them. His narrators look back on matters from Darwinian evolution and modern American art history to a reexamination of our country's culture during the Vietnam War (during which time a massive sell-off to foreign interests began to reshape the economy). Here an autobiographical presence is less evident than in the later '60s and '70s work, certainly less active in shaping each novel's form. In a similar way Vonnegut's essays of the 1980s, most of which are woven into the almost seamless text of *Fates Worse Than Death*, take a more relaxed attitude toward autobiography's shape-taking power. Unlike the pieces in *Wampeters* and *Palm Sunday*, these writings do not use references to the author's life as a way of surprising the reader, disarming expectations, or slipping the otherwise confining gears of good rhetoric. Instead, like the novels Kurt Vonnegut was writing at the time, they use autobiography in its simplest, most obvious manner: that of reminiscence. As with parts of *Bluebeard* and *Hocus Pocus*, the tone can become almost elegiac, most obviously so in the lovely essay on his family's long-ago summers in a string of cottages along Indiana's Lake Maxincuckee. Similar essays on his father, his sister, his first wife, his old war buddy, and others (all of them long dead) are not so much collected as drawn upon as first drafts for what now becomes an even more integral book than *Palm Sunday*. Instead of categorical sections, Vonnegut prepares a series of numbered chapters, the substance of which lies not in any specific topicality but rather in the posture he takes throughout, which is to look back— not in anger, but with a growing sense of peace. When not elegiac, this peacefulness is achieved by gentle self-mockery, as in the conclusion to his coverage of a particularly tragic and atrocity-filled African war. "The photograph at the head of this chapter shows me in Mozambique, demonstrating muscular Christianity in an outfit that might have been designed by Ralph Lauren," the author remarks. "The aborigines didn't know whether to shit or go blind until I showed up. And then I fixed everything" (175). That his conclusion is set apart in parentheses, a radically unconventional way to end an essay, underscores Vonnegut's understanding that in retrospect there was nothing at all that he could do.

Throughout his three volumes of nonfiction prose, Kurt Vonnegut maintains a consistency of method, the key to which is an artful inconsistency. Like even his earliest novels, there is a sense of rambling to his line of development—not hopelessly disordered, but arranged in ways other than the straight line of rational logic, making wide-sweeping lateral moves so that otherwise overlooked materials (often autobiographical) can be brought in, and most effectively so that having outflanked his readers, as it were, he can make his rhetorical move along a less guarded approach. Thus his essays work best when they are long, allowing him to amass a wide range of topics and opinions on which he can touch almost subliminally, just as in his novels odds and ends from widely various sources will recur often enough to give his narratives an uncanny sense of deep order. Within the continuity of *Fates Worse Than Death* he has familiarized readers with so many of his attitudes that he can bounce several of them together in a sentence or two with the multifaceted effect of a fancy combination pool shot. For example, halfway through the volume he has established in individual pieces how strategic bombing is inhumane, how politicians sometimes don't have best interests at heart, how nations are artificial and ineffective ways of human organization, how chance encounters with old hometowners are as meaningful as any other systematic structure, and so forth. Notice how so many of these points come together in a brief aside to fellow novelist John Updike, who before speaking in Indiana asked Vonnegut for some local names and topics: "I added that George Bush's making Dan Quayle the custodian of our nation's destiny, should Bush become seriously impaired, was proof to me that Bush didn't give a damn what became of the rest of us once he himself was gone. There's a bomber pilot for you" (94).

As with this comment on President Bush, Vonnegut's overall method is to personalize, to look past obscuring technicalities in order to see the human dimension and, most important, to express that dimension in familiar, trustworthy terms. For his writer's career, this method has shown success in both his fiction and nonfiction, whether in parallel fashion or through an intermixture of generic techniques. In *Timequake*, novel and essay are united in a new form by which the author presents neither fiction nor nonfiction, but rather the autobiography of a novel. Here matter and manner are mutually reenforcing, for the narrative about a ten-year jumpback and subsequent replay of a decade's history is told not as a story per se but as an account of how Vonnegut struggled with a more conventional version of these doings, scrapped it, and recrafted the volume as a summary of the original story within the context of everything else happening in the writer's life during this time.

Like all of Kurt Vonnegut's work, *Timequake* faces the audience of strangers to convey, in an interesting, entertaining, and trustworthy manner something important and worthwhile. In this work's case, the message involves the value of art in making the otherwise troublesome experiences of life more rewarding. The manner used to express this point encompasses Vonnegut's wide reach for materials from his own life and his countrymen's shared popular culture. Like all of his prose that he has allowed to be collected, it satisfies this firmly agnostic author that he has done his job in a way of which even God must approve.

WORKS CITED

Vonnegut, Kurt. "All the King's Horses." *Collier's* 11 February 1950: 18–19, 63–65. (Included in *Welcome to the Monkey House*.)

———. "The Big Space Fuck." *Again, Dangerous Visions*. Ed. Harlan Ellison. New York: Doubleday, 1972. 246–50. (Included in *Palm Sunday*.)

———. *Bluebeard*. New York: Delacorte, 1987.

———. "Brief Encounters on the Inland Waterway." *Venture* (October/November 1966): 135–38, 140, 142. (Included in *Wampeters, Foma, and Granfalloons*.)

———. *Cat's Cradle*. New York: Holt, Rinehart & Winston, 1963.

———. "Der Arme Dolmetscher." *Atlantic Monthly* (July 1955): 86–88.

———. "Epicac." *Collier's* 25 Nov. 1950: 36–37. (Included in *Welcome to the Monkey House*.)

———. "The Euphio Question." *Collier's* 12 May 1951: 22–23, 52–54, 56. (Included in *Welcome to the Monkey House*.)

———. "Excelsior! We're Going to the Moon! Excelsior!" *New York Times Magazine* 13 July 1969: 9–11. (Included in *Wampeters, Foma, and Granfalloons*.)

———. *Fates Worse Than Death*. New York: Putnam's, 1991.

———. "The Foster Portfolio." *Collier's* 8 September 1951: 18–19, 72–73. (Included in *Welcome to the Monkey House*.)

———. *God Bless You, Mr. Rosewater*. New York: Holt, Rinehart & Winston 1965.

———. *Hocus Pocus*. New York: Putnam's, 1990.

———. "How to Write with Style." International Paper Company advertisement run nationally during May 1980. (Included in *Palm Sunday*.)

———. "The Hyannis Port Story." Written for *Saturday Evening Post* but first published in *Welcome to the Monkey House*.

———. "In a Manner Which Must Shame God Himself" (coverage of 1972 Republican National Convention). *Harper's* (November 1972): 60–63, 65–66, 68. (Included in *Wampeters, Foma and Granfalloons*.)

———. "The Latest Word" (review of The Random House Dictionary). *New York Times Book Review* 30 Oct. 1966: 1, 56. (Included in *Welcome to the Monkey House* as "New Dictionary.")

———. "Mnemonics." *Collier's* 28 Apr. 1951: 38.

———. "More Stately Mansions." *Collier's* 22 Dec. 1951: 24–25, 62–63. (Included in *Welcome to the Monkey House*.)

———. *Mother Night*. Greenwich: Fawcett, 1961. New York: Harper, 1966 (second edition, with a new introduction).

———— . "My Visit to Hell" (coverage of the war in Mozambique). *Parade* 7 Jan. 1990: 16–17. (Included in *Fates Worse Than Death*.)

———— . "Oversexed in Indianapolis" (review of Dan Wakefield's *Going All the Way*). *Life* 17 July 1970: 10. (Included in *Wampeters, Foma, and Granfalloons*.)

———— . *Palm Sunday*. New York: Delacorte, 1981.

———— . *Player Piano*. New York: Scribner's, 1952.

———— . "Report on the Barnhouse Effect." *Collier's* 11 Feb. 1950: 18–19, 63–65. (Included in *Welcome to the Monkey House*.)

———— . "Science Fiction." *New York Times Book Review* 5 Sept. 1965: 2. (Included in *Wampeters, Foma, and Granfalloons*.)

———— . *The Sirens of Titan*. New York: Dell, 1959.

———— . *Slaughterhouse-Five*. New York: Delacorte / Seymour Lawrence, 1969.

———— . "Thanasphere." *Collier's* 2 Sept. 1950: 18–19, 60, 62.

———— . "There's a Maniac Loose Out There." *Life* 25 July 1969: 53–56. (Included in *Wampeters, Foma, and Granfalloons*.)

———— . *Timequake*. New York: Putnam's, 1997.

———— . "Torture and Blubber." *New York Times* 30 June 1971: 41. (Included in *Wampeters, Foma, and Granfalloons*.)

———— . *Wampeters, Foma, and Granfalloons*. New York: Delacorte / Seymour Lawrence, 1974.

———— . "Welcome to the Monkey House." *Playboy* (January 1968): 95, 156, 196, 198, 200–201. (Included in *Welcome to the Monkey House*.)

———— . *Welcome to the Monkey House*. New York: Delacorte / Seymour Lawrence, 1968.

———— . "Yes, We Have No Nirvanas." *Esquire* (June 1968): 78–79, 176, 178–79, 182. (Included in *Wampeters, Foma, and Granfalloons*.)

———— . "You've Never Been to Barnstable?" *Venture* (October 1964): 145, 147–49. (Included in *Welcome to the Monkey House* as "Where I Live.")

Vonnegut, Mark. *The Eden Express*. New York: Praeger, 1975.

CHAPTER TWO

VONNEGUT AND
AESTHETIC HUMANISM

David Andrews

We are here to help each other get through this thing,
whatever it is
——Dr. Mark Vonnegut, epigraph to *Bluebeard*

Pictures are famous for their human-ness, and not
their pictureness.
——Kurt Vonnegut,
quoted in Klinkowitz, *Vonnegut in Fact*

It is infinitely better not to know anything about art
than to have the kind of half-knowledge which makes
for snobbishness. The danger is very real. There are
people . . . who understand that there are great works
of art which have none of the obvious qualities of
beauty of expression or correct draughtsmanship, but
who become so proud of their knowledge that they
pretend to like only those works which are neither
beautiful nor correctly drawn.
——E. H. Gombrich, *The Story of Art*

In *God Bless You, Mr. Rosewater* (1965), a character in a Kilgore Trout novel asks the question that haunts so many Kurt Vonnegut novels: "'What in hell are people *for*?'" (21). The question remains unanswerable because it assumes an ultimate design within which humans have a meaningful, crucial function—an assumption that dissatisfies skeptics from Hume to Vonnegut.[1] In the absence of such ultimacy, Vonnegut grants humanity a wholly practical, humanistic purpose. People are *for* people—or, as Eliot Rosewater proposes to tell twin infants, "'There's only one rule I know of, babies . . . God damn it, you've got to be kind'" (93). Because it seems so arbitrary, however, Eliot's single commandment seems made for breaking. Were *Rosewater* a Barthelme story, the infants might respond by objecting that Eliot, in eliminating divine design, has eliminated the ultimate foundation for altruism. Why be kind? Who says?

Vonnegut says—and *Rosewater* is, after all, his design. By consistently answering the unanswerable question in Rosewater's way, Vonnegut has been implicitly answering a more focused question all along: What are the arts for? Predictably, Vonnegut's answer is that they are for people. The latter answer is satisfactory for the same reason the former is not. The unanswerable question is flawed in that it implies an erroneous analogy between people and manmade things, which have originary purposes only insofar as they have creators. As such a creator, Vonnegut assigns the rules for his artificial worlds; as a result, Rosewater's kindness imperative is, within his world, a species of absolute. Outside that world, it amounts to just another artificial construct, a lie. But it is an ethical lie, one unlikely to worsen humanity's plight. This is in keeping with Vonnegut's belief that "writers should serve their society," each writer proving himself "a good citizen" through the fabrication of things "that would tend to make people gentle" (*Conversations* 45, 72, 19). These may sound like the prescriptions of a didactic, potentially inartistic writer, but it would be a mistake to infer that Vonnegut thinks his admittedly simple purpose is simply accomplished—a point that *Bluebeard* (1987), his eleventh novel, makes clear.[2] Though all of Vonnegut's works are informed by his humanism, *Bluebeard* is unique among them in that it alone discloses through its literal, ideational content the actual complexity of Vonnegut's aesthetic and his view of art history. As a set of concepts, this moral-aesthetic viewpoint is revealing in its idiosyncrasy and worthy of scrutiny. What gives *Bluebeard* its power and its elegance, however, is the novel's unified structure, which realizes this complex viewpoint in a wise and decidedly crafty manner.

Before turning to an examination of *Bluebeard* and related texts, it is useful to break Vonnegut's moral-aesthetic viewpoint into a set of basic concepts. If art is explicitly humanistic, it must be solidly rooted in the contingent world, its positive value gauged by its relatively utilitarian, experiential, and ethical functions. For Vonnegut, a successful artwork, whether a novel or a painting, is never autotelic in the art-for-art's-sake sense. Rather, such an artwork is always for things external to itself, that is, for creators and perceivers. In this regard, art has two primary positive effects on creators and perceivers: therapeutic and communicative. The act of creation itself has the potential to be immediately therapeutic. Still, since creation is typically solitary, this is not the effect with the greatest humanistic value. Insofar as art forges a bond between creator and perceiver—a bond that, among its virtues, possesses a secondary therapeutic value of its own—art's communicative function is most important to Vonnegut. Naturally, the act of reading or interpreting art, whether literary or otherwise, supplies this effect most readily.

In other words, it is incumbent upon the artist to *express* himself to someone else. If this modest purpose is combined with a basic understanding of the three enduring artistic theories (the mimetic, the expressionist, and the formalist), *Bluebeard*'s position on abstract expressionism and its historical skirmishes with representationalism will come into focus. In Vonnegut's aesthetic, the expression of ideas and emotions is art's goal, with mimetic (or representational) and formalist (or abstract) techniques the instruments of this goal. If the artist expresses himself, his choice of technique is relatively unimportant. This is in keeping with the idea that art, a physical artifact, is in itself unimportant.[3] For Vonnegut, art does not possess intrinsic value; rather, it refers to humanity's intrinsic value.[4] Still, an artist must make formal choices, and these should be dictated by his inborn gifts (as *Bluebeard* proves, the author is a firm adherent of the idea of "talent"), by the idea or feeling he means to express, by his medium, and by his audience. Finally, the artist, however talented, is responsible for his expressions and must express ideas and images deemed likely to increase the world's store of available gentleness.

This is how art should work, but what Vonnegut and *Bluebeard* do best is dissect the various historical processes that corrupt art. These corruptions all turn art against its ideal humanistic purpose and exemplify in a specifically artistic context the author's ongoing ambivalence toward technology and other forms of artifice, which often betray the idealistic pursuits that spawn them. (That Vonnegut regularly refers to artworks as machines, as "gadgets" on which to "tinker," is instructive [e.g., Reed and Leeds 36].) The example of Felix Hoenikker in *Cat's Cradle* (1963) is relevant in that he unites science and art by equating an autotelic truth with an autotelic beauty. For Irving Langmuir, Hoenikker's real-life model, "any truth . . . was beautiful in its own right, and he didn't give a damn who got it next" (*Conversations* 233). Because Hoenikker pursues the truth with disinterest—a largely post-Kantian attitude that connects "pure science" with "pure art"—he considers the practical consequences of his science irrelevant. Through his research, Hoenikker separates himself from human experience and thus sacrifices his conscience—a Faustian process that Vonnegut's artists frequently duplicate. Sensibly, though, Vonnegut realizes that the pursuit of a true beauty through art is unlikely to lead to the annihilation that results from Hoenikker's pursuit of a beautiful truth through science:

> . . . he was allowed to concentrate on one part of life more than any human being should be allowed to do. He was overspecialized and

became amoral on that account. It would seem perfectly all right to
see a musician vanish into his own world entirely. But if a scientist
does this, he can inadvertently become a very destructive person.
(*Conversations* 234–35)

The above does not, however, suggest that Vonnegut perceives zero danger in
aesthetic solipsism. The undeniable historical impact of artists like Leni Riefen-
stahl, who defends her film *The Triumph of the Will* (1935) in purely aesthetic,
amoral terms (Sontag, "Fascinating" 83–87), argues against any blanket dispen-
sation for artists. Furthermore, if scientists provide a greater potential for catastrophe than artists, the corruption of art and aesthetics can lead, albeit on a
much smaller scale, to indifference, isolation, despair, and suicide. Because *Bluebeard* devotes itself to these corruptions, only gradually moving toward the dis-
closure of the protagonist's humanistic masterpiece, it implies the affirmative
value of aesthetic experience largely via negative examples.

In brief, *Bluebeard* is the "hoax autobiography" and summer diary of the
former abstract expressionist and current Long Island hermit, Rabo Karabekian
(i). The son of Armenian immigrants, Rabo is a talented draftsman who during
the Depression serves as an apprentice to Dan Gregory, a commercial artist
whose sentimentality and popularity recall Norman Rockwell. After World War
II, Rabo abandons representational techniques, hoping to become a "serious
painter." This change in style is followed by a bizarre artistic fiasco—all of
Rabo's celebrated paintings disintegrate after he uses a faulty "miracle" paint,
Sateen Dura-Luxe (19)—and a series of financial coups owing to his relationship with the abstract expressionists, in particular Jackson Pollock and the fictional Terry Kitchen. In the novel's joyous climax, Rabo reveals that, during the
1980s, he has returned to a depictive artistic style in order to create a gigantic
and somewhat gruesome painting that he has hidden in a potato barn on his
Long Island estate.

This schematic of Rabo's stylistic shifts invites misreading. For several
critics, the novel's conclusion privileges mimetic techniques and undercuts formalist techniques.[5] In this view, Rabo's final painting, which combines representationalism with dramatic subject matter (the events of May 8, 1945, as witnessed by a prisoner-of-war), demonstrates the author's simultaneous rejection
of Gregory's unrealistic realism and the abstract expressionists' austere formalism. That is to suggest that in his first phase Rabo's failure pertains to the subject matter—which, despite its virtuosic verisimilitude, is insufficiently true to
life—while in his second phase, his failure involves the technique itself. Though
this reading would seem a satisfying interpretation of Rabo's overall development, it falsifies *Bluebeard*'s details and simplifies Vonnegut's aesthetics. Though
Bluebeard does register Vonnegut's reservations about abstract expressionism, it
also registers his admiration for the paintings of Pollock and Kitchen (83, 164).
Such admiration is consistent with his interest in artistic revolutionaries such as
Matisse, Picasso, Braque, Klee, and others, all of whom manipulate relatively

abstract techniques to expressive ends.[6] Indeed, though subjected to scathing commentary (82–83), not even Gregory's paintings are categorically dismissed. Predictably, it is specifically the expressive content, not the illusionist techniques, of his paintings that Vonnegut appreciates (albeit by way of Rabo, another of his transparent alter egos). Thus Gregory captures "the excitement of the single moment" through pictures "vibrant with the full spectrum of his own loves, hates, and neutralities" (147, 146–47). What Rabo lacks in his first two phases is a similar ability to express himself. In the first phase, he has the natural talent with which to express himself, but relatively little self to express. In the second, he has enlarged himself through experience, but his talents are thwarted by external forces. In both phases, his artistic life and family life—for Vonnegut, the two are practically identical—are frustrated by his immaturity.

Under Gregory, Rabo learns to "counterfeit" reality, naïvely following his master's directive to "make a super-realistic painting" by drawing "everything the way it really is" (131, 133). Rabo obliges with a picture to make Van Eyck proud:

> The bone was bone, the fur was fur, the hair was hair, the dust was dust . . . and the water dripping from the skylight in my painting was not only the wettest water you ever saw: in each droplet, if you looked at it through a magnifying glass, there was the whole damned studio! (146–47)

This painting represents the culmination of Rabo's first mimetic phase. Though his style is similar to his master's, their aims clearly differ. Depicting objects in banal and almost random detail, Rabo places much less emphasis than Gregory does on the emotive, subjective side of the creative process. In terms of expressiveness, Rabo's painting is even blanker than those of the photorealists of the 1970s. Painters such as Cottingham and Goings give viewers mundane, amazingly literal pictures of diners, store fronts, and shopping malls, but their paintings often convey an arch, condescending opinion of the objects conveyed (e.g., Hughes 364). Metaphorically speaking, Gregory and Cottingham are like photographers, one sentimental, the other affectless, who articulate their human subjectivity through framing and lighting. By contrast, Rabo is like "a reasonably good camera" that takes detailed pictures in whichever direction it is pointed (44). *Bluebeard* does not, then, valorize mimetic techniques if they imply detail for detail's sake—which is not surprising considering that in mid-career Vonnegut agrees "with Kilgore Trout about realistic novels and their accumulations of nit-picking details" (*Breakfast* 740).

Taken to extremes, mimesis and abstraction thus become equally formalistic, equally inhuman. To be fair, though, Rabo's first failure to express himself is not entirely his fault. Young and inexperienced, he has talent but few ideas. To accent the relationship between his character's age and aesthetic, Vonnegut situates two formative experiences at significant moments in Rabo's career. The

first is his sexual initiation with Marilee Kemp, Gregory's mistress. After Rabo
puts the finishing touches on this "sexual masterpiece" (164), he is ejected from
Gregory's home, his career as a realistic painter effectively halted by the realities of the Depression (177–83). This interruption is extended by World War II,
during which he practices his illusionist techniques in a camouflage unit (2).
Rabo undergoes his second formative experience at the close of hostilities,
when, as a prisoner of war, he witnesses from "the rim of a great green valley"
an "[u]nforgettable" sight (198–99): the release of prisoners on V-E Day. These
events, one a spontaneous sexual masterpiece, the other the raw stuff of an artistic masterpiece, would seem bookends to his maturation, with the second providing the enduring images through which he may finally express his subjective awareness. Regrettably, the accidents of world history, art history, and
personal history prevent Rabo from expressing himself in paint for forty years.

In art history's simplistic conventional narrative, the Holocaust, coupled
with European modernism's emphasis on innovation and abstraction, gave
painters the impetus to look for a new visual grammar with which to express
new realities (Hughes 298–99). Putatively responding to this impetus were such
legends as Pollock, Gorky (an Armenian emigré), de Kooning, Rothko, Kline,
Gottlieb, Still, Newman, and Guston, among others. Vonnegut, however, does
not wholly accept this conventional view, as suggested by his comparison of
Rabo with Pollock and Kitchen. Having failed as a realist, Rabo adopts the
abstract expressionists' formalistic bent because he lives in New York, understands the drift of art history (44), and longs for playful, painterly companionship (45). Unfortunately, these external factors, variously social and historical,
are at odds with Rabo's talents, so the untraditional methods they inspire stifle
his response to World War II. Vonnegut further emphasizes this through his
depiction of Pollock and the fictional Kitchen, neither of whom can draw. It is
significant that Vonnegut disparages neither painter for poor draftsmanship.
Rather, he implies that they opt for abstraction for internal reasons, ones having little to do with World War II or "new realities." Each has the painter's traditional need to express himself through paint, but unlike Rabo, each lacks the
painter's traditional talents. They have *no choice* but to experiment with untraditional methods until they discover their gifts—as if to imply that all people
are gifted in one way or another.

Ironically, then, abstract expressionism frustrates Rabo's expressive tendencies during his second creative phase. Of Rabo, Pollock, and Kitchen, only
Rabo *chooses* his style. This may explain why Rabo's style, which recalls Newman's cold chromatic abstraction (or color-field painting) and Reinhardt's
colder minimalism, is the least expressive of the three. His paintings, silent and
aloof, consist of huge monochromatic fields split into two by Newmanesque
"zips," that is, vertical bands of tape. Rabo interprets these bright stripes as
souls, each evoking its separate narrative (202).[7] Naturally, his arbitrary interpretation is unlikely to come across to his viewer—especially since he gives his
painting titles "*meant* to be uncommunicative," titles like "Opus Nine" and

"Windsor Blue Number Seventeen" (35; Vonnegut's italics). Even Newman gave his works titles meant to evoke the painting's intended content—though some of these, for example, "Vir Heroicus Sublimis," seem overblown. Unlike Newman and other abstract expressionists,[8] Rabo accepts the radical formalist position that his paintings should be autotelic, "about nothing but themselves" (229). Consequently, he at first regrets "seeing stories" in his paintings, interpreting his intuitive perceptions as evidence that he is still at heart a hack:

> But I had a secret, which I have never told anybody before: "Once an illustrator, always an illustrator!" I couldn't help seeing stories in my own compositions of strips of colored tape applied to vast, featureless fields of Sateen Dura-Luxe. This idea came into my head uninvited, like a nitwit tune for a singing commerical, and would not get out again; each strip of tape was the soul at the core of some sort of person or lower animal. (202)

That Rabo is embarrassed by his artistic inclinations suggests he is more interested in belonging, in adhering to the aesthetic ideology of a school, than in expressing himself in paint. Unfortunately, his particular talent does not lend itself to this particular school. Indeed, the contrast between the self-consciousness of Rabo and the spontaneity of Pollock and Kitchen could not be more overt. As action painters, Pollock and Kitchen belong to an earlier, less academic phase of abstract expressionism, one Vonnegut depicts as playful, decorative, and expressive of the artist's unselfconscious delight at happening upon his natural gifts. As an abstract expressionist, Rabo is a polemicist, "a talker instead of a painter" (164). In contrast, Kitchen with his spray rig, like Pollock with his dancing paintsticks, is a "real painter, so he hardly talked at all" (165). The joy of painting is their thing, and their vibrant paintings (which in his "author's note" Vonnegut refers to as "the mudpies of art" [i]) express that childlike joy, doing the talking for them. Ergo, Vonnegut does not *ipso facto* disapprove of abstract expressionism and its techniques. Rather, he specifically disapproves of Rabo's embarrassed retreat into a cold, silent aesthetic, one that betrays his lived experiences by first betraying his inborn gifts.

Rabo's abstract expressionist paintings are not strictly anti-humanistic insofar as they are the product of his human relationship with the painters who serve as his extended "synthetic family" (7). But even here Vonnegut disapproves insofar as Rabo uses one set of human relationships as an immature way of escaping another set, i.e., his first wife, Dorothy, and the two sons he names for painters, Henri (Matisse) and Terry (Kitchen). This leads, first, to a distinction that Vonnegut draws between the literary and the visual, and second, to his perception of art's perilous fluctuation between the aesthetic and the anaesthetic. It is typical of artists like Gregory, Kitchen, Pollock, and even Rabo's father, a cobbler who makes bejeweled cowboy boots, to get so involved in the act of creation that "the whole rest of the world dropped away" (138). To some degree, Vonnegut views this solitary obsession as a natural and necessary aspect of the creative process—and an aspect with considerable therapeutic potential. According to Vonnegut, the painter "gets his rocks off while actually doing the painting. The act itself is agreeable" (qtd. in Reed 207). The implication is that he does not find writing equally agreeable. Indeed, he has been known to use graphic art as a restorative after the rigors of writing (Reed 206).[9] This implication is further supported by his novels. In Vonnegut's work, creators who find a similar relief in the act of creation are typically visual artists like Salo, the Tralfamadorian robot in *The Sirens of Titan* (1959) who relieves his boredom through sculpture, becoming more human in the process (240). For the writer, by contrast, the creative act is typically a task to be finished—and sometimes an afflictive task, at that—so completion and reception afford the greatest joy. Hence Rabo contends in *Bluebeard* that if a painter were fired into space in a capsule, he would need only his art materials for enjoyment, whereas Circe Berman, a Judy Blume-type writer, would require a "finished, proofread manuscript . . . along with somebody from her publishing house" to achieve similar pleasure (151).

Unfortunately, an artist may abuse the pleasures of creation such that they become a permanent anaesthetic escape instead of a temporary aesthetic restorative. Art then becomes a hindrance to human expression rather than its vehicle. This is true of Rabo's father, who numbs himself to the world, becoming "a perfectly contented, self-sufficient zombie," by making "perfectly beautiful cowboy boots" (64, 62). Similarly, the fascinations of his spray rig help Kitchen escape his father. Eventually, he becomes such a solipsist that when Rabo looks into his eyes, "there wasn't anybody home anymore" (63). For Vonnegut, the fact that Kitchen's paintings may be superior to those of Pollock and Rothko cannot atone for the anti-humanistic function of his creative acts. Rabo is *Bluebeard*'s prime example of aesthetic escapism. He uses abstract expressionism to forget his family—and the inutile, inexpressive paintings that result lack the usefulness of his father's boots and the essential "*human wonder*" of Kitchen's paintings (281; Vonnegut's italics). "I had a very hard time getting the hang of civilian life after the war," Rabo admits, "then I discovered something as powerful and irresponsible as shooting up with heroin: if I started laying on just one color of paint to a huge canvas, I could make the whole world drop away" (138). As a consolation, anaesthetic, and escape from human responsibility, *his* painting is, therefore, very much like his drinking, a point he later denies (281).

Vonnegut is not entirely unsympathetic to this anaesthetic use of art, and naturally, perceivers are as apt to resort to it as creators. And certainly, his belief that writers should provide people with "better lies," with fictions engineered to console and entertain, is well documented (*Conversations* 78; see also 12, 77; Harris 135; Merrill and Scholl 146). Nevertheless, Vonnegut takes a balanced approach in his own fictions, mixing jokes and comforting lies with discomfiting realities, for he knows that left unrestricted, the lie can exacerbate the suffering it was meant to relieve. The only people for whom he prescribes total escape into fiction are the "dumb people, who are in terrible trouble" because their limited intellects make them unfit to deal with despair in any other way (*Conversations* 91; see also Merrill and Scholl 147). The rest of us are obligated to remain sensitive to reality, resorting to aesthetics and anaesthetics on a temporary basis only.

The best example of such a helpless moron is Billy Pilgrim of *Slaughterhouse-Five* (1969). Pilgrim is relieved of his painful memories of war by the science fiction of Kilgore Trout, and, in particular, by his Tralfamadorian notion of time.[10] Vonnegut refers to these ideas as "horseshit"—albeit of "a useful, comforting sort" (*Conversations* 77). Though it seems everything that can be said about this conception of time has already been said in the criticism, it is useful to point out that the Tralfamadorians have a peculiarly aesthetic—and as it happens, anaesthetic—perspective. The Tralfamadorians perceive history as they would a painting, that is, "at a glance," and construct novels reflective of this timeless, nonlinear view (*Slaughterhouse* 51–52). Inhuman aesthetes, they encourage Billy to focus on "pleasant moments" and to take a dispassionate, aesthetically disinterested attitude toward time and memory (*Slaughterhouse* 65). That is, after all, how one appreciates artworks; since the Tralfamadorians view the universe as a similarly predetermined structure, they approach the two in identical ways. If these notions act as a salve, helping Billy cope with despair, they also have obvious drawbacks, the most crucial of which is the abandonment of ideas Vonnegut considers essentially human: free will, conscience, moral action, and so on. (Hence the Tralfamadorians do not prevent the destruction of the universe, since that "moment is *structured* that way" [*Slaughterhouse* 65; Vonnegut's italics].) In resorting to the Tralfamadorian aesthetic, then, Billy becomes inhuman himself—like the alien robots, and like Winston Niles Rumfoord, the chrono-synclastically infidibulated source of this "beautifully detached viewpoint" in *The Sirens of Titan* (155).

That Billy must sacrifice aspects of his humanity is for Vonnegut a sad but necessary act of self-preservation. A larger, if somewhat comic, danger inheres in his desire to preach Tralfamadorianism on television (*Slaughterhouse* 106). This represents a danger insofar as Billy's unwittingly irresponsible words might encourage others to passively accept future horrors akin to that of Dresden. As Trout learns in *Breakfast of Champions*, artists are responsible for their ideas (614–15)—which explains why no Vonnegut novel is particularly comforting. Indeed, Billy-*qua*-preacher presents much less of a threat than the wholly unscrupulous artist who manipulates the masses by numbing them with sentimental consolations or stimulating them with romantic lies.

Gregory is such an artist. An Armenian immigrant himself, Gregory is Horatio Alger in the Ayn Rand mold, having risen to become "the highest paid artist in American history" by dint of his talent, discipline, and self-confidence (49). Vonnegut emphasizes Gregory's cynicism by comparing his best-selling children's books to those of Circe Berman. Under the *nom de plume* of "Polly

Madison," Circe writes frank, realistic works "a dozen universes removed" from those illustrated by Gregory (57). His drawings, which Rabo refers to as "commercial kitsch" (141), are realistic in technique and detail, but their thrust is to flatter America's unrealistic notion of itself as a thriving, homogeneous nation of Anglo-Saxons. His work ranges from Rockwellesque sentimentality to Riefenstahlesque romanticism, with the former encouraging Americans to accept with complacent serenity the fascist European violence encouraged by the latter. For Vonnegut, Gregory is unforgivable not in his condescension toward his audience, or even in his manipulation of it, but in his complete lack of sympathy for it. To him, Americans are "'[s]poiled children . . . begging for a frightening but just Daddy'" (132). Since painters are "'the justices of the Supreme Court of Good and Evil,'" (134), they must, according to Gregory, present their audience with lies tailored to serve the good of society. The latter would resonate with Vonnegut's idea of the writer's social obligation if Gregory did not explicitly associate "the good" with war and machinery and "the evil" with the human body (134). Thus he creates pictures that refute Rabo's naïve prewar belief that "nobody could ever be fooled by romantic pictures and fiction and history into marching to war again" (140). Fittingly, Gregory dies in the service of his ideal "Daddy," Mussolini.

Vonnegut identifies Gregory's antimodernism as a species of antihumanism through which politics and aesthetics intertwine. In Gregory's view, artists should rule the masses from above by practicing a single, uniform aesthetic akin to the neoclassicism prescribed by Hitler and the social realism prescribed by Stalin as antidotes to the "degenerate" pessimism of modernism.[11] Like those dictators, Gregory would destroy the bastions of modern art, beginning with its capital, the Museum of Modern Art (132). In critical honesty, however, it should be noted that Gregory is Bluebeard's beauty spot, a tin villain whose unnuanced characterization is as caricatured in its depiction of fascism as Gregory's own illustrations. Vonnegut enjoys much greater success depicting through his narrator the ways in which modernism and art history betray art's humanistic purpose.

The true if subtle villain of Bluebeard is the word "serious," which at first seems innocuous, but which slowly gathers resonance as the novel continues. For Vonnegut, ideas like "serious art" and "the serious artist" are products of the vast techno-economic processes shaping art history—processes that are the common ancestor of Gregory's popular antimodernism and the Abstract Expressionists' elitist modernism. On one hand, modernism's ideology of "the serious" has resulted in the wonders of Picasso, Braque, Matisse, Klee, Pollock, and others. On the other, it has reduced the number of people willing to create art—which for Vonnegut and John Dewey should be "a record and celebration of the life of a civilization" (Dewey 326)—by rewarding, often with preposterous sums of money, geniuses, derivative specialists, and impressive charlatans. It has also reduced the audience for art by encouraging a novelty for novelty's sake that intimidates viewers through calculated shock and obscurity

(157; see also Gombrich 502; Beardsley 283–313; Hughes 373–76). On a more personal scale, Vonnegut suggests that failure as a "serious artist" may cause an artist like Rabo to submit to a debilitating self-consciousness, which in turn precipitates the betrayal of natural gifts and the false perception of a Platonic split between body and soul. Success may be worse. Vonnegut suggests that success as "a serious artist" may drain the playfulness from the work of a great but limited artist like Pollock, leaving him with few options. Together, these problems lead Rabo and Pollock to depression, with Rabo living in isolation and Pollock committing virtual suicide.

To begin with, the association of "serious art" with pain, alienation, and increasing abstraction is in Vonnegut's construction of art history a clichéd response to technical innovations. Without such innovations, the artist might still have a vital place in society like a farmer or a software designer, and "serious art" would not have unquestioned ideological value—does anyone, after all, attach elitist pretensions to software design? Instead, the artist has been ghettoized in competitive, self-destructive enclaves—with Greenwich Village, and the Cedar Tavern in particular, being Vonnegut's primary example. It is no accident, then, that Rabo Karabekian's defining characteristic is loneliness. After his mother dies, Rabo scrambles from one "family" to another but never quite feels at home. Compounding this loneliness are his artistic gifts, which, in conjunction with the romantic cliché of the artist as a tortured, talented *isolato* in rebellion against bourgeois convention, automatically set him apart from ordinary America. Like Vonnegut, Rabo is elegiac in longing for a rosy, bygone era during which the artist had an organic social function:

> I was obviously born to draw better than most people, just as the widow Berman and Paul Slazinger were obviously born to tell stories better than most people can. Other people are obviously born to sing and dance or explain the stars in the sky or do magic tricks or be great leaders or athletes, and so on.
>
> I think that I could go back to the time when people had to live in small groups of relatives—maybe fifty or a hundred people at the most. And evolution or God or whatever arranged things genetically, to keep the little families going, to cheer them up, so that they could all have somebody to tell stories around the campfire at night, and somebody else to paint pictures on the walls of the caves, and somebody else who wasn't afraid of anything and so on. (74–75)

Though Rabo does not claim to be a latter-day Dürer, he does claim that he would, had he "'lived ten thousand years ago . . . have wowed the cave dwellers of Lascaux, France'" (252–53). Unfortunately, he perceives human history as a gradual drift, then a quick jerk, away from this integration of artist and community. Technological innovations like "the printing press and radio and television" have made "simply moderate giftedness" obsolete since modern communications have put distant communities in touch with such "world champions" of art as Gregory (76). Mere talent is no longer enough; now an artist must be an *auteur* of supreme talent, shocking originality, and total aesthetic commitment. The invention with the most stunning impact on art history is the camera:

> I could catch the likeness of anything I could see. . . . But cameras could do . . . what I could do. And I knew that it was this same thought which had sent the Impressionists and the Cubists and the Dadaists and the Surrealists and so on in their quite successful efforts to make good pictures which cameras . . . could not duplicate. (43–44)

Having had it impressed on him by Gregory and Bauerbeck, another representational painter, that he would never amount to anything more than "a reasonably good camera" (44), Rabo abandons his "boyhood dream of being an artist" (43).

But technology betrays Rabo in a more devastating way. He resumes the dream upon meeting the abstract expressionists in Greenwich Village after the war, but by then his dream has morphed into the pursuit of a specifically "serious art" (44). Since "seriousness" has at that point come to be routinely if naïvely equated with abstract methods, he abandons his natural talents. "[N]ot drawing and forgetting everything I knew about art," Rabo recollects, seemed like "the magic key to my becoming a serious artist" (253). The resulting paintings, which command what Vonnegut considers "grotesque prices" in an art market dictated by a few influential critics such as Clement Greenberg and Harold Rosenberg (i), have a limited, specialized audience, which further alienates painters like Rabo from ordinary society. In *Bluebeard*, this notion of "ordinary society" is more than just another abstraction. Its ranks include Rabo's first wife, Dorothy, not to mention the servants and hangers-on who share his estate decades later—all of whom are open in expressing their antipathy for Rabo's art collection. Nevertheless, Rabo finds success, as measured by friendship and financial gain, only to experience his most humiliating reversal when his paintings disintegrate due to a faulty miracle, Sateen Dura-Luxe. Art and technology again combine to isolate Rabo, who embarrasses the abstract expressionists by becoming a comic footnote to art history. He keeps his money and art collection but loses his reputation as a serious modernist artist. Worse, he loses his painter friends, "since the ridicule my own paintings attracted and deserved encouraged Philistines to argue that *most* painters were charlatans or fools. But I can stand loneliness, if I have to" (9).

But does he really have to? Rabo remains aware throughout his life that he is drawn to Gregory, Bauerbeck, and especially the abstract expressionists by loneliness first, art second, seriousness third—yet ironically, it is his desire for seriousness that reinforces his loneliness and enervates his art. When he visits Bauerbeck, for example, he looks forward to joining the other art students because they "seemed to be a happy family, and I needed one" (180). Yet despite his consciousness that the value of aesthetic experience is measured in human terms, Rabo internalizes the idea of artistic "seriousness" and its corollaries through his artistic rejections. Upon asking Bauerbeck for "lessons in how to be a serious painter" (179), he relearns the lesson learned from Gregory, that is, that merely painting well is not enough. Rabo comes to Bauerbeck looking for a family and leaves thinking he must paint seriously, that is, with "*soul*" (146), to be accepted into such a family.

Abstract expressionism and his "zips" provide a temporary solution. The irony of Sateen Dura-Luxe, then, is more peculiar than it first seems. By causing his emblem of the soul to flake away, *the paint itself* seems to laugh at Rabo's self-defeating search for seriousness. It is a laugh that reverberates for decades. Years later when a woman offers Rabo the remains of "Windsor Blue Number Seventeen," she tells him that she recognized the massive canvas from an art-appreciation course in which the professor used before-and-after slides of Rabo's painting "'to lighten up the course,'" the rest of which "'was so *serious*'" (261; Vonnegut's italics).[12] This final aesthetic rejection by a brand of paint—which doubles as a social rejection in that it severs his relationship with the abstract expressionists, for whom he has in effect sacrificed his first wife and two sons—ends Rabo's quest for seriousness. This would seem like an ameliorative development if it did not also curtail his painting career for decades. Rabo, then, gives up on seriousness not because he has learned to question its ideological value but because he has come to accept that as a "[s]erious artist" he will forever remain a "[f]loparoo" (232).

Though Rabo seemingly understands the historical processes that enmesh him, for most of the book he is unable to transcend these processes. Aesthetically, his internalization of modernist ideology weakens his artistic production as a prelude to halting it altogether. Socially, this ideology leaves him bereft of family and friends alike. Worse, it leaves him ill-equipped to form new relationships. Rabo's self-consciousness, i.e., the social residue of past artistic desires, apparently determines his "life as a museum guard" (8). By the time Circe contaminates his sterility with liveliness, he has lost his abstract expressionist-era playfulness—and not even Circe in her mammoth bossiness conquers his stiffness easily. When she recommends he resume his painting "since it used to give [him] such pleasure," Rabo responds in a way she cannot yet understand: "'I have had all I can stand of not taking myself seriously'" (151). Rabo delivers these arch, exquisitely anal replies—which contrast sharply with his naturally free-and-easy prose style—to a number of Circe's entreaties. Thus his refusal to dance: "'I am not going to sacrifice my one remaining shred of dignity on the altar of Terpsichore'" (179). What Rabo in his mammoth self-absorption cannot yet understand is that Circe dances and plays pool as a way of dealing with the loss of her spouse. Her dabblings in dance, like Vonnegut's in paint, are primarily therapeutic. Luckily for Rabo, Circe later explains that "talking loud and brassy, telling everybody what to do" also has this beneficial side effect (285). In the end, her aggressive snoopiness is the key to unlocking the potato barn and with it the self-consciousness that has so shriveled his life. By refusing to show Circe the potato-barn painting or even to demonstrate his drawing talents, Rabo claims he is "'clinging to his dignity and self-respect as best he can'" (259). But after he explains that he plans to reveal his potato-barn painting posthumously so that he will not "'be around when people say whether it is any good or not'" (267), Circe correctly identifies his self-consciousness as cowardice. Cowed, he shows her the painting; from then on an unending stream of visitors enlivens his estate (269).

A closely related consequence of this internalization process involves the false, Platonic split that Rabo comes to perceive between the body—which Rabo, in the typical fashion of a Vonnegut narrator, refers to as "meat"—and the soul. If Rabo's quest for seriousness has the ill-consequence of alienating him from art and society, it has the further ill-consequence of alienating him from his physical self. In the usual reading, *Bluebeard* culminates with Rabo's successful reconciliation of body and soul (e.g., Kopper 583). This makes sense, considering that in the closing paragraph, Rabo thanks his body and then says, "Oh, happy Soul. Oh, happy Meat. Oh, happy Rabo Karabekian" (287). Still, if this interpretation is broadly correct, it is also crudely inadequate to Vonnegut's nuanced treatment of the body-soul distinction and its dualistic twin in the aesthetic sphere, the form-content distinction. Vonnegut implies that Rabo's mistake, as conditioned by dogmatic, imprecise role models, is to conceive of these dualisms as each consisting of two absolute, Platonic terms rather than of two relative, conceptually expedient terms. This leads Rabo to the false conclusion that the terms of each dualism are separable conceptually, ethically, and aesthetically, which in turn contributes to the inhibiting self-consciousness previously discussed. Though Rabo never fully understands the nature of his error, he indirectly overcomes it at the end through his highly self-conscious scheme to hide his painting, which eliminates his potential audience and thus, ironically, frees him to paint unselfconsciously.

In "On Style" (1965), Susan Sontag notes that though "[e]veryone is quick to avow that style and content are indissoluble," in the practice of criticism, "the old antithesis lives on, virtually unassailed" (15). The reason, she suggests, is that the distinction has practical value, allowing critics to communicate more precisely. Yet once it is forgotten that "form" and "content" are pragmatic and relative terms, that is, different ways of talking about the same thing rather than true Platonic antitheses, the distinction becomes pernicious. This is the lesson to be drawn from Rabo's experience with Gregory and Bauerbeck, two of the worst art critics in recent American fiction. As a youth, Rabo does not consider the soul as such until his teachers explain his essential unseriousness in terms of the essential soullessness of his paintings. When Gregory tells Rabo that his painting lacks soul, he means that its expressive content is relatively slender. Unfortunately, he fails to explain that "expressive content" is contingent on practicalities—for example, astute creative choices and astute viewer reception—and not on the artist's possession of a transcendent, Platonic soul (146). Bauerbeck compounds Gregory's error by associating content (hence the artist's soul) with the truly miserable cliché of romantic pain (181). The latter rejection disheartens Rabo, whose disaffection with his body derives from his assumption that his talents are purely physical. Rabo then proceeds to seek a purely formal art because he has been led to think he has little soul hence little talent for content. That this thought causes him to betray his talent for representation is *Bluebeard*'s saddest aesthetic irony.

Abstract expressionism, then, is the stone with which Rabo attempts to kill three birds. It gives him an artificial family; it allows him to be "serious" in an era in which seriousness is equated with abstraction; and it obviates content altogether, since in his estimation abstract expressionist paintings are autotelic, "about absolutely nothing but themselves" (8). If the last idea is the furthest reach of dualistic, formalistic rhetoric, it is no more ludicrous than the dualistic, contentualist rhetoric of Rothko, Gottlieb, and Newman—whose manifestoes recall Schopenhauer's definition of art, a theory combining two essentialist warhorses, Plato's Idea and Kant's thing-in-itself (Schopenhauer 184–85). In other words, these painters considered their art content distilled, with their theories forming an aesthetic so extreme it might be termed "the decorative sublime":

> We are for flat forms because they destroy illusion and reveal truth. . . . It is a widely accepted notion among painters that it does not matter what one paints as long as it is a well painted. This is the essence of academicism. There is no such thing as good painting about nothing. We assert that the subject is crucial and only that subject-matter is valid which is tragic and timeless. (qtd. in McCarthy 170)

Beware those secret Nietzscheans who contend that illusion destroys illusion! These ideas exactly oppose Rabo's autotelic idea—although in their recourse to absolutism the two are identical. De Kooning is more sensible. He claims that abstract expressionism, which is relatively inexpressive due to the extremity of its abstractions, diminishes content until it is "tiny—very tiny, content" (qtd. in Gaugh 116). Very tiny, yet still crucially there—an idea Marilee supports by noting that the abstract expressionists "have failed to paint pictures of nothing" (231). Like de Kooning's, Vonnegut's idea is sensible. There is no going beyond content or beyond subject matter—or even, for that matter, beyond representationalism. Despite his embarrassed, ultimately sterile retreat into putatively autotelic forms, Rabo all but gathers this same sensible idea through his inescapable identification of tiny, vertical souls, that is, forms of content, in his abstract expressionist paintings.

Rabo should not credit absolutes, but he does so anyway largely because his rejections have been framed in those terms—which is to say that Rabo's belief in those who reject him contributes to his isolation. Because they spend their time painting rather than participating in "the blather of art" (44), the truly gifted abstract expressionists do not credit dualistic rhetoric, as suggested by a conversation between Rabo and Kitchen:

> "I can't help it," I said. "My soul knows my meat is doing bad things, and is embarrassed. But my meat just keeps right on doing bad, dumb things."
>
> "Your what and your what?" he said.
>
> "My soul and my meat," I said.
>
> "They're separate?" he said.
>
> "I sure hope they are," I said. I laughed. "I would hate to be responsible for what my meat does."
>
> I told him, only half joking, about how I imagined the soul of each person, myself included, as being a sort of flexible neon tube inside. All the tube could do was receive news about what was happening with the meat, over which it had no control. (246)

Kitchen does not understand Rabo's dualistic distinction because he is not a self-conscious painter. Like Pollock, his gift for abstract expressionism, a gift variously registered as "soul" and "content," is physically spontaneous. Ironically, Rabo does not manifest a similarly gifted, similarly physical spontaneity until he experiences a "vision . . . of human souls unencumbered, unembarrassed by their unruly meat" (265). This inspires Rabo not in its valorization of the soul but in its valorization of unselfconsciousness. Not until he has come up with a highly artificial plan to eliminate his audience, however, is he able to curtail his self-consciousness, giving his physical talents the free play necessary to express his soul, that is, his subjective attitude toward his lived experiences. Thus his treatment of V-E Day is relatively spontaneous. "'My soul didn't know what kind of picture to paint,'" Rabo admits, "'but my meat sure did'" (287). This permits just two interpretations. Either Vonnegut is celebrating the dualistic ascendancy of the body or, far more probably, the indivisibility of the body-soul unity, with "body" and "soul," like "form" and "content," being two different ways of talking about the same irreducible thing.

The saddest aspect of Rabo's self-consciousness is its lack of necessity. He grasps only in retrospect the evolution of modernist ideology, but he has clues all along that this ideology is flawed. One important, long-forgotten clue comes by way of the tailor and secret painter, Isadore Finkelstein. Embarrassed by his "unambitious" realism when in the presence of the abstract expressionists (239), Finkelstein hides his paintings until his death. Thus he is an analogue for the older Rabo, who, in hiding his painting, fails to recall the lesson in the tailor's paintings. (Indeed, Rabo is wearing a suit made by Finkelstein when he decides to hide his gigantic final painting [265].) After inspecting these paintings, the young Rabo admires not only their quality but also that, regardless of his technique or his "seriousness," Finkelstein "enjoyed paint [and] appreciated reality." Instructive is an earlier conversation between Finkelstein and Rabo:

> At the end of that evening, I remember, he said to me: "I can't
> get over how passionate you guys are, and yet so absolutely *unserious*."
> "Everything about life is a joke," I said, "Don't you know that?"
> "No," he said. (238; Vonnegut's italics)

Finkelstein's problem is Rabo's. Art history intimidates and isolates, remitting art "to a separate realm, where it is cut off from association with the materials and aims of every other form of human effort, undergoing, and achievement" (Dewey 3). If an artwork is not a serious masterpiece, if its technique is neither innovative nor trendy, it is a secret shame under no circumstances to be shared lest the artist risk being labeled an "exhibitionist" (75). Yet Finkelstein learns here from Rabo, an ironic source to say the least, that "passion"—that is, a sincere, even *soulful* love of painting—is not to be confused with "seriousness"— that is, a self-conscious, ambitious attitude toward painting. One may love painting, it seems, even in a playful, exuberant, affectionately human way.

Rabo is not the only one to lose sight of art's exuberance to great ill consequence; the same proves true of Pollock. Rabo's seriousness results from his failures as a painter and his abilities as a draftsman, but, in Vonnegut's view, Pollock's seriousness results from his successes as a painter and his inabilities as a draftsman. Though Pollock died in a car crash in 1956, Vonnegut interprets his drunk driving as tantamount to a death wish and his accident as tantamount to suicide. Thus the factors spurring his self destruction may to some extent be applied to the other abstract expressionists who self-destruct, including Gorky (1948), Rothko (1970), and the fictional Kitchen.

Unlike Rabo, Pollock's playfulness inheres in his abstract expressionist works as well as his relationship with fellow painters. Recalling the early 1950s, Rabo notes that "[e]verything we said [then] was a kind of joke. I still don't understand how things got so gruesomely serious for Pollock and Kitchen after only six more years" (237). Vonnegut supplies the answer to this question in his "author's note" and in several interviews. In a reference to Pollock, Vonnegut implies that a painter's financial success contributes to the problem: "Tremendous concentrations of paper wealth have made it possible for a few persons or institutions to endow certain sorts of human playfulness with inappropriate and hence distressing seriousness" (i). In other words, the "serious" money being paid for paintings leads painters to betray the playful intentions of paintings originally perceived as therapeutic "mudpies." Pollock, it seems, has the bad luck to be favored with gifts favored by art history:

> . . . people are doomed to be the sorts of artist they are. I wrote an
> introduction to a special Franklin Library edition of *Bluebeard* . . . it
> says, essentially, why I think Jackson Pollock was so unhappy at the
> end of his short life: he lacked maneuverability, because he was in
> fact trapped both by society and by his own particular talent into
> doing what he did. He was rendered unmaneuverable, one, by the
> response of society, which was, "Hey, these things are extremely

> valuable. You've got to keep doing this." But the other problem was
> that he didn't have that many options. The fact was that he could
> not draw very well. (*Conversations* 265)

Thus Rabo's warning to "[b]eware of gods bearing gifts!" (188). The blessing is
a curse in that painters like Pollock, an unacquisitive soul who prefers the initial
playfulness to the ancillary cash, have no second blessing. Their style is dictated
by a singular gift. Once that style is drained of its joy due to the judgments of
art history and the laws of supply and demand, they have no way of recapturing
that joy. To a degree, the same applies to Rabo. As an abstract expressionist, he
claims to be a painter with "*options*" (256; Vonnegut's italics). Rabo later recognizes, however, that he never had any options as far as abstract expressionism was
concerned (82). Unlike the doubly gifted de Kooning and Guston, who alter-
nate freely between abstraction and figuration, Rabo is restricted by his talent to
mimetic techniques. This is his disaster, for unlike Pollock, he actively courts
seriousness and society's approval. The gods of art history are not on his side.

As David Rampton puts it, Rabo's solution to his particular quandary as
an artist limited by his particular talents is to turn "his back on the entire movement in modernist art criticism, from Clive Bell to Herbert Read to Mark
Rothko, which systematically and inexorably rejected both the narrative and
representational dimensions of visual art as irrelevant" (21). Rabo dares to be
irrelevant and hence "unserious" by returning to representational techniques,
but he does so with a difference so significant that this return is far more than
a return to the past, whether his own or art history's. The difference is that his
final painting—which he refers to as a "whatchamacallit" (269), as if to empha-
size that it is unclassifiable by extant terminology and thus radically original—
shows that his talent for draftsmanship has been deepened, not abandoned,
through his discovery of his closely related talent for narrative. Though he
describes his painting as the serendipitous product of his "meat," Rabo does
seem to be responding to an *a priori*, hence a fully cognitive, insight into Gregory's shortcomings as a painter:

> But let's . . . focus on the works of Gregory. They were truth-
> ful about material things, but they lied about time. He celebrated
> moments. . . . But he lacked the guts or the wisdom, or maybe just
> the talent, to indicate somehow that time was liquid . . . and that all
> moments quickly run away.
>
> Let me put it another way: Dan Gregory was a taxidermist.
> He stuffed and mounted and varnished and mothproofed sup-
> posedly great moments, all of which turn out to be depressing
> dust-catchers. . . .
>
> Let me put it yet another way: life, by definition, is never still.
> Where is it going? From birth to death, with no stops on the way.
> Even a picture of a bowl of pears on a checkered tablecloth is liq-
> uid, if laid on canvas by the brush of a master. (82–83)

The foundation of his later aesthetic, this concept informs Rabo's "whatchamacallit," a.k.a. "Now It's the Women's Turn," and his autobiography, a.k.a. *Bluebeard*. It is interesting to note how directly this concept opposes the Tralfamadorian aesthetic, which once again suggests Vonnegut's misgivings about Billy's anaesthetic. Whereas the Tralfamadorians write novels that so dispense with time that they are perceived, like paintings, "at a glance," Rabo paints a painting that so revives narrative time that it is, like *Bluebeard* itself, filled with birth, death, and the full range of its creator's thoughts and prejudices. Plainly, it cannot be taken in "at a glance," meaning it must be read like a human novel. Further, unlike Tralfamadorianism, an inhuman aesthetic designed to console, Rabo's aesthetic focuses on the human experience of time as a line from birth to death. Thus it is humanistic and life affirming without being an unrealistic anaesthetic.

There is a sense in which Rampton is mistaken, however, about Rabo's having simply turned his back on abstraction. I began this essay by arguing that Rabo's reversion to representationalism does not imply Vonnegut's dismissal of abstract expressionism, and this is borne out by the way in which Rabo introduces Circe to "the whatchamacallit." Just as his idiosyncratic perception of his "zips" imply that all art is somewhat representational, this scene implies that all art is somewhat abstract. While describing the moment he turns on the lights, Rabo reminds his reader that they "would be seeing the picture compressed by foreshortening to a seeming triangle eight feet high, all right, but only five feet wide. There was no telling from that vantage point what the painting really was—what the painting was all *about*" (267; Vonnegut's italics). From this angle, Rabo's painting, which viewed frontally is "so realistic it might have been a photograph," elicits a gasp of approval from Circe, who describes it as a "'very big fence . . . every square inch of it encrusted with the most gorgeous jewelry'" (268). Like Edith Waltz of *Deadeye Dick* (1982), Circe has waged "a holy war against nonrepresentational art" (*Dick* 217); here Rabo persuades her that abstract works can be both expressive and pleasing in a decorative sense, for her thematically pertinent perceptions of the fence and the jewelry, in tandem with her sheer human "wonderment" (267), are effects calculated by the painter. Vonnegut reminds his reader of this abstract dimension as the pair leave the barn:

> I took one last look at "Now It's the Women's Turn," which was foreshortened again into a seeming triangle of close-packed jewels. I did not have to wait for the neighbors and Celeste's schoolmates to arrive before knowing that it was going to the most popular painting in my collection.
> "Jesus, Circe!" I said. "It looks like a million bucks!"
> "It really does," she said. (283)

The irony in these plain-spoken statements is as "close-packed" as the abstracted jewels. From a nonfigurative vantage, Rabo's painting literally "looks like a million bucks," while from a more literal vantage, it figuratively "looks like a million bucks." Both viewpoints provide an ironic contrast with his previous paintings, some of which were once worth a million dollars—though none of them looked it.

Rather than a rejection of abstract expressionism, then, Rabo's painting is a synthesis of his two immature phases—though its abstract dimension, in accord with his gifts, is secondary. The same is true of the Rabo's "other" masterpiece, *Bluebeard* itself, which suggests that his insights into Gregory's narrative shortcomings, along with his discovery *while painting* his "whatchamacallit" of his own narrative gift, have made him susceptible to Circe's recommendation that he write his life story. As it turns out, the autobiography is a realistic narrative with an extremely pleasing, tightly focused abstract structure. It is to the latter that I now turn, for I think it crucial to remember that *Bluebeard* could not make an impact on the strength of its ethical and intellectual depth alone. Like any successful novel that develops a coherent moral-aesthetic viewpoint, *Bluebeard* succeeds because it fulfills its aesthetic principles through the words and structures that reveal them. As it implies art must be, *Bluebeard* is superbly expressive, and its primary tools as an expressive artifact are both mimetic and narrative, which is entirely appropriate given the primary talents of its two authors, Vonnegut and Rabo. Nevertheless, *Bluebeard* also implies that the greatest art registers its fascination with human experience not through "pure" or exclusivist techniques but through techniques that bridge the imaginary gap between merely expedient concepts like "representationalism" and "formalism." *Bluebeard* satisfies this requirement through the degree to which its abstract structures, its jeweled patterns and crafted motifs, are unified by a single theme, the longing for community, which creates an overall unity of narrative and pattern unparalleled in Vonnegut's oeuvre.[13]

Though an abstraction, artistic unity is important to Vonnegut's aesthetic. Vonnegut perceives a direct connection between compositional unity and the theme of community. Unity thus has a dual function in *Bluebeard*, being at once a formal goal and a thematically significant aspect of a narrative whose focus is Rabo's yearning for community. The connection between unity and community is a third idea, that of "audience." As Vonnegut contends in interviews, "the secret of unity in art—in a painting or a book or a piece of music—is to do it in order to please one person . . . that's how to achieve unity. It's a great mistake to open the window and make love to the world" (*Conversations* 289).[14] In other words, artists should not compose for a *type* of audience, and certainly not for a mass audience in the cynical fashion of Gregory. The whole will be more tightly focused, more "of a piece," if it is guided by a single, specific relationship throughout. Because artists are judged by the unity of their compositions, following this principle makes them better artists—a point Circe makes to Rabo in discussing Marilee's letters:

> "You were her *audience*," she said. "Writers will *kill* for an
> audience."
> "An audience of *one?*" I said.
> "That's all she needed," she said. "That's all anybody needs.
> Just look at how her handwriting improved and her vocabulary
> grew. Look at all the things she found to talk about, as soon as she
> realized you were hanging on every word. . . . That's the secret of
> how to enjoy writing and how to make yourself meet high stan-
> dards," said Mrs. Berman. "You don't write for the whole world, and
> you don't write for ten people, or two. You write for just one per-
> son." (59–60; Vonnegut's italics)

A sexist as a naïf, Rabo fails to perceive this aspect of his relationship with Marilee and becomes "bored being her audience" (63). A significant proof of his
maturation, then, is his ability to rectify this mistake with Circe, from whom he
learns the value of an audience not through sermonizing alone but also through
the fact that she becomes his audience-of-one during the composition of *Bluebeard*. Not only does Circe encourage him to write *Bluebeard*, she also snoops
through it during its composition, offering commentary and criticism (e.g., 37).
As if to recognize the role she has played in shaping *Bluebeard* into a whole,
Rabo dedicates it to Circe: "This book is for Circe Berman. What else can I
say?" (vii). A further proof of his maturation is the reciprocal nature of this relationship. If Rabo finds an audience in Circe, she finds an audience in him as
well. As mentioned, Circe thinks it therapeutic to boss Rabo and snoop
through his unfinished book. This relieves her of the pain associated with the
death of her husband and former audience, Abe Berman ("I don't put anything
down on paper which Abe Berman wouldn't find interesting and truthful"
[60]). When Circe finds Rabo, she is a writer without an audience of-one, just
as Rabo has been a painter without an audience-of-one since he stopped mail-
ing sketches to Marilee. More than obvious is that Circe is grooming Rabo to
fill Abe Berman's role, a role inextricably emotional and aesthetic. (Considering that Rabo [1916–88] dies shortly after finishing *Bluebeard*, Circe's snooping
is itself an unfinished book.)
    Which clarifies two ideas. First, as gauged by its degree of internal coher-
ence or unity, *Bluebeard's* aesthetic quality is an indirect expression of Rabo's
regard for Circe, his intended audience, just as the quality of Vonnegut's *Bluebeard* is an indirect expression of his regard for whomever his intended audience was in writing the novel. Ergo, if mass-production techniques have forced
art to yield its vital place in extended families, as love's visible secretion, art may
still have a vital place in today's fractured communities of nuclear families. Second, in *Bluebeard* Rabo (along with Vonnegut) achieves an astonishing degree
of internal coherence, thus emphasizing his love for his intended audience to
the point of braggadocio, by using as his unifying principle the idea that human
beings require community. Though Rabo is unaware of it when he begins, his
single aim as a writer is to communicate to Circe the process by which he finds

his way home after a long, lonely period of wandering. While writing *Bluebeard,*
Rabo develops in a literary medium the narrative gifts discovered while painting "Now It's the Women's Turn."[15] He has, however, many nonnarrative, relatively abstract "options" when it comes to achieving this essentially narrative
aim. For as it happens, *all* of the novel's major abstract patterns are organized by
his yearning for community.

Naturally, there are far too many patterns in *Bluebeard* to test this itali-
cized assertion in any encyclopedic way—which, if anything, verifies the
novel's Byzantine quality. Some of these, including the gender motifs and the
fairy-tale allusions, have been dealt with elsewhere and require no comment.
Others, like the tripartite pattern of stylistic shifts, have been dealt with here—
and by now it should be obvious that only Rabo's final style succeeds in
expressing anything substantial to an audience-of-one (though in regard to the
painting, Circe is by necessity an *unintended* audience-of-one), which is the
surest way for an artist to find his way home. In the space left, I will concentrate on two other abstract patterns that interlock through the idea of community: the meaningful asymmetry of the overarching plot structures and the
intricate system of Homeric motifs.

As with several of Vonnegut's novels, *Bluebeard*'s format resembles a non-
fictional collage.[16] Since dadaism and surrealism and the happenings, it has
become a truism that collage is effective due to its initial illusion of random-
ness. Seemingly an *ad hoc* technique resulting in disunity, the technique actually
creates an art of radical juxtaposition that allows the artist to tap unexpected,
hence extremely effective, sources of thematic unity. The main determinant of
the collage format in *Bluebeard* is Rabo's tendency to shift quickly between two
different narrative structures, that is, the story of his life and of his summer. As
the following three points suggest, this temporal shiftiness is hardly random.

First, the categories of Rabo's alienation, as revealed and classified by his
life's story, are systematically disrupted and resolved through his relationship
with Circe Berman, as recounted by his summer diary. Vonnegut uses collage
techniques to elicit these subtle correspondences. Second, though the two narratives proceed according to divergent time scales, they converge via asymmetrical climaxes. The autobiography inexorably leads to the cathartic but socially
alienated moment when Rabo decides to paint his "whatchamacallit." An artist
who for practical reasons gives up on his audience, Rabo, a "hermit," resorts to
painting for therapeutic purposes only. His "Renaissance," then, is both positive
and depressing (265), his view of art's affirmations having shriveled in tandem
with his view of life's affirmations. The diary, however, is no less inexorable in
leading to the carthartic but communal moment when Circe views the
"whatchamacallit." By way of collage, the diary's climax surrounds and encapsulates the autobiography's climax, which occurred two-and-a-half years earlier
(264–68). Thus the shrunken, antisocial view of art's value entertained by Rabo
while painting his final canvas is not for a single page allowed to blot out the
rehabilitated, social view of art's value entertained by Rabo while viewing his

painting with Circe. As Rabo comes to realize, art's truly climactic therapy lies not in solitary creation but in communal expression. Finally, through his deft use of collage, Rabo proves his literary artistry. By superimposing one plot structure over another, he becomes a master of narrative time, embodying through absract structures his core belief "that time was liquid . . . that all moments quickly run away" (82).

Vonnegut often distinguishes between authors who respond directly to life and those who respond to life by way of art history. Whereas he places himself in the first category, he places Barth, Barthelme, and Borges in the second because they concentrate "on what we could call 'literary history,' in the sense that they're responding to literary experiments in the past and are refining them" (*Conversations* 215; see also 177). From the author of *Bluebeard*, a novel obsessed with art history, this might seem disingenuous if he did not clearly intend his distinction as a relative and expedient hedge against extremism. Just as Rabo should not have separated himself from society, art, and body, literature as a whole "should not disappear up its own asshole" (*Conversations* 185). On the other hand, Vonnegut's opposition to aesthetic separatism does not place him in the ranks of anti-intellectual, antihistorical, anti-aesthetic authors. Obviously, his works are intellectually and historically oriented. Less recognized is that his works are all distinctly mannered and richly allusive. *Bluebeard* achieves the greatest density in this regard, approaching Joycean or Nabokovian extremes, which is significant considering the author's fear of exclusivist, potentially antihumanistic techniques. There is logic in the novel's particularity. Vonnegut obviates his suspicion of extremism by putting *Bluebeard*'s obsessively literary elements at the service of themes and plots that argue against separatism, aesthetic or otherwise. The best example of this strategy may be the novel's Homeric motifs, which suggest that *Bluebeard* is as obsessed with literary history as it is with art history.

A few efficient paragraphs must suffice. The master theme of both *Bluebeard* and *The Odyssey* is the longing for community. Homer's major supporting themes are the laws of hospitality—in essence, primitive codes guiding social relations—and the difficulties of homecoming. The least hospitable host in *The Odyssey*, hence the paragon of misanthropy and incivility, is Polyphemus, the Cyclops, a gigantic, one-eyed hermit who threatens to eat his guest, Odysseus (Homer 214–29). Vonnegut makes Rabo one-eyed and has him refer to himself as a "Cyclops" and a "hermit" so as to refer to that force in his character that inclines toward Cyclopean isolation—and to label that characteristic essentially negative. Naturally, the figure most obsessed with home is Odysseus, who is a more complicated character than Polyphemus in that he begins as an error-prone hero before developing into a virtuous superhero. Before finding his home community, Odysseus must first learn the laws of hospitality through trial and error—with the crucial help of female deities such as Athene and Circe. Thus Vonnegut makes Rabo Odysseus's analogue so as to refer to that positive force in Rabo that longs for home. Unfortunately, as with Odysseus,

Rabo's homeward tendency is attached to immature impulses that complicate his journey. The joker in this deck of allusions is the rather pointed gender reversal. Though both works offer sexist perspectives, *The Odyssey* verges on misogyny, whereas *Bluebeard*, hoping to correct what Vonnegut considers one of Western culture's seminal mistakes, verges on misandry. Thus, in *The Odyssey*, Circe, a bewitching host, turns Odysseus's men into pigs until he forces her to stop, inspiring her lust and aid in the process (Homer 234–48). By contrast, in *Bluebeard*, Circe, a bewitching guest, forces Rabo to stop being the pig he has long been. Since lust has informed his problem, notably with Marilee (211–16), there is no question of his having sex with Circe (284). Her aid is asexual.

Before finding his home, which he ironically, or not so ironically, finds within his own house, Rabo must also learn the laws of hospitality. More like Polyphemus than Odysseus, he must learn them through his role as a host. Once a helpless guest himself (of Gregory, of Edith, etc.), the older Rabo has long opened his doors, including refrigerator doors, to strangers and hangers-on. For all that, he has only *seemed* like a good host, having alienated guests and servants alike by paying attention to them mainly through unintended insults. Instructive is the case of his housekeeper-cook, Allison White, and her daughter, Celeste. In contrast with Odysseus, who knows the value of good servants, Rabo admits his self-absorption in admitting he thinks of his housekeeper only when paying her (126). More interesting is his relationship with Celeste, whose friends abuse his hospitality, thus recalling Penelope's suitors. Rabo considers himself a good host for tolerating Celeste, who "lives here and eats my food, and entertains her loud and willfully ignorant friends on my tennis courts and in my swimming pool" (7). Throughout the summer-diary sections, Rabo harps on Celeste's ignorance, thinking it an index of cultural decline. He even tests her knowledge of Western culture (90), which in his view begins with Homer and culminates in the abstract expressionists. Rabo assumes that Celeste's ignorance of the ancient and modern classics proves her insensitivity to insults, which ironically proves his own insensitivity. Celeste has a different form of knowledge—a knowledge Circe considers worth studying. This keeps Circe in touch with experience, which in turn makes her books interesting to people like Celeste, who has read them all, making Circe "'the Homer of the bubblegum crowd'" (187). And Celeste is perceptive enough to understand insults. When Allison and Celeste threaten to leave, Rabo is stunned they would sacrifice his hospitality, the "rooms with ocean views . . . the run of the property, and no end of free snacks" (124). As it turns out, Allison wants "to be a human being and not a nobody and a nothing" and Celeste no longer wants to be mocked as "stupid" (126, 127).

Though she is unfamiliar with his works, Celeste knows more about Homer than Rabo does. The kind of knowledge Rabo seems to value is an empty knowledge, a knowledge for knowledge's sake that only deepens his isolation. Like the value of art, however, the value of knowledge registers through practical social relations—and this truth is closer to the spirit of Homer than to that of abstract expressionism. Hence, despite his factual knowledge of Homer's works, as a host he is not true to the spirit of those works until he begins interacting in a sensitive, affectionate way with his guests. Though Rabo at one point comically accuses Circe of having taken "advantage of [his] hospitality" (122), it is only through her "divine intervention" that he finds his way home by first embodying the lessons of Homeric hospitality, which were designed not to enlarge an aesthete's arrogance but to improve social relations through a didactic form of entertainment (Knox 28–36). That he finally learns the value of cultural knowledge is suggested when he recalls "the joke at the core of American self-improvement: knowledge was so much junk to be processed one way or another at great universities. The real treasure the great universities offered was a lifelong membership in a respected artificial extended family" (175).

As with Odysseus, there is never any doubt that Rabo will learn the laws of hospitality and find his way home. His joyously self-referential first paragraph predicts this outcome, not to mention his triumph over the alienating ideology of seriousness:

> Having written "The End" to this story of my life, I find it prudent to scamper back here to before the beginning, to my front door, so to speak, and to make this apology to arriving guests: "I promised you an autobiography, but something went wrong in the kitchen. It turns out to be a *diary* of this past troubled summer, too! We can always send out for pizzas if necessary. Come *in*, come *in*." (1; Vonnegut's italics)

Rabo's welcome to the reader, at first a stranger, is as warm as Menelaus's welcome to Telemachus, who is likewise at first a stranger (Homer 125). Through metaphor, Rabo's first paragraph is transformed into an open door, with the reader figuring as a guest, the book as a home and a meal, and its author as a playful, accommodating host—which, by referring to the end at the beginning rather than to the beginning at the end,[17] achieves a thematically apt effect that might be termed "open closure." Ergo, Vonnegut manages to make his collage format, asymmetrical narrative climaxes, and Homeric motifs—all of which are highly literary elements with the potential to degenerate into modes of aesthetic separatism—into organic aspects of a thematically unified whole. Speaking summarily thus reductively, the function of this whole is to express in a pleasing fashion Vonnegut's belief that aesthetic experience should be a communal activity designed to increase human kindness, thus answering the answerable question, "what are the arts for?"

NOTES

1. This is the Argument from Design, a Panglossian theory that compares existence to artifice in order to explain away suffering through the idea of an overall plan.

The optimism of this theory has informed the work of Paley, Pope, and, more recently, Nabokov. Skeptics such as Hume and Vonnegut reject the Argument from Design as an inappropriate analogy inspired by wishful thinking.

2. The common misperception of Vonnegut as an anti-aesthete or anti-intellectual derives from more than the didactic, humanistic purpose he assigns art. (Insofar as these tags imply his opposition to aesthetic and intellectual extremism, they are, however, appropriate.) The primary source of these pejoratives is his clear, concise prose style. Vonnegut neither plays "Henry Jamesian games" nor aims for long, lyrically opaque paragraphs, and thus his prose has a "real simplicity" (*Conversations* 48). Still, that he "never had that much fun with language" alone indicates neither that his books are simplistic nor that he is a simpleton (*Conversations* 297), for verbal clarity entails neither compostional nor intellectual simplicity. If novels like *Slaughterhouse-Five* and *Bluebeard* are lucid, they are also structurally dense and metaphorically complex.

3. This emphasis on art's human impact rather than its formal composition is what marks Vonnegut as an instinctive adherent of the expressionist theory of art. Consider, for example, that expressionist theory regards an artwork's artifactual nature as secondary to its ideation, that is, its expressive content. Thus prominent proponents of this theory such as Benedetto Croce and R. G. Collingwood consider the artwork all but dispensable once it has transmitted the artist's intention (Cooper 145). Naturally, an emphasis on the human side of art can be abused just as much as an emphasis on the thingly side of art. If formalist theory leads to the emptiest abstract expressionist paintings by Barnett Newman and Ad Reinhardt, expressionist theory leads to the emptiest conceptualist works—many of which have no physical reality at all. Vonnegut is an aesthetic moderate, relying on mimetic and formalistic techniques where they further his expressive ends.

4. Vonnegut emphasizes the radically subjective, extrinsic value of art through Circe's "chromos." These strike a group of Soviets (who expect only abstract expressionist masterpieces) as indecipherable kitsch until Rabo informs them that the chromos are meant to evoke the tragedies awaiting the girls depicted. As a result, they apologize "for not understanding the true import of the chromos, and said, now that I had explained them, they were unanimous in agreeing that these were the most important pictures" (149). A similar event occurs in *Breakfast of Champions* when Rabo explains to a hostile audience the referential value of the "zip" in "The Temptation of Saint Anthony" (712–13). In both cases, once the audience is led to the human value of the artwork, it quickly appreciates that artwork and a tiny community is formed—and in both cases, it seems as if Rabo has put something over on his audience.

5. I should note exceptions, including Loree Rackstraw's recognition that *Bluebeard* "is sympathetic to all artistic endeavors" (137) and James Lundquist's assertion that the novel is not "an attack on abstract expressionism" (288). More common is the notion that William Rodney Allen repeatedly suggests in an interview, that is, that Rabo's shifts are progressive, with his final style given authorial sanction as an improvement on abstract expressionism (*Conversations* 265–69). This idea, though submerged, also informs the partisan tone of Cliff McCarthy's criticism of Rabo (165–176). Other critics like Rampton and Mustazza avoid the question of a privileged style altogether. Vonnegut has for his part insisted that this tripartite stylistic movement was intuitive (*Conversations* 267).

6. Vonnegut studied cubism while at the University of Chicago, examining "what it took to form a revolutionary group" (Klinkowitz, *In America* 13–14). In *Bluebeard*, the abstract expressionists form the "revolutionary group" and Paul Slazinger supplies the ideas about revolutionary groups formed by Vonnegut while at Chicago (191).

7. Harold Rosenberg claims that Newman's famous "zip," often mocked as emblematic of a crack between two doors, was "recognized by Newman as his Sign; it stood for him as his transcendental self" (qtd. in Hughes 318). Another source may be Dan Flavin, who as an abstract expressionist made installations out of neon tubes that seem to capture Rabo's weird view of souls as "low-intensity neon tubes" (202; see also Kopper 582–84). Rabo, of course, appears in several of Vonnegut's other works, including *Deadeye Dick* and *Breakfast of Champions*. Though the Rabo of *Breakfast* is not the Rabo of *Bluebeard*—the chronologies of the two works differ, so that Rabo defends his abstract paintings in *Breakfast* long after he has given up on them in *Bluebeard*—the two Rabos share the interpretation of the "zip" as a soul. Naturally, the ultimate source of this idea is Vonnegut himself, as suggested by *Slaughterhouse-Five*:

> I had outlined the Dresden story many times. The best outline I ever made, or anyway the prettiest one, was on the back of a roll of wallpaper.
>
> I used my daughter's crayons, a different color for each main character. One end of the wallpaper was the beginning of the story, and the other end was the end, and then there was all that middle part, which was the middle. And the blue line met the red line and then the yellow line, and the yellow line stopped because the character represented by the yellow line was dead. And so on. The destruction of Dresden was represented by a vertical band of orange cross-hatching, and all the lines that were still alive passed through it, came out the other side. (15)

Through an outline that resembles an abstract expressionist painting, Vonnegut makes decoration from horror. He recoils from this and from extreme or prettifying techniques in general, just as he recoils from the trivializing critics in *Slaughterhouse-Five* who consider art's function to be to "'provide touches of color in rooms with all-white walls'" (106) and from the trivializing beauty of Kubrick's *Dr. Strangelove*, which makes a visual delight of nuclear annihilation (*Conversations* 235).

8. Rothko, Newman, and many of abstract expressionism's particular influences such as Mondrian and Kandinsky, never intended to abandon content altogether through an autotelic formalism, as Rabo describes the abstract expressionists' intentions. See, for example, the passage attributed to Rothko, Gottlieb, and Newman midway through this essay, and Kandinsky's expressionist treatise *Concerning the Spiritual in Art* (1911), in which the artist asserts that color "directly influences the soul . . . the artist is the hand which plays, touching one key or another, to cause vibrations in the soul" (25).

9. This is not invariable. Vonnegut sometimes asserts the therapeutic value of writing, which enables writers to "treat their mental illnesses every day" (*Conversations* 109).

10. I am in accord with Merrill and Scholl, who in 1978 supplied the first accurate interpretation of Billy's relationship to Tralfamadore (142–50). Merrill and Scholl argue that Tralfamadore is a function of the escapist insanity induced in Billy by the

Dresden massacre, and that Vonnegut places clues to Tralfamadore's unreality throughout the work (see also Tanner 125–30). As Vonnegut notes, "all I was describing in
Slaughterhouse-Five was a very real *memory* process—and that fact is not often considered
in studies of that portion of the novel" (*Conversations* 214; Vonnegut's italics). Though it
cannot be verified, common logic says *Slaughterhouse-Five*, unlike *The Sirens of Titan*, is a
work of psychological fiction, not of science fiction—and that Billy's Tralfamadorian
aesthetic is an emotional anaesthetic unendorsed by Vonnegut except as a last resort.

    11. Vonnegut often expresses his admiration for modernism's revolutionaries
through references to the Armory Show (in *Bluebeard*, see 157; see also Reed and Leeds
5). He also likes to note the irony of Hitler's artistic background (e.g., in *Bluebeard*, see
180; see also *Dick* 5–9). Hitler, of course, had the greatest revenge of any artist *manqué*,
making his critics bend to his bankrupt taste by holding the "Day of German Art," an
anti–Armory Show elevating to high-art status fascist "Gregorian" kitsch.

    12. This is part of an elaborate joke related to the idea of seriousness. Rabo uses
Sateen Dura-Luxe, a paint noted for its endurance, to make paintings that "really would
outlive the smile on the 'Mona Lisa'" (258), Leonardo da Vinci's paragon of serious art.
But like the experimental paint Leonardo used to paint *The Last Supper*, another paragon
of serious art, Sateen Dura-Luxe quickly disintegrates—a simple joke. What makes it
"elaborate" is that the person who complains of the seriousness of an art course and
smiles at the joke in Rabo's paintings—a joke that Rabo, due to his internalization of
modernist ideology, cannot himself smile at—is named "Mona Lisa Trippingham" (262).

    13. It is a mystery to me why the critics are not in accord when it comes to the
unity of *Bluebeard*'s structure, a structure whose interlinked patterns I have only begun
to delineate in this essay. For example, Paul Skenazy calls the novel's collage structure
"fitful," and the novel as a whole "a rambling, gangly piece of work, meandering from
vignette to vignette and afraid of its own emotional material" (64, 65). But, as pointed
out in the body of this essay, it is a critical commonplace that the collage technique
depends on an illusion of disunity despite the fact that its now conventional purpose is
to locate unexpected sources of unity. Vonnegut is a master of this technique.

    14. Technically, this concept complicates my view of his aesthetic—that is, that
Vonnegut's formalistic tendencies are at the service of his expressionistic goal, not vice
versa—for it suggests that he expresses himself to an audience-of-one as an indirect way
of achieving his true goal, formal unity. But as Vonnegut is the first to admit, writers say
many things. To consider him more of a formalist than an expressionist defies logic.

    15. Is the reader to infer that Rabo, on finishing his painting, longed for a
medium that would lend itself naturally to his new narrative aesthetic, a medium that
would supply the stories behind the figures on his canvas? Such an inference is supported when Rabo notes he "at first made myself available in the barn to tell anyone
who asked what the story was of this person or that one, but soon gave up in exhaustion. 'Make up your own war stories as you look at the whatchamacallit,' I tell people"
(270). Through *Bluebeard*, Rabo is able to set down the stories behind many of the figures once and for all—as if the book were the painting's companion piece.

    16. For a fascinating overview of Vonnegut's nonfictional collage techniques, see
Jerome Klinkowitz's recent book, *Vonnegut in Fact* (1998).

17. This cross reference demonstrates the intricacy of the structural connections between Bluebeard's Homeric motifs and its moral-aesthetic ideas. Marilee interprets abstract expressionism in a traditional way as a cry of despair and frustration resulting from the horrors of World War II. In her view, the abstract expressionists' paintings "*write*, "The End"'" (229; my italics). This creates a curiously apt sort of closure. Marilee interprets this "end" as a reference to a time before subject matter existed; thus she calls the abstract expressionists "the Genesis Gang" (230). Though many aspects of the book question Marilee's view that the abstract expressionists were uniformly intent on eliminating subject matter from their paintings, Rabo, having inspired Marilee's view through his descriptions of the abstract expressionists, formally evokes this view by beginning his *written* artwork with the illusion that it begins before its beginning—and after its end. What makes this closure both "open" and "postmodernist"—with the latter referring in an artistic sense to a playful aesthetic that typically resists totalizing formal systems and in a chronological sense to a worldview situated at the end of Western culture thus far—is the absolutely perfect way it recalls through the theme of hospitality the openness that Western culture idealized during a time period traditionally associated with its birth.

WORKS CITED

Allen, William Rodney. *Understanding Kurt Vonnegut.* Columbia: U of South Carolina P, 1991.

Beardsley, Monroe. *Aesthetics from Classical Greece to the Present: A Short History.* 1966. Tuscaloosa: U of Alabama P, 1975.

Cooper, David, ed. *A Companion to Aesthetics.* 1992. Cambridge: Blackwell, 1995.

Dewey, John. *Art As Experience.* 1934. New York: Perigee, 1980.

Gaugh, Harry. *Willem De Kooning.* New York: Abbeville, 1983.

Gombrich, E. H. *The Story of Art.* 1950. Rev. 15th ed. New York: Phaidon, 1989.

Harris, Charles B. "Illusion and Absurdity: The Novels of Kurt Vonnegut." 1971. Merrill 131–41.

Homer. *The Odyssey.* Trans. Robert Fagles. New York: Penguin, 1996.

Hughes, Robert. *The Shock of the New.* 1981. New York: Knopf, 1991

Kandinsky, Wassily. *Concerning the Spiritual in Art.* 1911. Trans. M. T. H. Sadler. New York: Dover, 1977.

Klinkowitz, Jerome. *Kurt Vonnegut.* London: Methuen, 1982.

———. *Vonnegut in Fact: The Public Spokesmanship of Personal Fiction.* Columbia: U of South Carolina P, 1998.

Klinkowitz, Jerome, and Donald Lawler. *Vonnegut in America: An Introduction to the Life and Work of Kurt Vonnegut.* New York: Delacorte, 1977.

Knox, Bernard. Introduction. *The Odyssey*. By Homer. 3–64.

Kopper, Edward. "Abstract Expressionism in Vonnegut's *Bluebeard*." *Journal of Modern Literature* 17.1 (1994): 582–84.

Lundquist, James. "New Twists to Old Tricks." Rev. of *Bluebeard*, by Kurt Vonnegut. 1987. Mustazza 287–89.

McCarthy, Cliff. "*Bluebeard* and the Abstract Expressionists." Reed and Leeds 165–77.

Merrill, Robert. *Critical Essays on Kurt Vonnegut*. Boston: Hall, 1990.

Merrill, Robert, and Peter Scholl. "Vonnegut's *Slaughterhouse-Five*: The Requirements of Chaos." 1978. Merrill 142–51.

Mustazza, Leonard, ed. *The Critical Response to Kurt Vonnegut*. Westport: Greenwood, 1994.

Norrman, Ralf. *Wholeness Restored: Love of Symmetry as a Shaping Force in the Writings of Henry James, Kurt Vonnegut, Samuel Butler, and Raymond Chandler*. Frankfurt: Peter Lang, 1998.

Rackstraw, Loree. "Dancing with the Muse in Vonnegut's Later Novels." Reed and Leeds 123–43.

Rampton, David. "Into the Secret Chamber: Art and the Artist in Kurt Vonnegut's *Bluebeard*." *Critique* 35.1 (1993): 16–26.

Reed, Peter J. "Appendix: The Graphics of Kurt Vonnegut." Reed and Leeds 205–22.

Reed, Peter J., and Marc Leeds, eds. *The Vonnegut Chronicles: Interviews and Essays*. Westport: Greenwood, 1996.

Rose, Barbara. *American Painting: The Twentieth Century*. 1969. Rev. ed. Geneva: Editions d'Art, 1986.

Schopenhauer, Arthur. *The World As Will and Representation*. Vol. 1. 1818. Trans. E. F. J. Payne. New York: Dover, 1969.

Skenazy, Paul. "Poking Holes in the Social Fabric." Rev. of *Bluebeard*, by Kurt Vonnegut. 1987. Merrill 64–66.

Sontag, Susan. "Fascinating Fascism." 1974. *Under the Sign of Saturn*. 1980. New York: Anchor, 1991. 73–105.

———. "On Style." 1965. *Against Interpretation*. 1966. New York: Anchor, 1990.

Tanner, Tony. "The Uncertain Messenger: A Reading of *Slaughterhouse-Five*." 1971. Merrill 125–30.

Vonnegut, Kurt. *Bluebeard*. 1987. New York: Dell, 1988.

———. *Conversations with Kurt Vonnegut*. Ed. William Rodney Allen. Jackson: UP of Mississippi, 1988.

———. *Deadeye Dick*. New York: Delacorte, 1982.

————. *God Bless You, Mr. Rosewater.* 1965. New York: Dell, 1991.

————. *Kurt Vonnegut: Slaughterhouse-Five, The Sirens of Titan, Player Piano, Cat's Cradle, Breakfast of Champions, Mother Night.* 1969, 1959, 1952, 1963, 1973, 1961. New York: Heinemann, 1980.

Wölfflin, Heinrich. *Principles of Art History.* 1922. Trans. M.D. Hottinger. New York: Dover, 1950.

CHAPTER THREE

QUANTUM LEAPS IN THE
VONNEGUT MINDFIELD

Loree Rackstraw

Back in the early 1980s a visiting professor joined the Physics Department at my university for a temporary teaching appointment. I was startled to see his name on the list of new faculty that fall, because I had just finished reading an intriguing book by an author of the same name that had almost made it possi ble for me to comprehend the mysteries of quantum physics. The book, clearly directed toward readers whose eyes glaze over when exposed to mathematical formulas, had intensified my long-time fascination with the interrelationships of the sciences and the humanities. As an English professor, I had particular interest in the historical influence of cultural myths on everything from the development of political and economic systems to actual bodies of knowledge and worldviews. By the same token, it was clear that myths can change or new ones arise in response to both natural and historical events. Cultural myths seem to play an evolutionary function in that they can help persons or societies adapt to change.

My university's new physics professor, Fred Alan Wolf, was indeed the author of *Taking the Quantum Leap*, a volume that won him the American Book Award in 1982 for original science paperback. He very kindly visited my mythology class a couple times, and I read another of his books called *Star Wave*. Unlike some physicists I knew, he didn't find it offensive or silly to talk about relationships between myth and quantum physics. Of course there are many definitions of myth, but I was influenced strongly by the ideas of Carl G. Jung, who, unlike his mentor Sigmund Freud, saw the positive, energizing potential of the archetypal myth. Hence, I defined myth as a story about a profound mystery that is as close to truth as the teller can make it. With this definition, I argued that some aspects of quantum physics could qualify as myth. That made sense to Fred. What scientists call the "nonintuitive" or paradoxical nature of quantum mechanics, Fred called the "twilight zone."

When I mentioned that his explanation of "the 'new physics' of time" in *Star Wave* sounded very much like Billy Pilgrim's explanation of the Tralfamadorian view of time in Kurt Vonnegut's *Slaughterhouse-Five,* he said, "Sure, that's where I got it!"

Wolf's book acknowledges that time is indeed a profound mystery, one that lacks a clear metaphor or physical picture. While time appears as an independent variable in the equations of mathematical physics, time itself cannot be seen. One can observe space and motion, but not time. We may have a notion of "now" as opposed to a past or a future, but what we really experience are *events* in time rather than time itself. One can say the word "now," but "now" is not *present* or *here.*

He says we might come closer to observing time through what the Buddhists call "being-time," or a sense of "hereness."

> It does not need space, feeling, knowledge, sensation, emotion or others to be experienced. Here needs no object for itself.... Everything that is, is, was, and will be. It remains 'out there' forever. Things do not pass away in time. Every moment remains lifeless, motionless and frozen forever. We—that is, our being-time—sweep across the landscape of all experiences as an airplane passes over the Grand Canyon. Past, present, and future represent a map for the perusal of the all-seeing being-time. (20)

And here's what Billy Pilgrim in *Slaughterhouse-Five* reports from Tralfamadore:

> When a person dies he only *appears* to die. He is still very much alive in the past, so it is very silly for people to cry at his funeral. All moments, past, present, and future, always have existed, always will exist. The Tralfamadorians can look at all the different moments just the way we can look at a stretch of the Rocky Mountains, for instance. They can see how permanent all the moments are, and they can look at any moment that interests them. (23)

So file this as an anecdote to document a case of a mythic story invented by a fiction writer influencing the vision of a quantum physicist. Conversely, it suggests that Vonnegut himself has likewise shaped this and a number of other novels around concepts and insights deriving in part from the physical sciences.

Through his disarming play of mind and language, I believe he—like no other postmodern writer in the United States—has been able to present to mass audiences a new metaphysics of perception. His stories reveal how western language and institutions have structured our awareness of what is real and valuable in ways that can blind us to the dangers of our behavior as it affects the life of our planet.

Vonnegut's novels exemplify a sweeping new epistemology of dynamic wholeness and subjectivity that emerged in the mid-60s, one with global implications for life sustainability. And to this end, it suggests a happy synchronicity: the times were just right for the emergence of a highly popular fabulist with an extraordinary ability to reveal—in an unthreatening way—our naiveté about human objectivity and the limitations of knowledge founded on a materialist-mechanistic science.

To put his message and the method of his fictions into an academic setting would be to establish a broad curriculum. But the formal classroom and its logocentrism is suspect in his eyes. Instead, he lets his cartoonlike and often clownish antiheroes defamiliarize traditional ways of seeing and knowing. His novels cheerfully lure us into questioning the nature of being and reality: why is there something instead of nothing? How do we know? Such questions inevitably lead to a recognition of complementarity: we cannot "know" anything without being; but we largely invent our being, our sense of identity, by what (and how) we know. This seeming paradox is central to the concerns of postmodern theory that locate the generation of meaning and reality primarily in human consciousness. A controversial philosophy often accused of solipsism, its origins resonate with new theories growing out of the physical sciences in the early twentieth century.

This philosophy seems linked especially with the fields of quantum mechanics and particle physics that developed as new sciences in the 1920s based on old questions about the nature and behavior of matter at its smallest, most fundamental level. Building upon Einstein's recognition that matter is a form of energy, physicists discovered a force unaccounted for in Newton's grand seventeenth-century insights into the force called gravity. At the large, cosmic level, heat and light were irrelevant to Newton's quantification of the laws of motion. But at the microcosmic level, they are inextricably involved in a departure from laws of mechanical motion. And the technology required to observe nature at this infinitesimal level inevitably affects, or even determines, what one sees.

In his *Taking the Quantum Leap*, Wolf says "Quantum mechanics appears to describe a universal order that includes us in a very special way. In fact, our minds may enter into nature in a way we had not imagined possible. . . . Perhaps much of what is taken to be real is mainly determined by thought. The order of the universe may be the order of our own minds" (6).

This resonation with the postmodern philosophy of constructivism, which argues that reality is largely socially constructed, fuels my speculation that scientific insights can take on provocative powers we ordinarily attribute to mythology. Such powers were articulated in the concept of "paradigm shift," by Thomas S. Kuhn in his landmark history of scientific epistemology first published in 1962. Although confining his study to academic disciplines, his insights are now widely applied to an understanding of epistemological shifts in many areas. Central to his exposition is the same dilemma of the complementary nature of being and knowing that permeates Vonnegut's novels: one's cultural context (one might say the myths or worldviews by which one lives) plays a strong role in determining what one takes to be true or even real.

As a science historian, Kuhn perceived a pattern: major scientific models—metaphors or paradigms of nature—establish a kind of tradition that has the power to fundamentally shape the way scientists think and perceive, and strongly control the way they formulate new problems or hypotheses. The authority of this conservative tradition keeps scientific insights from evolving in a gradual, progressive way. Even if every possible attempt is made to accommodate the new into the old paradigms, the old finally yields and a new model emerges with new ways of solving problems.

Kuhn says this new model or "paradigm shift" occurs in all fields of human knowledge, and is often marked by a violent intellectual struggle. His postscript to the second edition of his book echoes the same issue Vonnegut and postmodernists raise about epistemology and ontology: "Scientific knowledge, like language, is intrinsically the common property of a group or else nothing at all. To understand it we shall need to know the special characteristics of the groups that create and use it" (210). That is, the new model of reality constitutes not only *what* is believed to be true, but also *how* one knows and perceives. Those outside the group defined by this paradigm will likely know and perceive by a different model, and perhaps claim a different truth or reality.

In this regard, comparative mythologist Joseph Campbell, building upon Jungian theory, understood myths to function in much the same way epistemological paradigms do—that is, as metaphors which shape human belief and its ways of knowing. He even speculated that it may be possible "to arrive scientifically at . . . an understanding of the life-supporting nature of myths . . ." (12). He believed mythic themes, like dreams, come from the unconscious wells of human imagination and are inspired by the energies of the body. As personifications of these empowering energies they can help a civilization sustain itself in harmonious accord with nature or with other social groups. He believed one of their most important functions is to help to reconcile the inner being of humans with changing external forces that constantly make new demands upon civilizations. Such themes express images of cosmic order, creative flowering, transformation, and sacrifice and rebirth, all of which can be recognized in Vonnegut's novels. Like him, Campbell warns that they are not to be confused with ordinary "facts" or "truth." Rather, they are to be seen as motivating powers of the body and of nature. As metaphors of spiritual potentiality in the human being, they "represent that wisdom of the species by which man has weathered the millenniums" (14).

Vonnegut the mythmaker, taking clues from the sciences, replaces the old picture of a purposeful cosmos set in an orderly pattern by a rational and just logos. Instead, he offers new "harmless untruths" about a paradoxical universe governed largely by chance and ongoing energy transformations of indifferent natural processes. Rather than offering principles of conduct in a world that seems to change with each new way we find to observe it, his stories comfort by making us laugh, by suggesting talent be used for creative expressions like dancing (*Breakfast of Champions, Jailbird, Bluebeard*) or making tasty recipes or music (*Jailbird*) instead of controlling, and by urging the practice of "common decency" instead of the impossibly ideal "love" (*The Sirens of Titan, Mother Night, God Bless You, Mr. Rosewater*) that so easily turns into its opposite. Instead of bureaucratic hierarchies that demean those who lack political or financial power (*Jailbird, Hocus Pocus*), Vonnegut envisions all life forms as interdependent and thus equally important and valuable (*Galápagos*). Most especially, protagonists in his novels and stories give us models of unselfconscious humility and whimsy as ways of adapting to the limitations of human awareness and its dangerous susceptibility to subjectivity.

Most of the readers of this essay are likely familiar with some of the early formative processes that evidently helped to imbue the awareness of Kurt Vonnegut: A Midwesterner with a heritage of German-American Freethinkers, and of parents who suffered substantial financial loss in the Great Depression. One of three children of an architect father and of a mother who committed suicide shortly before he sailed to Europe as an infantryman in World War II. Capture as a German P.O.W. during the Battle of the Bulge. Survivor of the Dresden firebombing during his incarceration in the underground meat locker of a slaughterhouse. Formal education in chemistry and anthropology, although a practitioner of journalistic writing beginning in high school and continuing through his employment as a publicist for General Electric. Marriage to a childhood sweetheart with whom he parented three children and adopted three nephews following the death of his sister. Kid brother to an eminent physicist and atmospheric scientist whom he idolized.

It was through lenses shaped by these kinds of experiences that Vonnegut viewed the emergence of what could be called an epistemological shift toward wholeness and subjectivity following World War II. By the mid-1960s it was marked by rebellions against status quo policies in institutions of education, government, and economics, giving rise to a variety of social and political movements involving minority rights, war and the arms race, and environmental concerns. It interrogated theoretical bases, principles, and methodologies in the natural and human sciences as well as in disciplines of the humanities. It assaulted theories and expressions of modernism in the literature, the visual and performing arts, and architecture, and gave us the now ubiquitous term "postmodernism."

Where was Vonnegut at the genesis of all this transformation? In the middle of America trying to get his antiwar novel written that would make another attempt at convincing readers of how dangerously vulnerable human awareness is to manipulation and mistakes in interpretation. In so doing, his *Slaughterhouse-Five* became a brilliant and accessible example of complex new insights into holism and the crisis of perception and meaning that were arising at the same time out of postmodern literary theory and quantum physics. In literary theory, deconstruction claimed that human consciousness is paradoxically incapable of objectively knowing truth, because it has invented or inscribed (differentiated) itself out of the "always already" whole of what Jacques Derrida calls the "trace" or "the play of signifying references that constitute language" (6). As the brain "wires itself" and expands, doubling in size four times during the life of a human,[1] the mind struggles to differentiate itself and "truth" out of the trace, a sea of interdependent textuality that sustains it and from which it can never escape.

Literary theorist Christine Froula says that Derrida's "description of the trace strikingly parallels certain themes that recur in attempts to translate the mathematical language of modern physics into conceptual terms. The spatial structure of the trace generates a metaphysics of time that follows that of relativity and quantum physics, challenging the phenomenological model of temporality which distinguishes human time-consciousness from cosmic time" (296). As physicist Martin Gardner puts it, " Space and time are like the two lenses in a pair of glasses. Without the glasses we could see nothing. The actual world, the world external to our minds, is not directly perceivable; we see only what is transmitted to us by our space-time spectacles. . . . We experience only our sensory perceptions: what we see, hear, feel, smell, taste, these perceptions are . . . shaped and colored by our subjective sense of space and time, as the color of an object is influenced by colored glasses or the shape of a shadow is influenced by the surface on which it falls" (156). Semiotician Robert Scholes, himself a critic of deconstruction, agrees that Derrida's theory is founded on the belief that because perception is coded by language that is always figurative rather than literal, perception is inevitably distorted and never accurate (181).

Likewise, quantum physics insists upon the uncertainty inherent in the act of human observation at the atomic, or most fundamental level of matter, because the object being perceived and the perceiving instrument (observer) interact with each other and inevitably change the nature of the object. After confirming the mathematical coherence of quantum mechanics, Werner Heisenberg said, "For the time being, we have no idea in what language we must speak about the processes inside the atom. . . . I assume that the mathematical scheme works, but no link with the traditional language has been established so far" (66).

Froula has argued persuasively that the linguistically based critique of Western metaphysics by Derrida has a number of parallels with modern physics, even though he doesn't explicitly acknowledge such links. Froula says,

"In both quantum physics and Derrida's 'grammatology,' the conceptual transformation of nature challenges the presumptions of linear language and puts
into question the representation of transcendence and the ontological, epistemological, and ethical assumptions attached to it" (288–89). That is, our language and system of grammatical logic appear incapable of representing the
paradoxical dynamics inherent in the natural world and cosmos that gave us
birth and of which we are an interdependent part. As Scholes says, "We 'make
sense' of the world around us only because we are linguistic or semiotic creatures, already shaped by our capacity for language" (181).

Vonnegut surely linked a number of his post-Dresden insights to the rev-
elations of atomic physics stemming from the revolutionary discoveries of Einstein, Heisenberg, Neils Bohr and others early in this century. His close relationship with his physicist brother, if not his public relations work at General
Electric after the war, gave him opportunities to comprehend the paradoxes
these discoveries revealed. And although he was not then familiar with the specific philosophy of Derrida (whose *Of Grammatology* was translated in 1976),
his novels such as *Sirens of Titan, Mother Night, Slaughterhouse-Five*, and *Breakfast
of Champions* reflect many of the same specific metaphysical concerns.[2]

Certainly an interrogation of the myopic arrogance of human authority
is central to his fictions. Likewise, Derrida's criticism was directed at powerful
institutions authorized by historical claim to the origin of truth and transcendent meaning inscribed by logos, the principle of order introduced by the
Greeks, and believed to structure the world and life of humanity. The logos was
articulated into divine status through language whose syntax and logic evolved
from a perception of the linear order of time with its apparent implicit causal-
ity. Social classes with access to institutions inscribed by such rationality had
self-perpetuating privileged status. The weakening of these privileged certain-
ties arose when the insights of postmodern physics made their way into cultural awareness and revealed that at its fundamental core, the universe becomes
and organizes itself through processes that are far from linear or logical.

Vonnegut's defamiliarization of the linearity of time reaches its finest
articulation in *Slaughterhouse-Five*, his story about finding the way to inscribe
the unspeakable absurdity of the firebombing of Dresden. I agree with Jerry
Klinkowitz that "How *Slaughterhouse-Five* achieves the timeless and spaceless
dimensions of Tralfamadorian fiction is Vonnegut's major formal achievement" (72).[3]

In his excellent "reader's companion" to this novel, Klinkowitz says, "The
formal achievement of *Slaughterhouse-Five* is its restructuring of the reading
experience . . . [which] allows its readers to come as close as humanly possible
to experiencing all of its disparate episodes at once" (86). The result "gives readers the chance to experience the world in fresh new ways, and not be prisoners of any one culture's typical forms of description" (105).

I would only go a step further, and suggest that this novel, because of its
mass appeal, played a significant role in the epistemological shift of a whole

generation of readers worldwide. In language that all can comprehend, through the curious amazement of the friendly Tralfamadorian extraterrestrials in *Slaughterhouse*, we can grasp the irony that humans, by nature and accident, have evolved as participants in the undifferentiated flux of the cosmos through a special mediation process of language development that enables us to define ourselves as distinct and purposeful. This process is a dynamic, one that evolved through the interdependent functioning of our neurologically created and developed consciousness and our self-invented system of signs and institutions. Together, they give us the comforting illusion that we travel rationally through time toward meaningful goals. The danger of that illusion (which Western worldview sees as "truth") is that it blinds us to the disastrous potential of those goals as they affect the life of our planet.

In *Slaughterhouse*, Vonnegut gives us a fictional analogy of this complex evolutionary development. We find time-tripping Billy Pilgrim, transported from the chaos of World War II to a Tralfamadorian time warp where he learns about books that can be read all at once with no beginning, middle, or end, and no causes or effects. From thence, he time-trips on a childhood visit to the absolute darkness of Carlsbad Caverns where he doesn't even know whether he is still alive. Then, comforted to see the ghostly luminescence of the numbers on his father's radium dial watch, he is transformed from total darkness to the light of the German prison camp where he parades with fellow prisoners past "starving Russians with faces like radium dials" to a shed where his name and serial number are recorded in a ledger that makes him legally alive (77–78).

Billy's experience of the timeless chaos of war and the undifferentiated darkness of the womblike cave can be read analogously as the state of primordial humanoids on the verge of inventing a sense of time and language. Armed with these tools the evolving *Homo sapiens*, like the efficient and self-directed warriors around Billy, can construct a sense of identity and purpose. They can differentiate German and Russian from American, and establish institutions that give them a sense of power and order, a place of stability in space. However, note that Billy time-trips from the dark cave into the light of a *prison* camp signaling the limits to his awareness. We might see this as a parody of Plato's cave allegory with its ascent out of shadowy illusion into the light of the "true" world above.

Indeed, until he finds his new Tralfamadorian vision, the world of personal identity and purpose is utterly beyond Billy's comprehension in the meaningless chaos of his cosmic odyssey. Particle physicists say almost everything in the universe is composed of an electron and two quarks, one called "up" and the other "down" (Lederman 51). Billy, a pilgrim unstuck in time, endures his particle state with quantum jumps into the wilderness of one moonscape after another. Alienated from his fellow soldiers by his ridiculous attire and the missing heel of one shoe he shuffles "up-and-down, up-and-down," or is distributed in timeless space like an electron wave/particle.

But there are those curious and friendly Tralfamadorians under whose prison dome he occasionally finds himself, and whose "books" seem to be comprised of "brief clumps of symbols separated by stars" (76). The Tralfamadorians tell him that "each clump of symbols is a brief, urgent message describing a situation, a scene. We . . . read them all at once, not one after the other . . . the author has chosen [the messages] carefully so that, when seen all at once, they produce an image of life that is beautiful and surprising and deep. There is no beginning, no middle, no end, no suspense, no moral, no causes, no effects. What we love in our books are the depths of many marvelous moments seen all at one time" (76). Indeed, it was to approximate this kind of "narrative" that Vonnegut structured his novel.

This description could be read as a spin-off of the assumptions of Max Planck, likewise a pilgrim, who blazed an early path in 1900 to quantum physics by puzzling over the relationship between light and energy. Recognizing a deep connection between lines of the visible light spectrum and chemical elements that give off light when heated, he found that "radiation was emitted in discrete bundles or 'packets' of energy" which he identified as "quanta" (Lederman 148). He devised a formula, perhaps not unlike the Tralfamadorian novel, that provided a way to detect the fundamental nature of the universe of which we are a part. It reveals a nature beautiful and deep, and most certainly full of surprises. One of the surprises, of course, is that human consciousness appears to be inextricably bound up with its nature.

It's useful to know that Planck's work led quantum mechanics to a flowering of paradoxical answers in its effort to understand the fundamental structure and behavior of the subatomic universe. It gave us Heisenberg's uncertainty principle, which revealed the wave/particle duality or complementarity of the atom's electron (While the electron continues to act like a particle when it's being detected, its distribution in space between measurements follows wavelike probability patterns). The wave-particle duality appears in all matter, including light, but "the more we determine or define a system in terms of the one of these complements, the less we know about the other" (Lederman 169–71). After the historical debate among European physicists in 1927, the accepted version of Neils Bohr's "Principle of Complementarity "leads to this conclusion: reality is "one unbroken wholeness that appears paradoxical as soon as we observers attempt to analyze it. We can't help but disrupt the universe in our efforts to take things apart" (Wolf, *Quantum Leap* 120). In other words, there is no "objective" reality separate from ourselves "out there."

Billy Pilgrim's visit "out there" to the Tralfamadorians (who can see in the fourth dimension) gives him a new way of understanding how humans participate in the invention of "reality," and with that a purpose: to let people back on earth know they aren't seeing things as they really are. After the war he becomes an optometrist prescribing corrective lenses and telling people about the nature of time. He explains that: "It is just an illusion we have here on Earth that one moment follows another one, like beads on a string, and that once a moment is gone it is gone forever" (23). Instead, Billy can give them the comforting message that people only appear to die. He is not afraid of his own death and he knows there is no way to prevent the accidental end of the universe, because the moment is structured that way.

Within the context of his life under the Tralfamadorian prison dome, Billy's emergence from the darkness of Mammoth Cave as a child, to the bright lights of the German prison camp give the reader a nonthreatening and humorous way to recognize the reality-creating function of human perception with its biologically and culturally created lenses. *Slaughterhouse* is replete with numerous other examples, such as the safety Billy (as a terrified soldier) feels by limiting his vision of the outside world "to what he could see through a narrow slit between the rim of his helmet and his scarf from home" (36); or the hilarious picture of a drunken Billy in the dark of the back seat of his car trying to find the steering wheel (40); or "the gruesome crucifix" that had hung over his bed as a child, bought by his mother who, "Like so many Americans . . . was trying to construct a life that made sense from things she found in gift shops" (33). I have written elsewhere about the complex and paradoxical function of awareness in Vonnegut's novels, especially as it is developed in *Breakfast of Champions*.[4]

But the prison context (which can be found in most of his early novels) points to another recognition he wishes to leave with his readers: human perception seems inevitably bound by the paradoxical nature of the cosmos itself. If one can presume that the Tralfamadorian book is a playful spin-off of quantum mechanics, it is to alert us that the human invention of linear time is what convinces us that the undifferentiated cosmos is really an orderly, purposeful universe. It's that same invention of time and language that has allowed us to construct myths and religions that can help us adapt to powerful biological and cosmic transformations, but also can help us justify destructive behavior and comfort ourselves that we can escape the inevitability of death. Ironically, Billy (and Vonnegut himself) survived the Dresden firebombing only because he was in an underground prison, signaling the mythic manifestation of a protective womb. Billy's rebirth from the prison is to alert us to the paradox that our myths can backfire and fool us into justifying cataclysmic wars, inhumane civilizations, and global economics that destroy the natural environment upon which we depend for survival. As Vonnegut has said many times, he is the only person who profited from the moral zero of the Dresden bombing.

The Heisenberg uncertainty principle may be seen today as a cliché by philosophers of epistemology and constructivism. But *Slaughterhouse-Five*, written in the mid-sixties, was not written with a readership of philosophers in mind. Indeed, quantum mechanics and deconstruction are still theories that tax the average person's counterintuitive intelligence (even English professors). Vonnegut's early practice as a professional journalist may have helped to shape his insistent use of unimposing language and style to express complex ideas and paradoxes like those issuing from the sciences. But another reason for putting insights of scientific and philosophic disciplines into accessible "lowbrow" language and playful style may be, in part, his recognition that academic knowledge, with its arbitrary disciplinary specialization, belies the "unbroken wholeness" of the cosmos in which we are participating organisms. To see through the lens of only one specialized body of knowledge is to be like Billy Pilgrim snugly viewing war from the narrow slit between his helmet and his scarf from home.

In the long process of coming to terms with his personal experience of war and the Dresden firebombing, which enabled the writing of *Slaughterhouse-Five*, Vonnegut seems to have come to a refined perception of his authorial role, which he articulates explicitly in his often quoted wish in *Breakfast of Champions* for a culture of humane harmony. In his resolve to "shun storytelling" he "would write about life. Every person would be exactly as important as any other. All facts would also be given equal weightiness. Nothing would be left out" (210). Like Billy, we can be comforted to know that the message of the new physics and cosmology is that the elements of Earth are the same as those of the entire universe. We are all made of "star stuff." Copernicus was right that "We are not special."

The only thing that makes us "special," which Vonnegut also makes explicitly clear in *Breakfast of Champions*, is that we, along with other forms of earthly life, possess *awareness*. And with awareness comes the potential for creativity and free choice. Just as he literally ascended from the Dresden cave prison to write *Slaughterhouse-Five*, Vonnegut the author is "literally" present in *Breakfast of Champions* to be "reborn" when fictional artist Rabo Karabekian interprets his prize-winning abstract painting of "the unwavering band of light" that represents "awareness . . . all that is alive and maybe sacred in any of us" (220). This is, of course, the image of the column of light that towered over the mass slaughter of Dresden after the firebombing.[5] Vonnegut has been spreading his survival insights ever since, hoping to make sure that we remember how fragile and easily manipulated our awareness is and how naïve and cruel our free choices can be. Nonetheless, even though it gets us in a lot of trouble, it's what makes us human. If we can be humbly aware of its limitations, it can give us the capability for creative renewal for ourselves as well as for the life of our planet. And it is through our conscious creativity that we may manifest and experience a mythic sense of our participation in the generative processes inherent in the cosmos. When we are in accord with these universal processes we, too, may recognize our sense of awareness as a sacred aspect of the universe.

Vonnegut is a master at "doing" the "word"—that is, at creating a world of words that is "about" inventing a fictional world. Having made his authorial presence explicit in *Slaughterhouse-Five* and in most of the novels that follow including his last, *Timequake*, he draws attention to the creative process itself. As his metafictional world shifts in its many "meanings," it invites us as readers to be aware of our function as participants with him in that invention, to be conscious of our roles in the whole creative process of imagining.[6] Each reading of a good novel yields mutual transformations in both the reader and the text. Apparently the print on the page has not changed. Rather, one's inventive consciousness is participating in the "contextuality" of the reading experience. To "see" through Vonnegut's (sometimes reflecting)[7] lenses the ambiguity, the blur between actual life and the life of fiction, and between reading and inventing the story, is to become more humbly aware of the fiction of our own lives. To "see" Vonnegut's invented authorial godhead "at work" inventing the story before our very eyes, is to be linked to the generative processes of the novel's world with all its contexts and contradictions.

Likewise, this holistic interrelationship among the reader, the text, and the author as it generates the story parallels the generative processes of the cosmos itself. Jerome Bruner notes that our central nervous systems have evolved so that the brain stores "neural models of the world" that seem to influence what we perceive: "perception is to some unspecifiable degree an instrument of the world as we have structured it by our expectancies" (47). There is a growing school of thought that the evolutionary structurings and processes of our minds are homologous to the structurings and processes of the cosmos. Some of these multidisciplinary views are summarized in a 1984 text for the general reader called *Looking-Glass Universe* by John Briggs and F. David Peat. Essentially they say that our brains evolved from the cooperative processes of the universe, what Nobel Laureate Ilya Prigogine calls a "universe of interwoven autonomous dissipative structures." They agree that "mind is somehow implicated in that *whole* process and is not strictly localizable in the brain" (267)—even as the wave potential is somehow implicated in the electron of Bohr's quantum view, and as the whole context of mythic and cultural expression is implicated in the single novel.

As an important interpreter of Prigogine's complex ideas, Erich Jantsch said the self-organizing evolutionary processes of this universe stem from the primal energies of the Big Bang. They are characterized by the dynamic, multilevel complementarity of novelty (random chance) and confirmation (determination), the same processes that he thinks comprise art: "The creative process wherever it unfolds, in art or science or merely in natural and effective living, falls together with the dynamics of evolution." He could be speaking of Vonnegut's reflexive novels when he says that "The self-organization dynamics of the creative work—its mind—and human self-organization dynamics—the human mind—are two sides of one and the same evolutionary process; they form a complementarity.... Creativity is not a state but a process" (291). Jantsch suggests that as we participate in this creative process, we are minding ourselves just as the universe is minding itself.

I believe Vonnegut's fiction functions as myth to attune the reader to this dynamic "minding," the precarious dance of human consciousness between complementary tensions of chance and determination, the creative balance between adaptation and autonomy, all the while implying the ambiguities between inner and outer, between self and the cosmos. By reflecting on his narrative process of self-invention, by our participation in the linking back to the source, we may become aware of the basic wholeness of the evolving universe, the indistinguishable context for our participation and choices within it. This is not to transcend the world, then, as in some religious doctrines, but rather to be in accord with or at one with its open, creative processes. It is not to see some static super model of the cosmos, but rather to honor the unfolding web of interrelations, the evolutionary connectedness of everything, including ourselves.

Cosmologist Brian Swimme and cultural historian Thomas Berry, in an effort to articulate new insights of postmodern sciences, envision the universe as an unfolding story. They describe its self-organizing evolution as "a single multiform development in which each event is woven together with all others in the fabric of the space-time continuum" (21). They warn that "Human language and ultimately human consciousness need to be transformed to understand in any significant way what is intended" if humans are to enter fruitfully into the web of relationships within this primordial activity (24). It is such a transformation that I believe Vonnegut's novels can provide for the consciousness of his many readers, and which may account in part for his wide readership and popularity.

For as long as humans have celebrated the stories we call myths, they have provided ways to adapt creatively to the challenges of this primordial activity. Readers of Kurt Vonnegut's myths are given new corrective lenses that can make the transformation of consciousness and language less frightening and more fruitful.

How, then, is one to live fruitfully in the face of the undifferentiated flux and paradoxical, if creative, processes of our cosmos? Vonnegut suggests a sense of levity and an adaptive mode of behavior. Western tradition, particularly that celebrated in the United States, has long embraced the model of the stalwart and principled tragic hero whose noble stance takes him—AND his country and followers—into oblivion. In contrast, Vonnegut has aimed at helping us see nobility in the unselfconscious comic protagonist like Billy Pilgrim who does his best to bumble through the contradictions of life. He is an antihero who has a sympathetic respect for the bizarre even as he tries to dodge the cruel bully. He is kind rather than righteous. Billy's pilgrimage helps us recognize our limitations in comprehending an absurd universe, but at the same time, it encourages us to keep trying to expand our awareness and to appreciate the humane comforts of a community in which each member is valued. It's a model that could make the human pilgrimage into the next millennium more viable.

In a commencement speech he delivered in May 1998 at Rice University, Vonnegut urged the graduates to value teachers who made them excited to be alive, to develop interests other than money, to appreciate and strengthen communities, and to take notice of those moments when they are happy. It might have been Billy Pilgrim talking.

NOTES

1. See Robert B. Livingston's *Sensory Processing, Perception, and Behavior* for a lucid discussion of the neurological, cultural, and memory influences on the development and functioning of sensory processing.

2. `Joseph Sigman's "Science and Parody in Kurt Vonnegut's *The Sirens of Titan*" provides an excellent discussion of Vonnegut's use of Einsteinian relativity and quantum mechanics in that novel.

3. It seems especially ironic that this and other of his early novels were demeaned with the pejorative label of "science fiction," when he nonetheless was able to articulate—in his middle-class Hoosier American language—the profound paradoxes that had confounded some of the most brilliant thinkers of the century who were at a loss to articulate their "nonintuitive" discoveries to the general public.

4. See my "Vonnegut's Faustian Daemon and the Paradox of 'Awareness,'" in Marc Leeds and Peter Reed, eds., *Kurt Vonnegut: Images and Reflections*.

5. See a full explication of this image as used in this and other Vonnegut novels in my "Dancing with the Muse in Vonnegut's Later Novels" in *The Vonnegut Chronicles*.

6. See my "Dancing with the Muse in Vonnegut's Later Novels" for a full discussion of the generative motif in Vonnegut's metafiction, and a somewhat different take on this theme from that discussed in Leonard Mustazza's *Forever Pursuing Genesis*.

7. See *Breakfast of Champions* and *Deadeye Dick* for the use of this image, likely to suggest the reader's participation with the author in inventing the story.

WORKS CITED

Briggs, John, and F. David Peat. *Looking-Glass Universe*. New York: Cornerstone Library/Simon, 1894.

Bruner, Jerome. *Actual Minds; Possible Worlds*. Cambridge: Harvard UP, 1986.

Campbell, Joseph. *Myths to Live By*. New York: Bantam, 1972.

Derrida, Jacques. *Of Grammatology*. Trans. Gayatri Chakravorty Spivak. 1967. Princeton: Princeton UP, 1976.

Froula, Christine. "Quantum Physics/Postmodern Metaphysics: The Nature of Jacques Derrida." *Western Humanities Review* 39.4 (Winter, 1985): 287–313.

Gardner, Martin. *The New Ambidextrous Universe: Symmetry and Assymetry from Mirror Reflections to Superstrings*. 3rd rev. ed. New York: W.H. Freeman, 1990.

Heisenberg, Werner. *Physics and Beyond: Encounters and Conversations*. Trans. Arnold J. Pomerans. New York: Simon, 1980.

Jantsch, Erich. *The Self-Organizing Universe*. Oxford and New York: Pergamon, 1980.

Klinkowitz, Jerome. *Slaughterhouse-Five: Reforming the Novel and the World*. Boston: Twayne, 1990.

Kuhn, Thomas S. *The Structure of Scientific Revolutions*. 2nd ed. Enlarged. Chicago: U of Chicago P, 1970.

Lederman, Leon, and Dick Teresi. *The God Particle: If the Universe Is the Answer, What Is the Question?* Boston: Houghton Mifflin, 1993.

Livingston, Robert B. *Sensory Processing, Perception, and Behavior*. New York: Raven, 1978.

Mustazza, Leonard. *Forever Pursuing Genesis: The Myth of Eden in the Novels of Kurt Vonnegut*. Lewisburg: Bucknell UP, 1990.

Rackstraw, Loree. "Dancing with the Muse in Vonnegut's Later Novels." *The Vonnegut Chronicles: Interviews and Essays*. Ed. Peter J. Reed and Marc Leeds. Westport: Greenwood, 1996. 122–43.

———. "Vonnegut's Faustian Daemon and the Paradox of 'Awareness.'" *Kurt Vonnegut: Images and Representations*. Ed. Marc Leeds and Peter J. Reed. Westport: Greenwood, 2000. 51–66.

Scholes, Robert. "Tlon and Truth: Reflections on Literary Theory and Philosophy." *Realism and Representation: Essays on the Problem of Realism in Relation to Science, Literature, and Culture*. Ed. George Levine. Madison: U of Wisconsin P, 1993. 169–85.

Sigman, Joseph. "Science and Parody in Kurt Vonnegut's *The Sirens of Titan*." *Mosaic: Journal for the Comparative Study of Literature and Ideas* 19.1 (Winter, 1986): 15–31.

Swimme, Brian, and Thomas Berry. *The Universe Story: From the Primordial Flaring Forth to the Ecozoic Era—A Celebration of the Unfolding of the Cosmos* San Francisco: Harper, 1994.

Vonnegut, Kurt. *Breakfast of Champions*. New York: Delacorte/Seymour Lawrence, 1973.

———. *Deadeye Dick*. New York: Delacorte/Seymour Lawrence, 1982.

———. *Slaughterhouse-Five*. New York: Delacorte/Seymour Lawrence, 1968.

Wolf, Fred Alan. *Star Wave: Mind, Consciousness, and Quantum Physics*. New York: Macmillan, 1984.

———. *Taking the Quantum Leap*. San Francisco: Harper, 1981.

VONNEGUT'S GOODBYE: KURT SENIOR, HEMINGWAY, AND KILGORE TROUT

Lawrence R. Broer

> Our purpose is not to make up anyone's mind, but to make the agony of decision making so difficult that you can escape only by thinking.
>
> —Fred Friendly

> The fateful question for the human species seems to me to be whether and to what extent their cultural development will succeed in mastering the disturbance of their communal life by the human instinct of aggression and self-destruction.
>
> —Sigmund Freud, *Civilization and Its Discontents*

Kurt Vonnegut's has been a career of exorcisms—of a demonic war, of family alienation, of hostile critics, of a potentially disabling pessimism, and, more recently, in *Timequake*, of his tormenting alter ego, his career-long nemesis, Ernest Hemingway. At least symbolically, Hemingway has been as important and certainly as unsettling a force in Vonnegut's fiction as Dresden, or as the science fiction writer Kilgore Trout, or as that gun-loving nut of a father who in

Timequake Vonnegut says looked like Trout himself. Here as elsewhere—in *Happy Birthday Wanda June*, *Palm Sunday*, *Deadeye Dick*, *Bluebeard*, and *Fates Worse than Death*—Vonnegut views Hemingway as an artist of the highest order, as a superb craftsman with an "admirable soul" the size of Kilimanjaro (*Fates* 62). Amazed by Hemingway's "brushwork," the simple language, the power of omission and repetition, and paradoxically finding Hemingway's bullfighting stories among his favorites, Vonnegut applauds the "much deserved Nobel Prize" (*Fates* 9). In *Timequake*, Vonnegut even emulates Hemingway's love of elemental experience, such sensuous pleasures as taking food and coffee, enjoying a cooling drink on a hot day, spending a lazy day fishing, or simply "sleeping and waking up," declaring that one mission of the artist is to make people appreciate being alive.[1] Vonnegut waxes Hemingwayesque when he quotes from *Our Town*, "Oh, earth, you're too wonderful for anyone to realize you" (21).

Yet it is to separate himself from Hemingway, to damn, not praise, that Vonnegut usually speaks of his fellow artist-warrior. While admiring Hemingway's best stories, Vonnegut scorns the Hemingway mystique, his idealization of valor and physical prowess. If Hemingway's soul is large, it is also in Vonnegut's critique a soul corrupted by a primitive delight in the killing of animals and so-called arts of war. It is probably with Hemingway in mind that Vonnegut quips in *Timequake*, "I can't stand primitive people. They're so stupid" (109). In *Timequake*, but especially in his prolonged treatment of Hemingway in *Happy Birthday Wanda June* and *Fates Worse Than Death*, Vonnegut decries Hemingway's passion for blood sports, so alien to his own conservationist sympathies. Viewing the shooting of big animals for pleasure as inhumane and outdated, Vonnegut asks us to imagine nowadays boasting of killing three lions, and reporting delight at the prospect of killing a fourth one. As to the glamour of big game hunting, Vonnegut explains that "It is predicted that the last East African elephant will die of starvation or be killed for its ivory in about eight years (*Fates* 7). Vonnegut also looks askance at what he calls "the greatest reward" for a character in a Hemingway story, the "celebration of male bonding," the feeling one man has for another in the neighborhood of danger (*Fates* 9). Vonnegut shares the view of a female friend that it was ridiculous that men had to get out of doors and drink and kill before they could express something as simple and natural as love (9).

It is in *Happy Birthday Wanda June,* self-described as "a simple-minded play about men who enjoy killing and those who don't" (1), that Vonnegut delivers his most impassioned assault upon what he calls "the part of Hemingway which I detested—the slayer of nearly extinct animals which meant him no harm" (viii). The bully ghost of Hemingway permeates the character of Harold Ryan from first to last—from such surface resemblance as their favorite pastime of twitting weaklings, their sexual attitudes about male and female roles,[2] their open joking about death—to more revealing spiritual parallels in their attitudes toward death and killing, and toward a defiant, chin-protruding brand of heroism. Both Harold Ryan and Hemingway hold honor, pride, and the demonstration of worth through physical strength as ultimate male priorities, and killing as noble behavior. Harold Ryan boasts that as a professional soldier he has killed perhaps two hundred men, and thousands of animals as well (2). He relishes matador-like displays of manhood—choices between fighting and fleeing—and as a soldier in the Abraham Lincoln Brigade during the Spanish Civil War, glories in his nickname "La Picadura—the sting."

By contrast, Norbert Woodly, whose age difference from Harold matches that of Vonnegut and Hemingway, ridicules what he calls Ryan's "heroic balderdash," calling Ryan a living fossil, as obsolete as cockroaches or horseshoe crabs (182). Finding it disgusting and frightening that a killer should still be a respected member of society, Woodly articulates Vonnegut's moral outcry from *Player Piano* to *Timequake:* "Gentleness must replace violence everywhere, or we are doomed" (2). As opposed to Harold Ryan's association of manhood with toughness and physical challenge, Woodly says he wants to cry whenever he comes into a room containing animal heads, "a monument to a man who thought that what the world needed most was more rhinoceros meat" (*Happy Birthday Wanda June* 10). "Any one of these poor dead animals," he tells Harold, "was a thousand times the athlete you could ever hope to be. Their magic was in their muscles—your magic is in your brains" (21). Woodly plays a violin in a doctor's quartet, was a stretcher bearer in the Korean War, doesn't play sports, always takes the path of least resistance, uses his brains instead of his muscles, and attempts to change people with the weapons of compassion, unselfishness, and maudlin concern (7).

Vonnegut continues in *Timequake* to challenge what he sees as Hemingway's relatively romantic treatment of war and death, his hardboiled pose that mixes heroism with physical valor, and killing with honor. Contrasting his own Purple Heart for frostbite, this country's second lowest decoration, with Hemingway's War Cross and Silver Medal of Honor for being shot, Vonnegut accuses Frederick Henry of *A Farewell to Arms* of getting Catherine Barkley pregnant to prove his manhood, declaring that the novel really proclaims Hemingway's detestation of civilian life, of marriage (81). The tears Henry sheds are those of relief for having been saved from an unglamorous life of civilian responsibilities—getting a regular job, a house, life insurance. Despite Hemingway's vivid depiction of the horrors of war, Vonnegut suggests that Frederick and Catherine have too many wonderful experiences, thus representing the most popular story a writer can tell about a good-looking couple having a really good time copulating outside wedlock, and having to quit for one reason or another in the full blush of romantic feeling (80–81).

Vonnegut portrays his own more sardonic version of war through several stories by Kilgore Trout, a soldier-artist who shares both Vonnegut's and Hemingway's military background. In Trout's account of Albert Hardy, Vonnegut's World War I soldier not only has his penis shot off like Jake Barnes in *The Sun Also Rises*, his body is atomized, and his penis, his "ding-dong," is blown into oblivion (79). In a Trout story that appears to parody the ending of *A Farewell to Arms*, reflecting what Frank McConnel calls the "stylized brutality" of Hemingway's depiction of war and bullfighting, the Knights of the Round Table are equipped with Thompson submachine guns. Probably with Frederick Henry in mind as Lancelot, and Catherine as Guinevere, Lancelot, the "purest in heart and mind," puts a slug through the Holy Grail and makes "a Swiss cheese of Queen Guinevere" (xiii). Vonnegut shares with Trout a real-life, similarly anti-heroic tale about his friend David Craig. Craig shoots a German tank with a bazooka, but no Germans pop out of the turret, no one celebrates. As if again parodying Frederick Henry's convenient exit from humdrum domesticity, Kilgore Trout concludes that at least the tank's occupants died in glory, that David Craig's true heroism was in sparing his victims "years of disappointment and tedium in civilian life" (80).

It would take a book to properly explain why the author Frank McConnel calls the most recognizably Hemingwayesque of the new generation of writers to emerge after World War II should speak so frequently and disdainfully of Hemingway's humanity. We might speculate that Vonnegut draws apart from Hemingway just as Hemingway had done from his immediate mentor, Sherwood Anderson, to better define his own stylistic identity. Or we might wax Freudian, citing the fact that, as McConnel explains, every artist must kill or castrate his artistic father before he can function on his own, especially the symbolic father who liked to be called "Papa" (163). Vonnegut, himself, suggests in *Fates* that differences in their respective cultures and war experience made Hemingway his natural adversary. Explaining that they were divided by booms and busts and wars radically different in mood and purpose and technology, which separated not only himself from Hemingway but the first half from the last half of the twentieth century,[3] Vonnegut declares that while only twenty-three years apart in age, the difference might have been a thousand years (*Fates* 60). In particular, Vonnegut attributes their differences in temper to the differences between World War I and World War II, and between both of these wars to the war in Vietnam. The nature of true battle stories by Americans was utterly debased by World War II, he explains, "when millions upon millions of us fought overseas and came home no longer needing a Hemingway to say what war was like" (*Fates* 62). Vonnegut suggests that the nightmare of hydrogen bombs and the atrocities of the Nazi death camps necessarily created a new historicist sensibility, one that no longer believed that dishonor was a fate worse than death, since the military death of one man might easily mean the death of everything (*Fates* 144). What made the Vietnam soldier particularly "spooky," Vonnegut explains, is that he never had illusions about war, never had Hemingway's need to return from war with the shocking news that war was repulsive, stupid, and dehumanizing (*Fates* 146).[4] Rather the Vietnam veteran was the first American soldier to know from childhood that war was a meaningless butchery of ordinary people like himself, and that death was plain old death, the absence of life. This is precisely what Harold Ryan's wife Penelope reminds Harold of in *Wanda June* when she accuses him of confusing heroism and honor with killing and death. "It is not an honor to be killed," she chides; "It is still just death, the absence of life—no honor at all" (174).[5]

The fact is that Vonnegut's repudiation of Hemingway—the thousand years he says divides them—may obscure their amazing artistic affinities. Vonnegut's summary of their common origins and experiences exposes but the tip of the iceberg: "We were born in the middle West, we set out to be reporters, our fathers were gun-nuts, we felt profoundly indebted to Mark Twain, and we were the children of suicides" (*Fates* 61). In his move East from Indianapolis to Barnstable, Massachussetts, Vonnegut was not a literal expatriate like Hemingway, but was certainly a spiritual disaffiliate. Vonnegut could be speaking for a disenchanted Hemingway when he asks in *Timequake*, "Why did so many of us bug out of a city built by our ancestors, where our family names were respected, whose streets and speech were so familiar, where there was the best and worst of Western Civilization" (130). Parallels extend even to the fact that both writers experience serious writer's block that prevents them from completing works in progress. Vonnegut explains that it was only after a ten-year silence that Hemingway produced *Across the River and into the Trees* and *The Old Man and the Sea*, the first of which was widely panned, and the second of which Vonnegut, himself, debunks in *Timequake*. When Vonnegut asks a commercial fisherman what he thinks of *The Old Man and the Sea*, the fisherman calls Santiago "an idiot," insisting that Santiago should have "hacked off the best chunks of meat and put them in the bottom of the boat, leaving the carcass for the sharks" (xi).

Reminiscent of Hemingway's abortive efforts to complete his famous Land, Sea, and Air novel, Vonnegut explains that in the winter of 1996 he found himself the creator of a novel that did not work either, a novel that refused to be written (*Timequake* xiii). But as if to undercut the heroism of Santiago's adventure at sea, Vonnegut says about his own unwieldy fish, "Filet" the thing, improvise, reinvent (xiii), which produces *Timequake II*, a "stew" made from the best parts of *Timequake I*. Perhaps it is this capacity for reinvention that Vonnegut has in mind when he says that "the suicide Ernest Hemingway" (51) almost made it to sixty-two, while he, himself, has lasted to the age of seventy-three (xii). Hemingway wasn't an old man when he wrote *The Old Man and the Sea*, Vonnegut says, but "he obviously felt like one" (*Fates* 66), felt that his work, thus his life, was done (*Fates* 67). Wondering what he would have missed if his own thoughts of suicide had been as successful as Hemingway's, Vonnegut rejoices not only in the writing of at least four more books and some "swell" essays (183), but in the accomplishments of his children and in the birth of three more grandchildren (187). However strong his gloom, however disappointed in the economic and physical violence of his society, Vonnegut was not about to give up life for death, or to stop trying to protect nature, or to slow down, at least a little bit, crimes against "those Jesus Christ said should inherit the Earth someday" (*Fates* 189).[6]

Vonnegut's seemingly off-hand reference to gun-nut fathers and a family legacy of suicide—Hemingway's father, Vonnegut's mother—probes deeply into the works of both writers. But it was their experience as soldiers and their resultant wounds, Hemingway's physical one at Fossalta, Italy in World War I, Vonnegut's psychological one in Dresden, Germany in World War II, that constitutes their major bond and the strongest influence upon their respective careers. Though Vonnegut acknowledges that Hemingway was one of the best reporters of war the world has ever known, but not technically a soldier,[7] Hemingway's wound was at least the more visible of the two. At the age of eighteen, Hemingway was literally blown up by an Austrian trench mortar while serving as a civilian ambulance driver on the Italian front. As a lowly twenty-year-old Pfc., albeit an intelligence and reconnaissance scout, Vonnegut first was captured "in tact" during the Battle of the Bulge while looking for enemies, then forced to witness the hideous firebombing of Dresden. While Hemingway has described his own near mythic return from war in such major stories as "Soldier's Home" and "Big Two-Hearted River," Vonnegut explains that when *he* got home, his Uncle Dan clapped him on the back and bellowed, "You're a man, now." Vonnegut says that while neither he nor Hemingway ever killed anyone, he himself "almost killed his first German" (*Timequake* 70).

According to their fictional accounts—what Vonnegut calls "psychological stevedoring" (*Fates* 54)—Vonnegut and Hemingway's experiences of childhood alienation with cold and insensitive parents and with demoralizing war wounds were more alike than unalike.[8] If different in kind, their woundings were equally complex and psychologically damaging, indicating many kinds of disability,[9] and setting in motion the central themes of their fiction, both conscious and unconscious. Each writer develops a similarly despairing, naturalistic view of existence as perpetually warlike, and each creates literary heroes whose shattered consciousness and early flights from complexity and social responsibility reflect their author's own sense of vulnerability and disillusionment. Writing as therapy, each author makes what Vonnegut in *Slaughterhouse-Five* calls his "duty dance with death," a process of literary exorcism in which he attempts to overcome feelings of impotence and cynicism, and to discover a source of action, a set of values, that will result in a more positive, more integrated identity. When Vonnegut speaks in *Timequake* of Kilgore Trout's "ghostly childhood," and of nightmarish episodes of war and carnage, he evokes the essential experience of all of Vonnegut's and Hemingway's protagonists, the literary purging of which McConnel says allows both writers to come to terms with their experience of "apocalypse" (50). "These were memories," Trout says, "he could only exorcise by telling what they were" (50).

If we needed further convincing, reading the nonfiction prose confessions of both writers should persuade us that each author writes as a process of therapy, putting himself at the center of the stories he tells.[10] When Earl Rovit says that Hemingway was addicted to scraping at apparently unhealed wounds (185), he could not have better defined the dehumanized and fragmented condition of the Vonnegut/Hemingway hero or the therapeutic aspect of each writer's art. In their respective psychodramas, the authors invite us to follow the evolution of essentially one individual, the same person under different names, whose wounds, sins, and hopes for redemption carry over from one protagonist to the next, and are nearly always those of their creator. The experiences that shape the young manhood of Nick Adams shape as well the character of Frederick Henry and Jake Barnes. The childhood traumas that plague Rudy Waltz haunt as well his adult incarnation as Billy Pilgrim or Howard Campbell. And nearly always these fictional self-creations have their authors' history behind them—the wound, the psychic fragmentation, and the quest of the wounded soldier for positive values and for ways of ordering his life in a hostile, naturalistic world.

In both cases, then, the Vonnegut/Hemingway adolescent protagonist, the nearly catatonic hero of "Big Two Hearted River" or *Deadeye Dick*, survives ogreish, unaware, and nonnurturing parents only to experience the slaughter-house of war—the brutality of battle, the impermanence of love, and the impos-sibility of any metaphysical solution: Frederick Henry is physically as well as emo-tionally shot to pieces, and Billy Pilgrim emerges from his underground bomb shelter "a broken kite on a stick," headed for a mental hospital. The shock of war, particularly the meaningless deaths of Catherine Barkley and Edgar Derby, sepa-rate both Henry and Pilgrim from their senses, symbolized by the title of Hem-ingway's story, "A Way You'll Never Be." Both psychically maimed men are as Vonnegut describes Eugene Debs Hartke in *Hocus Pocus*, the counterpart to Hemingway's Colonel Cantwell in *Across the River and into the Trees*: "a seriously wounded" man both "physically and psychically" (116)—a potential "burned out case" (103) prone to "psychosomatic hives" (290) and dangerously tempted to "good ole oblivion" (119). The resultant feelings of futility and impotence of all of Vonnegut's returning soldiers, for example, Billy Pilgrim, Eugene Debs Hartke, Rabo Karabekian, differs little from the literal castration of Hemingway's Jake Barnes, a wound that ends the greatest of emotional consolations in an absurdist world. Now, for a long while, psychic survival for both sets of heroes depends on their ability to deflect pain and fear. Increasingly emotionally withdrawn, each shattered persona adopts masks that shield a vulnerable self, Hemingway's pseudo toughness, Vonnegut's alarming passivity, but which in either case creates a mind perpetually at war with itself. Both practice what McConnel calls a "studied for-getfulness" (169), an escape from complexity and social responsibility manifesting itself in Frederick Henry's "separate peace" and Howard Campbell's "Nation of Two"—a womblike condition in which a pair of lovers in a world gone mad attempts to survive by being loyal only to a nation composed of themselves.

The retreat from consciousness manifests itself also in each author's ironic, understated style—a screen of words, of short, ritualistic, declarative sen-tences that numb the protagonist's pain and protect him from further potential horrors. But as Wendolyn Tetlow explains about Hemingway's protagonists, despite the hero's seeming indifference to pain, the reader hears the silent screams just beneath the iceberg's surface.[11] We notice the typically Heming-wayesque understated features of tone in Howard Campbell's description of the shooting of Resi's dog in *Mother Night*:

> The old soldier came over, expressing a professional's interest in the sort of wound such a pistol might make. He turned the dog over with his boot, found the bullet in the snow. . . . He now began to talk of all sorts of wounds he had seen or heard of, all sorts of holes in once living things.
> "You're going to bury it?" he said.
> "I suppose I'd better," I said.
> "If you don't," he said, "somebody will eat it." (84)

This seems to parody lines from Hemingway's *Across the River and into the Trees*, when Colonel Cantwell reports a dead G.I. lying in the road, repeatedly run over by passing vehicles. "That was the first time I ever saw a German dog eating a roasted German kraut. Later on I saw a cat working on him too" (257).

If at war's end protagonists such as Frederick Henry or Howard Campbell have not completely burned out in the manner of Colonel Cantwell or Eugene Debs Hartke, they certainly are "tempted" by "good ole oblivion," a totally fatalistic view of their place in the universe. Anticipating the weary lament of Billy Pilgrim in a world whose destructive forces he cannot control ("So it goes"), Howard Campbell concludes that the world's brutality is something he too can do nothing about. About Hitler's treatment of the Jews, Campbell says, "It isn't anything I can combat—so I don't think about it" (*Mother Night* 38, 40). Frederick Henry's paralysis is enforced by the same fatalism that prevents Campbell from believing any longer in justice, or love, or God, and turns him into a lifeless robot. Looking ahead to Jake Barnes's declaration that he did not care any longer what life was about, Lieutenant Henry decides that all are victims, the good and the bad, the brave and the unbrave, of the mechanistic universe that snares and kills with impunity. Henry might have Campbell's image of history as a "huge steam roller" in mind when he concludes that there is simply no defense against the great and final foe—death. "Now Catherine would die," he says. "That was what you did" (*Farewell to Arms* 338).

This view of the hero threatened with annihilation, and emotionally disabled by fear and cynicism continues as the dominant strain in Hemingway's work up to *Death in the Afternoon*, and in Vonnegut up to *Breakfast of Champions*. Until then, the best the hero can do to combat feelings of helplessness is to seek out bogus substitute religions, dubious moral guides, and supposedly wiser beings who will teach the hero exactly how to live. While the Hemingway protagonist encounters real-life father figures like Pedro Romero or the white hunter, Robert Wilson in "The Short Happy Life of Francis McComber," Vonnegut's hero evidently hallucinates authority figures like Frank Wirtanen of *Mother Night* or the reappearing ominous Tralfamadorians of *The Sirens of Titan* or *Slaughterhouse-Five*. Hemingway's tutors preach physical toughness and stoicism, while the likes of Bokonon or Winston Niles Rumfoord indoctrinate the pliant protagonist with illusory promises of perfect peace and contentment. In

either case, the protagonist relinquishes his will to an imagined higher authority whose moral absolutism the protagonist believes will give his life the meaning it lacks.

But virtually at mid-career, in *Death in the Afternoon*, and in *Breakfast of
Champions*, Hemingway and Vonnegut take their protagonists in directions so
different that Vonnegut's fiction from *Breakfast of Champions* to *Timequake*
becomes not only a response to a world of violence and death but a rebuttal of
Hemingway's response. In what amounts in these respective spiritual manifestoes to a moral rebirth and new artistic faith, each writer now creates a hero
who feels as if he has learned the correct way to live in Hemingway's "nada"
and Vonnegut's "chaos," what Brett Ashley calls in *The Sun Also Rises* (1926)
"what we have instead of God" (245). Yet the ideologies that dominate the
worldview and behavior of these reformed heroes differ radically, and return us
to Vonnegut's essential quarrel with Hemingway as portrayed in *Happy Birthday, Wanda June*, the Hemingway who equates manhood with heroic comport-
ment, and who associates emotional and artistic integrity with the killing of
animals. Analogous to Vonnegut's appearance as himself in *Breakfast of Champions*, Hemingway assumes the role of his own newly created hero in *Death in the
Afternoon*, taking us on a tour of the world of the bullfight while expounding
on his own fatalistic philosophy of life. Nothing has happened in the years since
the writing of *A Farewell to Arms* to change the author's belief that man's
chances for survival are largely shaped by forces beyond his control. Death and
mutilation are just as prevalent in the bullring as in the world of Nick Adams,
Frederick Henry, and Jake Barnes. "They" turn on you here to kill and break
you as surely as they turned on Henry and Catherine in *A Farewell to Arms*. In
a universe as absurd at its core as Vonnegut's, Hemingway observes that the most
sincere and dedicated matadors are killed more frequently than others. But in
the symbolic life-and-death struggle of the bullring, Hemingway discovers an
antidote to the feeling of inner helplessness experienced by Frederick Henry
and Jake Barnes. By discharging one's pent-up aggressions on the object of the
bull, one achieves a cathartic release, a temporary, if not illusory, triumph over
death and the brute forces of nature.

Judging from Vonnegut's portrait of Hemingway in *Happy Birthday, Wanda
June* and *Fates Worse than Death*, what disturbs Vonnegut even more than the
praise of physical toughness is the sense of glory Hemingway takes in killing. In
Death in the Afternoon, Hemingway explains that what the Spanish mainly went
to see in the course of the bullfight was the pleasure of giving death, "one of the
most profound feelings in those men who enjoy killing" (233). The great matador, he says, must have a spiritual enjoyment in the moment of killing, a love of
killing for its own sake (232). Later in *Green Hills of Africa* (1954), on a violent
hunting expedition to the heart of the African jungle, Hemingway seems bent
not only on sharing the matador's great pride in braving physical danger, but in
killing cleanly and well, drawing his rifle sights on a buck and dispatching it with
accuracy and released tension that approximates the final sword thrust of the

matador. In Hemingway's execution of a kudu, his sense of triumph comes both
from adhering to the strict requirements of the hunt, and from killing well, with
"honor." When Hemingway shows displeasure over not having bagged the
biggest kill, his guide reminds Hemingway of what is most important anyway.
"You can always remember how you shot them," he says. "That's what you really
get out of it" (197). True to the caricature of Hemingway in *Wanda June*, the
Hemingway hero from here on out assumes the aggressive stance of the torero,
the matador/killer. Harry Morgan, Robert Jordan, Colonel Cantwell, Thomas
Hudson, and Santiago are all faced with the same problems of fear, violence, and
death that produce a state of emotional paralysis in Hemingway's earlier characters, but the disdainfully aggressive manner in which they now try to combat
these forces designates in Hemingway's view their moral superiority.

Just as Hemingway maps out the spiritual terrain of his more virile and
hardened hero in terms of the circumscribed world of the bullfight in *Death in
the Afternoon*, Vonnegut defines what he calls the "new me" in *Breakfast of Champions* in relation to the imaginative openness of the Museum of Modern Art.[12]
Playing himself, as Hemingway does in *Death in the Afternoon*, Vonnegut
describes *his* spiritual rebirth, the ascension of a more creative and optimistic
self, in terms of his recognition that he possesses an imaginative faculty capable
of resisting the mechanistic conditioning processes of a machine-ridden world,
and therefore of steering his own course as a person and as an artist. Vonnegut
comes to this awareness through the artistic vision of Rabo Karabekian, the
painter who later in *Bluebeard* emerges symbolically as the main regenerative
force in the author's spiritual evolution, and the end product of his artistic
metamorphosis. And what a resurrection, not the transformation of the impo-
tent Jake Barnes into the pugnacious soldier, Colonel Cantwell, but the
neutered Billy Pilgrim into the consummate artist, Rabo Karabekian. This most
alienated of men, with his hideous psychic wounds—the traumatized child, the
war-scarred soldier, the failed husband and father—has come through the fires
of Dresden to be symbolically reborn in *Breakfast of Champions*, then, as Rudy
Waltz says in *Deadeye Dick*, to be healed by music of his own making in the
novels of Vonnegut's "second career"—*Slapstick, Jailbird, Deadeye Dick*, and *Galápagos*. Conceived in the epiphanaic light of Rabo's painting in *Breakfast of
Champions*, Vonnegut writes of surviving his defeatist self by facing tormenting
family ghosts and his own destructive impulses, then by working out an
"esthetics of renewal"—the existential possibilities of authoring one's own
identity in life as art.

Reflecting Vonnegut's "rebirth," these self-inventors, priests, physicians,
artists of Vonnegut's second career are forecast in the earlier portrayal of Norbert Woodly in *Wanda June*, an artist-healer directly opposed to the aggression
and emotional stoicism of Hemingway's own reconstructed protagonists.
Though as wounded as Robert Jordan, or Cantwell, Morgan, or Hudson, these
heroes, Wilbur Swain, Walter Starbuck, Rudy Waltz, and Leon Trout do not
lapse into primitive modes of thought or action as a way of reordering their

decentered worlds. They do not kill anyone, or achieve "honorable" deaths as do the aforementioned protagonists by facing the on-rushing bull with bravado and strained shows of courage. Whereas Hemingway's heroes assert their masculinity, Vonnegut's heroes open themselves to the female within, to the more creative and gentle side of their nature, adopting kindness and restraint as moral priorities rather than a militant code of conduct that esteems physical toughness and stoical reserve.[13] "The old heroes," Penelope declares, "are going to have to get used to this—the new heroes who refuse to fight. They're trying to save the planet" (176). As if again to parody the "old" heroism of Hemingway's Santiago, Vonnegut in *Timequake* juxtaposes "two luckless fishermen in rowboats who are deadringers for the saints Stanley Laurel and Oliver Hardy" (209). It is perhaps in direct reference to Hemingway's lusty and brawny hunters and fishermen that Vonnegut quips that he used to go hunting for rabbits and birds "before Allie [Vonnegut's sister] cried so much he had to give it up" (131).

When Penelope announces to Harold that there is no time or place for battle anymore, no room for hunters or men of war in the vision of those devoted to saving the planet, she evokes the image of Vonnegut as shaman, a kind of spiritual medicine man who knows that unless checked our cruelty and aggression will take us the way of the mastodon and the megatherian. Functioning as the projective imagination of the life force, a creative evolutionist whose inspiration comes from George Bernard Shaw and Eugene Debs, Vonnegut argues that our only hope of saving the planet from destruction is by encouraging reflectiveness and the will to change. He would move us *up* the evolutionary ladder, not down, using our brains rather than our muscles to bring about change. It is on behalf of this saner, more evolved world that Vonnegut directs his satirical missiles at Hemingway, a world in which kindness, mercy, and respect for life has replaced the aggression represented by Hemingway's later heroes. Vonnegut believes that the world's chief source of agony, blood lusts epitomized by Harold Ryan, are not only self-destructive, but jeopardize the species as a whole. Unless human beings understand that the smallest acts of violence are connected to the world's larger, bloodier deeds, we are doomed to complete, as said in *Deadeye Dick*, "the suicidal flight we are on" (151). In *Timequake*, Vonnegut suggests just such a connection between Hemingway's own suicide and Western civilization's several attempts at suicide in World War I and World War II (205). Vonnegut stresses that the madness that executes beautiful kudu, that makes armaments, or worships guns emanates from mankind's heart of darkness—and he knows that the denial of responsibility for such violence: seeing it as inevitable, or playful, or honorable under any conditions—makes the deadly spiral circular and unending.[14]

To this end, Vonnegut associates Hemingway's primitivism in *Wanda June* with the mentality of Neanderthals, presently on earth in the form of men making change for peep shows, or recruiting Marines (20). Accused of being a "living fossil," Harold Ryan counters that since life is a survival of the fittest, you have got to fight from time to time or get eaten alive (17). Ryan echoes Hemingway's justifications for killing in *Green Hills of Africa*, that as a deeply primitive man who sees life as perpetually at war, he only gives what he takes, meeting aggression with aggression:

> I did nothing that had not been done to me. I had been shot and I had been crippled and gotten away. I expected always to be killed by one thing or another and I, truly, did not mind that anymore. (21)

Having only wounded his prey "instead of killing him quickly by breaking his neck as he had attempted" (183), Hemingway absolves himself from guilt by assuming the matador's "common sense" attitude toward killing and death. He reminds himself that since death is the inevitable climax to things anyway and since the natural devouring and self-devouring process that goes on nightly will continue with or without his participation, he might just as well indulge his primitive appetites as one who takes pleasure in the beauty of violence and death gracefully administered. It is in this same vein, adopting emotional blinders of sorts, that Hemingway reconciles himself to the more brutal aspects of the bullfight, seeing them as necessary to the symbolic life and death struggle with nature. "After a while," he says, "You never notice anything disgusting" (*Death* 81). This is what the would-be matador Jake Barnes says to Brett Ashley in *The Sun Also Rises* when she wonders how she will hold up during her first bullfight: "Just don't watch when its bad" (162).

What Vonnegut thinks about Hemingway's fatalism—Hemingway's acquiescence to a world of death and violence—is central to our understanding of Hemingway's symbolic role in *Timequake*. When in *Wanda June* Harold Ryan defends his brutality as an inflexible part of himself by insisting that this is the way God meant him to be, that this is the way his "particular clock is constructed," Norbert Woodly counters that, "We simply stop doing that—dropping things on each other, eating each other alive" (18). Woodly explains that what *is* inevitable is the necessary consequence of Ryan's aggression: "Let a radar set and a computer mistake a tank or a meteor for a missile, and that is the end of mankind" (19). That it is possible to understand and redirect the mindless conditioning processes that shape and control Harold Ryan's proclivities for cruelty and killing leads to the play's surprising climax, and focuses Vonnegut's quarrel with Hemingway here and elsewhere in Vonnegut's work. To illustrate that spiritual transformation is possible once one realizes that the reality of self and society are open to change, Vonnegut has Harold Ryan convert from a man of violence and cruelty to one of kindness and mercy. Ryan learns to laugh at his pretenses, and to believe that saving life is more important than saving face, suggesting that civilization may yet learn to do the same.

But in Vonnegut's latest parable about the seductive nature of deterministic belief, the author surprises us with an even more amazing feat of hocus pocus than that of Harold Ryan's conversion. I have argued earlier, in *Sanity*

Plea: Schizophrenia in the Novels of Kurt Vonnegut, that Vonnegut uses his father Kurt Senior, and that eternal harbinger of doom, Kilgore Trout, to purge himself of his more embittered and cynical self. In *Breakfast of Champions*, for instance, Vonnegut draws a direct line between his own demoralized condition and these two presences—the noxious Trout and the life-hating father—associated with disillusionment and death throughout his fiction. Equating his morbid father with machinery and mechanistic structures—timequakes, in effect—Vonnegut notes that when he was depressed to the point of suicide, he felt like that syphilitic standing underneath the "overhanging clock that his father had designed . . . eaten alive by corkscrews" and unable to fit together the world of self and the world of society (*Breakfast* 3). Then, from that void which he says is his schizophrenic hiding place from despair and cynicism, comes the wasted and saddened voice of Kilgore Trout, which Vonnegut says is also that of his father (181).

In *Deadeye Dick*, Vonnegut apparently achieves a major pinnacle in his personal, moral, and artistic evolution when he symbolically kills off this cynical father in print. As much a spiritual orphan as Hemingway's Nick Adams, Rudy Waltz frees himself from his father's destructive influence by writing a play, a process of exorcism and liberation, just as his father dies. No doubt Vonnegut's decision to remove the "Sr." from his name was just such an act of literary autogenesis. Later in *Bluebeard* Vonnegut and his renascent artist-hero Rabo Karabekian make a quantum leap in psychic healing when Rabo finally forgives his father for having been "the unhappiest and loneliest of men," bent upon self-innovation (31). Feeling at peace with himself about his father, he declares that *this* time he will forgive his father for good. In *Breakfast of Champions*, Vonnegut explains that as a similar act of cleansing and renewal, he was setting free his most cynical and moribund hero, Kilgore Trout, the liberation of whom amounts to the author's repudiation of his most pessimistic voice, the exorcism of a second fatalistic father. In effect, Vonnegut liberates Trout to celebrate his own disengagement from a mechanical relationship with his creator, who programmed him to write as he has. Only inertia had to be overcome, Vonnegut explains, before he could steer a more positive fictional course. Just as Vonnegut in *Breakfast of Champions* and Vonnegut's artist-angel Rabo Karabekian in *Bluebeard* emerge symbolically reborn in their awareness of themselves as artists in control of their lives and artistic creations, so now in *Timequake* it is the once-broken Trout—"this terribly wounded man" (*Breakfast of Champions* 234)—who overcomes apathy to assume the role of Vonnegut's shaman: the canary bird in the coal mine who values awareness and responsibility above all human virtues. This is the central story of *Timequake*, the successful efforts of that prophet of doom Kilgore Trout to negotiate the personal and artistic freedom Vonnegut had bequeathed to him in *Breakfast of Champions*.[15] Like Vonnegut after *Breakfast of Champions*, Trout will serve no longer as anyone's puppet, or put on any more puppet shows of his own. Just as Vonnegut had used Trout to dramatize his own view that he was a programmed writing machine, Trout's miraculous regeneration as Vonnegut's shaman measures the degree of optimism Vonnegut feels now about the efficacy of free will in the otherwise robot-populated world of *Timequake*. For a while, in *Timequake*, Trout, Kurt Senior, and Ernest Hemingway merge as one symbolic father figure—the voice of pessimism Vonnegut has battled in himself throughout his career.[16] It is by no coincidence that Trout dies at the age of eighty-four in the Ernest Hemingway Suite of the writer's retreat known as Xanadu, the city of imagination, or that the Trout whose cynicism drove his own wife and son from home, and led Leon Trout's mother to suicide, should speak to Vonnegut in the voice of Vonnegut's own father, Kurt Senior.

This most demoralized of Vonnegut's world-weary protagonists, Kilgore Trout, bears the same deterministic wound, the same legacy of childhood trauma, family insanity, deforming war experience, and depression that infects Kurt Senior and Ernest Hemingway with what Vonnegut in *Timequake* calls PTA, post–timequake apathy, a fatalistic malaise whose victims believe that their lives are as "unmalleable" (97), as irreversible as Harold Ryan's clock, impervious to change. Like Vonnegut's regressive, weak-minded characters in *Galápagos*, who have stopped giving a damn about what happens next, the robotic beings of *Timequake* appear to undergo a crisis in the year 2001, a freak of nature that "zaps" them back to the year 1991, and apparently compels them to repeat the last ten years of their lives. During such a rerun, people might think they were directing their own lives, but they really couldn't steer. In such a state of mind, rather than reinventing himself a la Harold Ryan and now Kilgore Trout, the Hemingway of *Timequake* remains death-bound and fatalistic. By contrast, it is precisely Kilgore Trout's new potential as a healer of self, then as a healer of others, that distinguishes Trout in his role as shaman, and that provides Vonnegut's most dramatic example yet of people as essentially fictional beings in stories they themselves create.[17] It is in their contrary recreations of self, Trout as humanist, Hemingway as ardent primitivist, that Vonnegut offers his final view of the disastrous effects of PTA on Hemingway's life and art, and of his own efforts to provide an iconography that turns war to peace, hatred to love, bigotry to compassion, rather than that which eggs men on to be even more destructive and cruel (*Bluebeard* 240).

No matter how successful Kilgore Trout's metamorphosis, his affirmation is neither easy nor simple. Vonnegut is not so naïve as to think that free will, his philosophic focus in *Timequake* and throughout his work, is ever complete, or that it solves all human problems any more than do those "big brains" in *Galápagos*. Remember Kilgore Trout's response to his author in *Breakfast of Champions* when Vonnegut sets him free? Yes, he cries, but can you make me young again? (*Breakfast of Champions* 295). At first, Trout's optimism is more tentative than triumphant, and even threatens to be cancelled when he worries, as in *Breakfast of Champions*, that his innate cynicism has made him unfit for the task of shaman, and that his proposals for reform go unnoticed in any case. Even when the timequake of 2001 quits and free will kicks in again, Trout is left "fibulating" with indecision, wondering whether the universe can or *should* continue to grow or die, whether free will is a blessing or a curse. Given the fact that he has previously only brought suffering to those around him and to his readers, should he, at his age, play "Russian roulette" with free will again, with the lives of others at stake (112)? Perhaps, he muses, the opportunities of free will for him are no longer relevant, and wonders further whether once and for all he shouldn't stop giving "a shit" what was going on, or what he was to do next. The equivocating Trout resembles the casualties of *Timequake* who have become so benumbed by PTA, so habituated to living in the mindless funk of a timequake that they are totally unprepared for the demands and responsibilities of free will. Hence, when Zoltan Pepper, one of Trout's fictional projections, realizes that it was "all of a sudden up to him to decide" (77) what to do next, he is run over by a fire truck whose driver is equally oblivious to the new reality. The inertia inspired by PTA leaves people used to taking directions from others accident-prone the world over. People get run over in traffic, fall down stairways, and, in despair, with a loss of self-respect, even commit suicide as in real life. "If self-respect breaks a leg," Vonnegut explains, "its owner has to shoot it. My mother and Ernest Hemingway and my former literary agent and Jerzy Kosinski and my reluctant thesis advisor at the University of Chicago and Eva Braun all come to mind" (*Timequake* 183). Vonnegut notes that independence of thought becomes especially dangerous in countries ruled by despots. He refers to the Nigerian "junta which regularly hangs its critics for having much too much free will" (174). Perhaps, Vonnegut wryly observes, the best thing to be when free will kicks in is a Mbuti, a pygmy in a rain forest in Zaire, Africa (151). Infected with PTA, the robotic beings of *Timequake* actually welcome their fate as machines rather than rebel. Relieved of responsibility for their actions, no one needs to apologize; in fact, no one learns from his mistakes. The painful complexity of human identity has ceased to be.

Given Trout's history of cynicism and defeatism, it is no surprise that like Vonnegut and like Vonnegut's other spiritually regenerated artist-heroes after *Breakfast of Champions*, Trout is still tempted to repeat his past, his familiar fatalistic tendencies as man and artist, just as people in a rerun following a timequake must do. In his story, "My Ten Years on Automatic Pilot," Trout concludes, "I didn't need a timequake to teach me being alive was a crock of shit. I already knew that from my childhood and crucifixes and history books" (93). In part, Trout still serves as Vonnegut's scapegoat, bearing his author's own burden of trauma and despair. It is Vonnegut, himself, who frets that scientists are finding more and more to make us believe that genes make us behave "this way or that," just as a rerun after a timequake would do (118), and Vonnegut, who in the very first pages of the novel creates a virtual litany of people like his mother and father and his sister Allie who hated life and secretly wished for it to end. Vonnegut acknowledges that both he and Trout are "polar depressives," people convinced that only 17 percent of people on the planet have lives worth living (141), and so susceptible to PTA that both are "black holes" to anyone who might imagine that he or she was their friend (28). As in *Breakfast of Champions*, Trout continues writing stories, notably sitting on Hemingway's bed in the Hemingway Suite at Zanadu, that threaten to infect his readers with his own disillusionment, causing them to believe that they can no more feel or reason than grandfather clocks (*Breakfast of Champions* 234). It is Trout's inadvertent mind-poisoning of Dwayne Hoover in *Breakfast of Champions* that now drives Dudley Prince nearly insane in *Timequake*. One such story concerns a scientist who kills himself when he realizes that the world of computer programming has done his thinking for him, deluding him into believing he was creative. Still another tale deals with the sardonic advice of the psychiatrist, Dr. Schadenfreude, who instructs his already suicidal patients that the planet is dying and that they are crazy for thinking that they matter.

But Kilgore Trout's narrative is no rerun. If Vonnegut and Trout are still susceptible to the potentially fatal pull of PTA, it is their hopeful voice inspired by their faith in the inviolability of human awareness that prevails in *Timequake*. Trout recognizes that it isn't a timequake dragging people through "knothole after knothole," but something else "just as mean and powerful" (46), the mind-crippling force of PTA, the moral sickness that steers the characters of *Galápagos*, who have stopped giving "a damn" (80), into an apocalyptic nightmare by military madmen. When Vonnegut describes the planet as "rigged with both natural and manmade booby traps" (*Timequake* 183), he identifies what Trout now renounces as a dynamite banquet, described in *Cat's Cradle* as a "wonderful idea" that proves to be "hideous in retrospect." While these superficially benign bargains came in a variety of packages, Trout sees that none is more dangerous than the mind-numbing belief that mechanistic structures such as timequakes, or Harold Ryan's aggression, are impossible to resist. As with Vonnegut's seeming advocacy of the consolations of smaller brains in *Galápagos*, the author presents us again with counterbalancing texts—the advantages of free will versus the attractions of determinism—that force us into a closer-than-usual examination of the devilish consequences of PTA. But reading closely, using *our* will and *our* "big brains," so to speak, we see that the petrified victims of PTA become as dehumanized as the twin computers in *Galápagos*, Gorbaki and Mandarax, pathological personalities with no more ability to feel or care about the future than "highly accurate clocks" (60). Just as Billy Pilgrim becomes lobotomized by the self-imprisoning fatalism of Tralfamadore, Trout observes that earthlings possessed by PTA became the "utterly amoral playthings" of those enormous forces of control that rob characters such as Billy and Paul Proteus of *Player Piano* and Jonah of *Cat's Cradle* of their dignity and self-integrity.

Judging from reviews of *Timequake* and from assessments of Vonnegut's artistic purposes in these collected essays, Vonnegut's critics, as if awakened from a timequake, no longer persist in reading Vonnegut as a writer of "pessimistic" or "defeatist" novels, but at long last appreciate the nature of his work as therapy, an autobiographical psychodrama in which he battles personal despair, and, as an avowed humanist and healer, warns against the perils of fatalism rather than affirms such a philosophy. If Vonnegut opens this book with a list of the living dead, which once would have included himself and Trout, he also speaks of Jesus Christ and the Sermon on the Mount, offering his usual prayer for mercy and respect, "For Christ's sake, let's help more of our frightened people get through this thing, whatever it is" (163). Vonnegut describes his novel as a "celebration" of the goodness, the creative genius of his brother, Bernie, and expresses eternal gratitude to his Uncle Alex for passing on beloved books to him, "reason enough to feel honored to be alive (157). He personally pronounces Kilgore Trout healed and whole. Poisoned with PTA, Hemingway and his mother may have killed themselves, "But not Kilgore Trout. His indestructible self-respect," Vonnegut declares, "is what I loved most about Kilgore Trout" (*Timequake* 183). Trout's hard won self-respect directs him to write stories that combine traditional humanism with the openness and philosophical pluralism of Pablo Picasso's paintings in the Museum of Modern Art, stories important for their humanness rather than their "pictureness." He will express his contempt for "cruel inventions," "irresistible forces in nature," and for fictions with absolute moral codes, closed scripts that privilege masculine authority and contain romantic plots like that of *A Farewell to Arms*. But he will resist "mainstream fiction" that makes heroes and heroines alike "feel like something the cat dragged in" (*Timequake* 63). Rather than encouraging a militant code of ethics such as Harold Ryan derives from the circumscribed and deterministic world of the corrida, he will create fictions that display his disgust with war and instead promote life-support systems like that of "extended families"— whose sense of human community causes even Dudley Prince's "rigor mortis to thaw" (*Timequake* 158).

The "rapture" Trout experiences in the power of choice to transform cruel vengeance to kindness and forgiveness is inspired by Rabo Karabekian's view that "Belief is nearly the whole of the Universe" (*Breakfast of Champions* 152). Trout sees that as explained by Einstein's observations in the novel's epilogue, all reality, all art, all science issues from the power of creative imagination, and therefore, that conceptions such as timequakes are but "obstacle courses" of our "own construction" (*Timequake* xiii). When Vonnegut announces in his preface that the only distinction between a rerun and real life are those the imagination makes, he underscores both the primacy and the existential responsibilities of creative will, the view that, whether as life or as story, a timequake is an artifice, an invention, whose qualities of heart and mind are ours to determine. Hence Vonnegut borrows Trout's term "manmade timequake" to explain that the very novel he writes is one whose soul and structure *he* designs, as imaginary as Xanadu, and therefore as open to reinvention as he desires. Whereas *Timequake I* fails to materialize, Vonnegut creates himself and Trout anew in the novel he chooses to call *Timequake II*, a work like a Picasso collage, or one of those imaginative recipes of Rudy Waltz in *Deadeye Dick*, that demonstrate that one can author one's existence in life as in a story rather than submit to the tyranny of prestructural systems of control. As Vonnegut has done in *Breakfast of*

Champions, Trout ignores "conventional paradigms"—what the "outside" world wants him to do, until he has "comprehended his own absorbing business, the story" (96). Trout thus finishes his own "long opposed" story about timequakes whether fate, or the universe, wants him to do so or not (97). Like Rudy Waltz, he becomes an artist at "ad libs," at improvisation when he sobs out loud during a play about beauty (203). He says nonsensical things on purpose, "Boop-boop-a doop, dingle-dangle, artsy-fartsy, wah, wah, and so on" (99). He cheers at the idiosyncratic possibilities of language by which he can change "Hickenbooper's Lockenbar" to "Lockenlooper's hickenbar, or Barkenhicker's Loopenlock (148), and delights in the flattened wheelchair transformed to a piece of modern art," *The Spirit of the Twenty-first Century*" (181). This is, in fact, the "spirit" of Rabo Karabekian's abstract or pessimist paintings in the Museum of Modern Art, which repudiates reality as an ordered and finished hierarchy, and invites the continuous reappraisal and resynthesis of the "mastery" reality paradigm.[18]

At the heart of Vonnegut and now Trout's understanding of both literary and real-life timequakes as open-ended existential ventures, Trout espouses his author's view of the mental life of human beings as inherently schizophrenic— that is, as capable of using their creative genius for harm as for good. "I believe in original sin," Vonnegut says, and "I also believe in original virtue. Look around" (*Timequake* 211). And he does, filling the novel with dichotomized people and conditions, "the best and the worst of Civilization" (12), humane impulses as well as destructive ones, existing within the same individual or insti- tution. Trout's story entitled "The Sisters B-36" perfectly illustrates his view of the complex potential of the human spirit for good or evil. We learn that what makes "Booboolings" the most "adaptable" creatures in the known universe is their "big brains," the human essence of which is imagination. But while Boo- boolings become hopeful, caring, and merciful when nurtured by such civiliz- ing influences as books, paintings, and music, they become insanely cruel and unfeeling when exposed to mindless television shows and computers. Hence one sister in the story becomes a picture painter; the other invents automobiles, flame-throwers, land mines, and machine guns. Trout recognizes that these alternative realities are never absolute, but are imaginative constructions with the power either to encourage or to distort our humanity. Vonnegut finds ample evidence of both irresponsible as well as humane creations. Perhaps with the earlier thwarting of his and Trout's humanistic zeal in mind, Vonnegut cites the example of Prometheus, who brings fire to human beings so they can be warm and cook, but who instead use fire to incinerate other humans in Hiroshima and Nagasaki (168). The physicist Andrei Sakharov, whose wife was a pediatri- cian, helped perfect a hydrogen bomb. The same great University of Chicago that gave up football in the name of sanity in 1942 allowed its vacant stadium to be turned into a bomb factory fifty-three years later, and commemorates the anniversary of the bombing of Hiroshima in the University Chapel.

But what heartens Vonnegut and Trout is their knowledge that freed of the conscience-numbing power of PTA, human beings become creatures with "options," capable of using the counterbalancing forces of creative will and imagination to convert destructive realities to humane ones. Hence, the scientist Leo Seren *apologizes* for his part in preparing the first atom bomb (4); and Andrei Sakharov evolves from an atom bomb advocate to one of the world's most ardent dissidents. Frank Smith, descendent of the notorious John Wilkes Booth, gives a stunning performance in Robert Sherwood's production of *Abe Lincoln in Illinois.* Vonnegut's brother Bernie, who once couldn't draw for "sour apples" and hated art, becomes a "poor man's Jackson Pollack." Vonnegut's son Mark writes a book about his going crazy in the 1960s, then graduates from Harvard Medical School, and has an exhibition of his watercolors. And Vonnegut's boyhood pal David Craig returns from killing Germans in World War II to become a builder in New Orleans (129). And of course Vonnegut, himself, transmogrifies from a car salesman who could not get a job teaching at Cape Cod Junior College to the successful author of *Slaughterhouse-Five*, a startling reversal of what humans did with Promethean fire.

In dramatic illustration of himself as a writer with "options," who intends to devote himself to reversing mankind's insanely aggressive tendencies, Trout tells a story in which he envisions himself as someone capable of steering the ship of destiny, the Bahia de Darwin of Galápagos, in an intelligent and merciful direction. Vonnegut explains that the name of the World War II bomber plane in Trout's story, "Joy's Pride," had a significant double meaning. It meant self-respect; it also meant a lion's family (8). Apropos of its schizophrenic potential, "Joy's Pride" was named in honor of a nurse in obstetrics, but is slated to drop an atom bomb on Yokahama. But the Trout who had once lured his own son Leon into the "blue tunnel of death" in *Galápagos* (159), and who confesses to Vonnegut that he had once "made sandwiches of German soldiers between an erupting earth and an exploding sky" (*Timequake* 10), exercises his "option" to be "merciful" (9). He instructs the pilot in his story to return to base, unused bomb and all.[19]

As he has done ingeniously with Rabo Karabekian in *Bluebeard* and Eugene Hartke in *Hocus Pocus*, Vonnegut stresses Trout's awareness of the interchangeability of life as fiction—that for better or worse reality can be made over by imagination as in a novel or play—by providing countless examples of both art and life as playful imaginative constructions. What was "actually" happening, Vonnegut reports, "might easily have been the ink-on-paper consequences of a premise for a story he himself had written" (111). He refers to Andrei Sakharov as a "real life *character* worthy of a story by Kilgore Trout" (5), and explains that his first wife, Jane, "may have felt like a character in a book by me, which in a sense she was" (116). Later Vonnegut describes a real-life war experience that merges with a fictional scene in *Bluebeard*, and says that he himself was "a character" in *Timequake I* (xiv). Real and fictional characters interact throughout the story. Kilgore Trout and Monica Pepper, for instance, sit on chairs once belonging to Henry James and Leonard Bernstein (47) and Monica and Vonnegut's sister Allie "were both pretty blonds, six-foot two" (32). But no single example anywhere in Vonnegut's work more compellingly illustrates life and art as similar creative ventures as does the illusion of Kilgore Trout as real in *Timequake*. While Vonnegut ironically foregrounds Trout's fictionality by announcing that "Trout doesn't really exist" except as the author's alter ego in several other novels (xiii), he talks to or about Trout constantly *as if* he were as real as Vonnegut, or Kurt Senior, or Ernest Hemingway, on whose bed he sits to write. "I have sabotaged a few of the thousands of stories he wrote," Vonnegut reports, "between 1931, when he was fourteen, and 2001, when he died at the age of eighty-four . . . in the Ernest Hemingway Suite of the writer's retreat Xanadu" (xiii). With myriad references such as, "I told Trout" (24), or "As Trout would point out to me" (78), or "That was Trout's idea not mine" (63), Trout assumes a real-life identity, independent of his creator, that climaxes his venture in self-creativity and his role as an anti-PTA advocate, a more caring man and writer. Mirroring his author's own self-doubts in *Breakfast of Champions*, Trout worries that he was destined to remain a character in someone else's book, somebody "who wants to write about somebody who suffers all the time" (*Timequake* 241). But his emergence as his own person, not merely his author's spokesman, is an act of free will, a "man made epiphany" (*Timequake* 19) whose magic surpasses even the arousal from death-in-life of Rudy Waltz, Rabo Karabekian, Eugene Hartke, and Kurt Vonnegut himself. Just as the reborn artist Rudy Waltz and Kurt Vonnegut confirm their wholeness and mutual liberation by coming face to face at the end of *Deadeye Dick*, so do Vonnegut and Trout when Vonnegut affirms Trout's healing mantra by calling out to him from the rear of the gallery where Trout addresses a "family" of artists: "You've been sick, Mr. Trout, but now you're well, and there's work to do" (212). As his "finale," Trout announces for a final time the magic of his mended soul and his rededication as a healer of others, what he calls that new and beautiful quality in the universe: "your awareness," which exists "only because there are other human beings" (213).

Ernest Hemingway wrote in *A Farewell to Arms* that people who survive terrible wounds are sometimes stronger in the broken places. In view of Vonnegut's portrait of Kilgore Trout and Ernest Hemingway at the end of their respective careers—Trout's evolution to his salubrious role as canary bird and a ripe old age of eighty-four, Hemingway's devolution to the blocked and despairing consciousness of the years following the Nobel Prize and the self-inflicted death at the age of sixty-one—the above seems better to describe Trout, or Vonnegut, than Hemingway. Some years ago I sent Vonnegut a story by Ray Bradbury about the death of Ernest Hemingway, entitled "The Kilimanjaro Device," which Vonnegut subsequently discusses in *Fates Worse Than Death*. It was a "made up" story, Vonnegut explains, about a person with a "magic" jeep who encounters a grizzled, terminally depressed Ernest Hemingway along a "wilderness" road near Ketchum, Idaho, and who offers Hemingway a lift to a better death than the one he was headed for (*Fates* 182). Afterwards Vonnegut wrote to me, "The Bradbury story brought a lump to my throat—I realize now that I see

Hemingway as a good man who blundered into a forest, and never got out again" (Letter April 2, 1990). The jeep is of course the liberating force of imagination, an acceptance of the feminine creative principle within themselves by which Vonnegut and Kilgore Trout have saved themselves from depression to create new, more humane, and artistically vital careers. Conversely, the "forest" is Hemingway's self-created machismo, mistaken as an irreversible timequake, a rigid and aggressive male persona whose militant code of ethics undermines Hemingway's personal and artistic growth and contributes to his tragic death. "We all see our lives as stories," Vonnegut writes in *Deadeye Dick*, "and the ends of those lives as epilogue." Hemingway, Vonnegut concludes, found his epilogue so uncongenial that he committed suicide (208), a form of "typography, a period," the only consistent conclusion to the "story" he carried in his head (*Fates* 67). "I place as much value on a period," Vonnegut says, "as on the painting careers of my father or my sister" (*Fates* 39).

Recent studies of Hemingway's declining years vindicate Vonnegut's view that the aggressive persona that Hemingway created for himself, informed by the walled-in world and stylized violence of the bullfight, left both the author and his inflexible machismo characters profoundly brutalized and divided within themselves. Trout, by contrast rewrites his timequake. He overturns the tragic impulse to cruelty and cynicism to share his author's feelings of personal harmony, the unity of body and soul, yin and yang, that enriches artistic possibilities, and reconnects him to community—the bonds of kinship, marriage, fatherhood, and friendship that Robert Jordan, Colonel Cantwell, Thomas Hudson, and Santiago so yearn for but never achieve. To borrow a page from Trout's Dr. Schadenfreude, Vonnegut has seemingly laid all ghosts to rest, said his good-byes to the demonized Fathers, and can rest in peace at century's end. Looking back from the year 2000, Vonnegut can conclude that it was all worthwhile. Like the builder Ted Adler he can ask with delight about his powers of invention and reinvention, "How the hell did I do that? (*Timequake* 129).[20]

NOTES

1. While Vonnegut has always cared deeply about the Earth, itself—this "lovely, moist, nourishing, blue-green ball"—he and his characters are relative newcomers to this capacity for sensuous experience. The Hemingway hero has always found compensation in sensual pleasures, what E. M. Halliday calls the hero's "passionate fondness for life."

2. Recent scholarship by such critics as Linda Wagner Martin, Linda Miller, Nancy Comley and Robert Scholes, and Mark Spilka has shown that gender issues in Hemingway's work are far more complex than earlier perceived.

3. See Lawrence Langer's excellent study of the historical forces behind the differences in the tone and mood that separate modernism from postmodernism, *The Holocaust and the Literary Imagination*. In my book in progress, *Writers at War: Vonnegut's Quarrel*

with Hemingway, I take a closer look at the ways in which Vonnegut's criticisms of Hemingway define essential shifts from the modern to postmodern mode. A telling example occurs in the contrast in tone between *A Farewell to Arms* and *Slaughterhouse-Five*. Both writers would agree to feeling inadequate to capturing the horrors they had experienced in war, as shown by their similar reductiveness of style. But Vonnegut's postmodern sensibility is expressed in the elaborate, absurdist, science fiction plot, and in the frivolity of tone that suggests that any attempt to confront the unacceptable in terms of conventional moral seriousness is foredoomed to failure by its pretense to epiphany (McConnel 170).

4. Frank McConnel says that this was a world in which men would for the first time begin wars knowing that their avowed ends would not be accomplished, a world that would produce a new kind of "anti-heroic hero" (169). One wonders how Hemingway, who said that the *only* thing to do with war was to win it, would have coped with the ambiguities of the war in Vietnam.

5. In *Happy Birthday Wanda June*, Penelope inquires into the sexual roots of Harold Ryan's obsession with heroism and death. She tells Harold that one reason men like war is that it allows them to manifest their fear and disrespect for women. The perversion of life-directed processes, of love and creativity, by the instinct to death and aggression is a major motif in the works of both writers, but it appears more consciously in Vonnegut's characters. Jake Barnes turns from his incapacity to make love to Brett Ashley, to seeking emotional satisfaction in the administering of death in the bullring. Mark Baldwin argues that Jake seeks to compensate for the limp or missing penis through the imposition of violence and the management of his friends (147).

6. It is worth noting that Hemingway and Vonnegut share populist sympathies, a respect for the world's have-nots whom Vonnegut refers to in *Timequake* as "sacred cattle," people who are "somehow wonderful despite their economic uselessness" (141). Vonnegut's social concerns, however, are obviously more direct and extensive.

7. James Jones, author of *From Here to Eternity*, told Vonnegut that he did not consider Hemingway a fellow soldier since Hemingway had never submitted to training and discipline either in World War II or in the Spanish Civil War (*Fates* 61). Vonnegut quips in *Palm Sunday* that Irwin Shaw's *The Young Lions* was such a good book that it made Hemingway mad. "He thought he had copyrighted war" (138).

8. Hemingway claimed that Philip Young was trying to put him out of business by psychoanalyzing him, arguing that Young had invaded psychic territory that belonged exclusively to him. By contrast, rather than feeling threatened, Vonnegut welcomed the psychoanalytical speculations of *Sanity Plea: Schizophrenia in the Novels of Kurt Vonnegut*. His willingness to deal openly and compassionately with painful family experience suggests that his mental health was well on the mend.

9. Linda Wagner Martin suggests how broadly the wound should be interpreted, how comprehensively it applies to the myriad losses—deaths of sorts—the hero suffers in a naturalistic world: deprivations of love, faith, country, family; of illusions of immortality, of a sense of personal significance, and of control over one's fate (5).

10. One should never assume uncritically that the protagonist of a Hemingway or Vonnegut work is necessarily the same person as the author, as if no strategies of authorial distancing were at work to establish the hero as an independent creation. It is best to

believe that while both writers invite us to view their fictional creations in light of their own values and attitudes, each, as Jackson Benson says of Hemingway, enlarged, subtracted, combined, transposed, and added new cloth to his underlayment of memory. I like what Robin Gadjusek says about Hemingway's complex reworking of life experience—that the heroes are simultaneously versions of the author and *other* than the author.

11. See also Frederick Busch's excellent discussion of the "muted screams," the "terror of silences" in Hemingway's work. Busch says that the choice of the Hemingway protagonist is either to fall prey to the terror of living, and therefore kill himself, or soldier on by finding ways to diminish the import of screams while performing with generosity, courage, and skill.

12. I refer here to the Museum of Modern Art in *Bluebeard*, the symbolic arena of Rabo Karabekian's artistic awakening.

13. Kathryn Hume notes that the increased affirmation of Vonnegut's protagonists after *Breakfast of Champions* correlates with their more sympathetic relationships with women. By contrast, studies by Rose Marie Burwell, Robert Flemming, Mark Spilka, and Nancy Comley and Robert Scholes indicate that the inflexible macho mask that suppressed the feminine side of Hemingway's nature accounts for the author's inability to complete works that required Hemingway to delve more deeply into that part of his psyche. These studies suggest that the denial of the female presence in others or in himself, the need to dominate rather than harmonize, impoverishes creative possibilities, and contributes to aggression. Gerry Brenner demonstrates that even Santiago remains "a cauldron of hostility," a man of "murderous potential," by repressing the female within himself (81, 82).

14. Robert Flemming and Rose Marie Burwell cite Hemingway's willingness to look at the darker implications of killing and the abuse of children and former wives in *Islands in the Stream* and *Garden of Eden*. They see the novels as a single tapestry that counts the cost of machismo to the artist and those whose lives, children, parents, lovers, comrades, even pets, are united with his own. Burwell recognizes a new degree of conscience, introspection, and self-criticism, thus gains in self-knowledge and integrity. Yet as a writer whose ethos and style in fact *denied* awareness, Hemingway and his characters fall short of an examination of their inner diabolism that conversely allows such protagonists as Rabo Karabekian and Kilgore Trout to achieve an integrated and peaceful spirit. Flemming and Burwell agree that Hemingway could not complete *Islands* or *Garden of Eden* precisely because these works demanded a more probing explanation of the author's psyche than he was prepared to give.

15. See Kathryn Hume's excellent discussion of Kilgore Trout's many transformations as Vonnegut's alter ego. She explains that Trout's fluctuating identity from novel to novel serves as a means of integrating potentially overwhelming fragments of Vonnegut's own psyche (186). But Trout has never been treated so factually or extensively as in *Timequake*. Details are filled in about his family background, even his conception on Dead Man's Rock (159).

16. Vonnegut and Hemingway would evidently agree that, as Rudy Waltz says in *Deadeye Dick*, their fathers were "bad fathers" to have. Vonnegut refers to his father in *Timequake* as "frankly vengeful" (144). He comments that Kurt Senior became a gun nut

and hunter in order to prove that he wasn't effeminate, even though he was in the arts, an architect and a painter. In *Bluebeard*, Vonnegut not coincidentally links his father to Ernest Hemingway by explaining their mutual belief that stored-up sperm made them more cheerful, brave, and creative (152).

17. James Cox observes that Hemingway, in fact, had a tendency to confuse his life with his art. Consistent with Vonnegut's view of Hemingway's death, Cox suggests that Hemingway's life was shaped by his fiction rather than vice versa (307).

18. Vonnegut's quarrel with Hemingway is in part a quarrel with modernism itself, with what Ihab Hassan describes as modernist privileging of authority, mastery, centering, order, and law, of which "the Hemingway Code is perhaps the starkest example" (Hassan 45). Yet, as with his connection to Hemingway, Vonnegut's relationship to modernism should be perceived both in terms of continuity and discontinuity, sameness and difference, unity and rupture, filiation and revolt (Hassan 88). Patricia Waugh would say that Vonnegut makes peace with realism, despite his occasional metafictional leanings (19), indicative of Todd Davis's view of Vonnegut in this volume as a "postmodern humanist" or "sardonic moralist," a moralist who dares the postmodern haze.

19. This scene reminds us of Billy Pilgrim's infrequent affirmative use of imagination in *Slaughterhouse-Five* when he reverses a destructive bombing mission in a war film. I partially concede here to Kevin Boon's argument that meaning and value in Vonnegut's "chaotic" universe is sometimes more indeterminate or complex than not. Despite the best efforts of Trout's bomber pilot, Trout's story ends apocalyptically as a crack in the ocean floor swallows everything in sight (10). (See note 18.)

20. Cynthia Ozick would call Vonnegut's response one of postmodern "self-surprise," as opposed to the modernist's pretense of "self-knowledge" or "self-anointment." When Vonnegut observes that his stories sometimes write themselves ("If I put the tip of a pen on paper, it would write a story of its own accord" (*Timequake* 92), he illustrates Patricia Waugh's point about metafiction that "the author discovers that the language of the text produces him or her as much as he or she produces the language of the text" (138).

WORKS CITED

Baldwin, Mark. *Reading* The Sun Also Rises: *Hemingway's Political Unconscious*. New York: Peter Lang, 1997.

Benson, Jackson, ed. *The Short Stories of Ernest Hemingway*. Durham: Duke UP, 1975.

Boon, Kevin. *Chaos Theory and the Interpretation of Literary Texts: The Case of Kurt Vonnegut*. New York: Edwin Mellen, 1997.

Brenner, Gerry. The Old Man and the Sea: *Story of a Common Man*. New York: Twayne, 1991.

Broer, Lawrence. *Hemingway's Spanish Tragedy*. Tuscaloosa: U of Alabama P, 1973.

――――. *Sanity Plea: Schizophrenia in the Novels of Kurt Vonnegut*. Tuscaloosa: U of Alabama P, 1994.

Burwell, Rose Marie. *The Postwar Years and the Posthumous Novels*. Cambridge: Cambridge UP, 1996.

Busch, Frederick. "Reading Hemingway without Guilt." *New York Times* 12 January 1992: 10–19.

Comley, Nancy R, and Robert Scholes. *Hemingway's Genders, Reading the Text*. New Haven: Yale UP, 1994.

Cox, James. "In Our Time: The Essential Hemingway." *Southern Humanities Review* 22 (1988): 305–20.

Flemming, Robert E. *The Face in the Mirror*. Tuscaloosa: U of Alabama P, 1994.

Gajdusek, Robin. "Artists in their Art: Hemingway and Velasquez—The Shared Worlds of *For Whom the Bell Tolls* and *Las Meninas*." *Hemingway Repossessed*. Ed. Kenneth Rosen. Westport, CT: Praeger, 1994.

Halliday, E. M. "Hemingway's Ambiguity, Symbolism, and Irony." *Hemingway: A Collection of Critical Essays*. Ed. Robert P. Weeks. Inglewood Cliffs: Prentice Hall, 1958.

Hassan, Ihab. *The Postmodern Turn: Essays in Postmodern Theory and Culture*. Columbus: Ohio State UP, 1987.

Hemingway, Ernest. *The Sun Also Rises*. New York: Scribner's, 1926.

———. *The Short Stories of Ernest Hemingway*. New York: Scribner's, 1927.

———. *A Farewell to Arms*. New York: Scribner's, 1929.

———. *Death in the Afternoon*. New York: Scribner's, 1932.

———. *Green Hills of Africa* New York: Doubleday, 1954.

———. *For Whom the Bell Tolls*. New York: Scribner's, 1940.

———. *Across the River and into the Trees*. New York: Scribner's, 1950.

———. *The Old Man and the Sea*. New York: Scribner's, 1932.

———. *Islands in the Stream*. New York: Scribner's, 1970.

———. *Garden of Eden*. New York: Scribner's, 1986.

Hume, Kathyrn. "Vonnegut's Self-Projections: Symbolic Characters and Symbolic Fiction." *The Journal of Narrative Technique* (Fall 1982): 177–90.

Langer, Lawrence L. *The Holocaust and the Literary Imagination*. New Haven: Yale UP, 1975.

Martin, Linda Wagner. *New Essays on* The Sun Also Rises. Cambridge: Cambridge UP, 1987.

McConnel, Frank. "Stalking Papa's Ghost: Hemingway's Presence in Contemporary American Writing." *Wilson Quarterly* 10.1 (1986): 160–73.

Ozick, Cynthia. "The Muse, Postmodern and Homeless." *Metaphor and Memory: Essays*. New York: Knoph, 1989. 136–39.

Rovit, Earl. "On Psychic Retrenchment in Hemingway." *Essays of Reassessment*. Ed. Frank Scafella. New York: Oxford UP, 1991: 181–88.

Spilka, Mark. *Hemingway's Quarrel with Androgyny*. Lincoln: U of Nebraska P, 1990.

Tetlow, Wendolyn. *Hemingway's* In Our Time*: Lyrical Dimensions*: Lewisburg: Bucknell UP, 1992.

Vonnegut, Kurt. *Player Piano*. 1959. New York: Dell, 1971.

———. *The Sirens of Titan*. 1959. New York: Dell, 1971.

———. *Mother Night*. 1961. New York: Dell, 1974.

———. *Cat's Cradle*. 1963. New York: Dell, 1975.

———. *Slaughterhouse-Five*. 1969. New York: Dell, 1972.

———. *Happy Birthday, Wanda June*. New York: Delacorte/Seymour Lawrence, 1971. New York: Dell, 1971.

———. *Breakfast of Champions*. 1973. New York: Dell, 1975.

———. *Palm Sunday*. New York: Dell, 1981.

———. *Deadeye Dick*. New York: Delacorte/Seymour Lawrence, 1982.

———. *Galápagos*. New York: Delacorte/Seymour Lawrence, 1985.

———. *Bluebeard*. New York: Delacorte, 1987.

———. *Hocus Pocus*. New York: Putman's, 1990.

———. *Fates Worse Than Death: An Autobiographical Collage*. New York: Berkley, 1992.

———. *Timequake*. New York: Putman's, 1997.

Waugh, Patricia. *Metafiction: The Theory and Practice of Self-Conscious Fiction*. New York: Metheum, 1984.

CHAPTER FIVE

YOU CANNOT WIN, YOU CANNOT BREAK EVEN, YOU CANNOT GET OUT OF THE GAME: KURT VONNEGUT AND THE NOTION OF PROGRESS

Donald E. Morse

> While civilization has been improving our houses, it has not equally improved the men who are to inhabit them.
> —Thoreau, *Walden*

> I don't have the feeling that we are going anywhere.
> —Kurt Vonnegut

At the end of the twentieth century, the heirs of nineteenth-century believers in progress ironically often appear within the ranks of science itself—the very disciplines from which Charles Darwin, James Hutton, and others tried to banish them. Some contemporary cosmologists, for example, trumpet their optimism about humanity's ability through the use of technology and ever-expanding knowledge to meet any coming crisis or to survive any challenge. Barrow and Tipler in *The Anthropic Cosmological Principle* speculate "that technology will continue to rise exponentially over billions of years, constantly accelerating in proportion to existing technology. . . . Over several billions years, intelligent beings will have completely colonized vast portions of the visible universe" (Kaku 308). Technology, like culture, is Lamarkian rather than Darwinian; that is, society and culture retain, as an inherited trait, technological and cultural innovations whereas humans can neither biologically inherit nor build on a previous generation's accomplishments. There is no absolute barrier to what they may accomplish through technology, but clearly there remains an absolute barrier to what humans can do physically in addition to the seemingly insuperable barrier to what they may become morally. Progress in technology thus does not equate with progress in humanity, despite a fuzzy popular linking of the two. Upon hearing that "they" were building a telegraph between Maine and Texas, Thoreau commented, "We are in great haste to construct a magnetic telegraph from Maine to Texas; but Maine and Texas, it may be, have nothing important to communicate" (*Walden* 36). Similarly, in novel after novel, Vonnegut raises Thoreau's question about distinguishing between means and ends. What, he asks in *Timequake*, is the actual function of the ubiquitous television set? He concludes that television contributes to the loss of imagination in contemporary society by replacing the printed book with an already fully formed image flickering on a screen. Books nurture the imagination, while television, along with other electronic forms of pre-formed images, helps kill it. "TV is an *eraser*," exclaims the narrator of *Timequake* in disgust (193). Television's ephemeral, constant stream of images along with its instant events replaces and erases history, art, and literature, damaging both individual and collective memory. A medium almost devoid of reflection, television exists exclusively in what William James calls, the "*specious* present" (609).

Furthermore, progress is not to be equated with motion, no matter how fast or extensive. In *The Sirens of Titan*, Malachi Constant rockets around the solar system like a high-speed yo-yo going nowhere—from getting rich to becoming poor, ricocheting off one planet to another, from being kidnapped on earth to arriving eventually on Titan then being shipped back on earth to die; he never really goes anywhere. His nonarrival becomes doubly ironic in light of his dubious lifetime wish to become a modern day Mercury carrying a really important message "sufficiently dignified and important to merit his carrying it humbly between two points" (17). His prayer appears answered for he does get to carry a message, but it proves to be what he neither wanted nor needed. For while his message, which lies at the heart of the novel, is truly an important one, it is hardly "dignified," nor is it really his since it means nothing to him. Rather than becoming Mercury, the messenger of the gods, he becomes a mere errand boy sent on a fool's task. Yet his belief in progress dies hard. Perhaps the best comment on such a foolish belief in *The Sirens of Titan* comes from Ransom K. Ferm who supplies the novel's epigraph:

> Every passing hour brings the Solar System forty-three thousand miles closer to Globular Cluster M13 in Hercules—and still there are some misfits who insist that there is no such thing as progress. (5)

Quod erat demonstrandum. If progress is measured in motion or in speed, then, of course, Ferm is right, but if it is measured in purpose or direction, then his words become bitterly ironic. Charging ahead on a course not chosen but randomly taken at an unregulated speed creates only the illusion of progress no matter how swift the movement. In *Galápagos*, Vonnegut suggests that such illusionary progress is a good example of humanity's penchant for driving at high speed on a superhighway that will end abruptly at the cliff edge of ecological or nuclear suicide. Once again, humanity has confused the means (high speed driving) with the end (survival of the species). One way out of this dilemma would be to extirpate that great big brain humans have or, at least, let it evolve into something smaller and hence less harmful to humans, other creatures, and the planet. Hence in *Galápagos*, Vonnegut sends humanity back to the sea to fish, but with a much more modest-sized brain.

Popular views of progress often equate it with increasing complexity as well as with motion and speed. The notion of life ever advancing toward more complexity comes about in part through misconstruing Darwin's observation that local adaptability to changed or changing conditions leads to the establishment of new species.

> Everybody knows that organisms get better as they evolve. They get more advanced, more modern, and less primitive. And everybody knows . . . that organisms get more complex as they evolve. From the first cell that coalesced in the primordial soup to the magnificent intricacies of *Homo sapiens*, the evolution of life—as everybody knows—has been one long drive toward greater complexity. The only trouble with what everybody knows . . . is that there is no evidence it's true [ellipsis in original]. (Lori Oliwenstein qtd. in Gould 212)

Reasoning from dead-end or unsuccessful experiments in evolving creatures, such as horses or humans, many placed human beings at the pinnacle of evolution as they once placed them at the pinnacle of creation. But substituting evolution for creation still leaves unresolved the problem of the absence of evidence for assuming that humans are indeed the goal of evolution rather than an adaptation to local conditions. As paleontologist, Stephen Jay Gould contends, "We are glorious accidents of an unpredictable process with no drive to complexity, not the expected results of evolutionary principles that yearn to produce a creature capable of understanding the mode of its own necessary constructing" (Gould 216).

In *Galápagos*, Vonnegut reverses the cliché of humanity marching ever onward and upward. Adapting to local conditions and taking advantage of accidents and serendipity, *exactly as evolution has always done*, humans in this novel return to the sea. Darwin's best examples of evolution occurring because of local adaptation also occurred on the Galápagos islands where he encountered isolated animals—like the humans in *Galápagos*—that had evolved into new species. Neither the strongest nor the most complex survived, but the fastest and best at adaptation. Rather than viewing species as superior or inferior, Darwin emphasized their differences, especially those differences that enabled certain species to survive changing conditions. The elephant that evolved into the wooly mammoth did so to survive in a new age of ice. To say that the wooly mammoth is somehow superior to his ancestor the elephant establishes an indefensible scale of value. Similarly, the animals of Australia evolved to live under incredibly difficult conditions of small erratic rainfalls, scarce food, and intense heat. The kangaroo, for instance, leaps rather than runs because leaping over long distances uses only a fraction of the energy that running does. The wombat and a sheep have about equal body mass, but one being perfectly adapted to scarcity requires only a small fraction of the other's daily intake of food to survive.

Galápagos describes a world in which only a tiny remnant of humanity remains not because a nervous finger on the nuclear trigger led to worldwide conflagration hence mutation (*Cat's Cradle* had described metaphorically a nuclear winter before the term became popular), but because the vast majority of humanity mysteriously becomes sterile and therefore fails to reproduce. Initially, such conditions appear more benign than, say, a world subjected to radioactive fallout, but they prove equally as effective as the Bomb in eliminating the human menace. This scenario, derided as too improbable by some critics, appears now, at the end of the twentieth century, as all too possible. Consider the large area in Siberia where the human and animal population is under threat of extinction from the huge amount of leaking nuclear waste deposits. For decades, the atmosphere there has been polluted with radiation. Should that waste leach into the Arctic Sea, as appears now possible or even probable, then the poisoning of all northern latitudes of the globe becomes a distinct possibility. The much-vaunted human technology could yet destroy all humanity. Stephen Jay Gould warns that

> accumulating technological "progress" need not lead to cultural
> improvement in a visceral or moral sense—and may just as well end
> in destruction, if not extinction, as various plausible scenarios, from
> nuclear holocaust to environmental poisoning, suggest. I have long
> been impressed by a potential solution . . . to the problem of why
> we haven't been contacted by the plethora of advanced civilizations

that ought to inhabit other solar systems in our universe. Perhaps any society that could build a technology for such interplanetary, if not intergalactic, travel must first pass through a period of potential destruction where technological capacity outstrips social or moral restraint. And perhaps no, or very few, societies can ever emerge intact from such a crucial episode. (223)

Vonnegut explores this issue of possible progress undercut by the misapplication or abuse of technology in *Deadeye Dick*. As in most of his novels, a belief in progress crashes into a barrier perhaps best described by C. P. Snow in his witty reformulation of the three laws of thermodynamics:

1. *You cannot win* (that is, you cannot get something for nothing, because matter and energy are conserved).

2. *You cannot break even* (you cannot return to the same energy state, because there is always an increase in disorder; entropy always increases).

3. *You cannot get out of the game* (because absolute zero is unattainable).

(Quoted in Kaku 304)

This barrier to progress becomes a leitmotiv in many Vonnegut novels, including *Deadeye Dick* where it becomes entangled with the understandable wish for a better world after World War II. During her luncheon with Rudy Waltz's family, Mrs. Eleanor Roosevelt shared her belief with the Waltzes that

there would be a wonderful new world when the war was won. Everybody who needed food or medicine would get it, and people could say anything they wanted, and could choose any religion that appealed to them. Leaders wouldn't dare to be unjust anymore, since all the other countries would gang up on them. For this reason, there could never be another Hitler. He would be squashed like a bug before he got very far. (*Deadeye Dick* 59)

But these brave and hopeful words are seriously undercut by subsequent events in world history as well as in the novel. Immediately after her visit, Rudy goes upstairs to the gun room and fires the shot heard round Midland City that kills the pregnant Mrs. Eloise Metzger. Rather than the brave new postwar world, Rudy enters a world where his random unthinking event exercises control— an absolute control—over him. As he painfully learns—*You cannot win, You cannot break even,* and *You cannot get out of the game.*

In *Deadeye Dick* the aptly named John Fortune Farm in Midland City becomes symbolic of true progress in the United States during this century. First, in the '30s the farm thrived, was self-sustaining and productive. During the Great American Depression, however, it became economically nonviable, whereupon the owner, Fortune, set off on a fruitless search for Shangri-La. In the '40s, the farm shifted from productive to destructive as the United States armed forces fighting in World War II used it for a tank proving ground. In the '60s, the farm, transformed once more, became "Avondale," an archetype of suburban tract housing, made up of the "little shitboxes," as Rudy describes. Abruptly, in the '80s, the farm disappeared from the map altogether when it, along with all of Midland City, became a test area for the neutron bomb. There's even speculation that the bomb was dropped under orders of the United States government, since Midland City was classified as the least objectionable place on which to test such a weapon (234). "What I showed happening to Midland City," comments Vonnegut, is "the indifference of our government to the closing down of these towns." The example he gives of such a destroyed town or city is Terra Haute, Indiana:

> The last business just closed down there—Columbia Records closed down its plant . . . permanently. . . . [T]his place has got twenty-seven churches, . . . a railroad yard, it's got all this, and it might as well have been neutron bombed, and so there was that analogy. . . . If a neutron bomb did go off accidentally in Terra Haute, it would be on the news for about three days because the feeling is that these people weren't really of any importance. (Reed, Interview 9)

Like Vonnegut's Midland City, Terra Haute, a once viable Indiana town with a most livable environment, becomes consigned to the scrap heap by American progress—a huge mistake in Vonnegut's eyes, but like so many mistakes this one has no single cause and no clear force or person to blame. Like so much that is radically changing the face of America, Terra Haute's fate was decided in a corporate boardroom far removed from the actual city itself. The neutron bomb becomes an apt symbol for this kind of progress measured by corporate bottom lines.

The destruction of viable human environments, such as Terra Haute or Midland City, is not a new story in the United States. In 1620, the Pilgrims, upon first viewing the shore of the New World, saw not a green and pleasant land, but only wilderness and savages. They quickly set about destroying both by utilizing their vastly superior technology and replaced them with more familiar "civilization." In *Slapstick*, Vonnegut reverses that movement from nature to city, from savage to civilized by creating an Eden in the wilderness— or in as much wilderness as modern Vermont allows—and peopling it with a primitive-appearing, simian-like, monstrously tall Adam and Eve. At the same time, Vonnegut again appears to reverse a popular evolutionary stereotype. Here, the cliché of humans progressing up and away from apes becomes challenged since these innocent great apes are distinctly superior to ordinary humans (Mustazza 140–41). Armed only with astronomical intelligence quotients, the zygotes thrive in this idyllic setting and, when together, complete one suprahuman person. When together, they write a work critical of Darwin's theory of evolution and a "precocious critique of the Constitution of the United States" (52), learn ancient and modern languages, and master calculus. Apart, each becomes "stupid and insecure" as each feels as though his or her "head were turning to wood" (87). Progress in the person of an embittered psychologist proves the modern snake in the garden and condemns them to separation and exile. Thus they are expelled forever from paradise. Worse, they are separated. *Slapstick* suggests that if a genius should appear, humanity would treat her or him not as a potential means to genuine social, political, or cultural progress, but as a pariah. Collective wisdom would conspire to throw him or her out, not just out of Eden, but out of the human community by confining her or him to a mental ward.

The new millennium will change neither humanity nor its inability to progress. Speaking of Earth, a guest on a talk show in *Hocus Pocus* notes, "We could have saved it, but we were too doggone cheap" (143). People will continue to follow "the complicated futility of ignorance" (*Hocus Pocus* 14), so events and people in the new century, in the new millennium, will continue much as they have in this century. The result will not be progress toward enlightenment or toward a new heavenly city or toward a better life, but toward Apocalypse. In Vonnegut's universe, help is not on the way to Earth and, therefore, humans have to realize they are alone and must, of necessity, become their own best resource.

Unlike in Arthur C. Clarke and Stanley Kubrick's *2001*, in Vonnegut's millennial novel, *Hocus Pocus*, humans will not travel to other parts of the universe in the new century, nor will they receive help from some mysterious source outside themselves, this planet, or this solar system. The hero of *Hocus Pocus* "is a graduate of West Point and a veteran of the Vietnam War, a thoughtful but not tormented man who killed many human beings on the orders of his Government and dispensed many official lies as an information officer" (McInerney 309), and learned firsthand that war is meaningless butchery of ordinary people like himself. Eugene Debs Hartke's ironic name combines that of Eugene Victor Debs, the great social reformer, with that of Indiana Senator, Vance Hartke, who in 1968 narrowly won reelection having bravely campaigned against the Vietnam War—one of the very few congressmen who dared do so. Like Howard Campbell in *Mother Night* and Walter Starbuck in *Jailbird*—like Miguel Cervantes—Hartke writes his book in prison, the very place where the novel was born. Like so many prison writers, he must use whatever scraps of paper come to hand.[1] It was on just such scraps of paper in 1963—actually on the edges of pages of *The New York Times*—that Martin Luther King Jr. wrote his *Letter from Birmingham Jail*, his prophetic call to resist and end racism in America. *Hocus Pocus* itself proves a ringing denunciation of American racism as well as the Vietnam debacle, but, unlike King, its author is no prophet. Typical of many prison narratives, Hartke's impulse to write is very tentative. The unnamed editor of *Hocus Pocus* speculates: "It is . . . likely . . . that he [Hartke] began this book impulsively, having no idea it would become a book, scribbling words on a scrap which happened to be right at hand" (vii).

Another of Vonnegut's single-book authors, Hartke questions the sanity of his time. Were not those in charge of Vietnam, for instance, a little like the governor and his wife in the second part of *Don Quixote*; that is, people so caught up in their delusions derived from fiction that they produced fake events for real people to participate in, rather than for actors on stage or television to act out or for characters in a novel to follow (an issue first explored at length in *Breakfast of Champions*)? Hartke, like the Knight of the Woeful Countenance, became the victim of someone else's script, speaking someone else's lines, himself offering encouragement in a futile enterprise: "I was a genius of lethal hocus pocus!" he exclaims (154). Like Eliot Rosewater, Walter Starbuck, and Dr. Wilbur Swain, Hartke wanted to help his fellow humans through a life of service. His first career choice was journalism, but he ended up at West Point training to be a professional soldier. During his career, he kills dozens and dozens of his fellow humans—all quite legally, as he repeatedly points out. Some of those killings were regrettable, such as the incident where he "pitched a grenade into the mouth of a tunnel one time, and killed a woman, her mother, and her baby hiding from helicopter gunships which had strafed her village right before we [Hartke and others] got there" (252). Like Eliot Rosewater's killing of the unarmed firemen in World War II, this incident is, of course, unintentional, if clearly "unforgettable" (252).

Eugene Victor Debs (1855–1926), four times candidate for president of the United States, received almost a million votes as a third party candidate in 1920. In 1922 Debs chose as his epitaph "While there is a lower class I am in it. While there is a criminal element I am of it. While there is a soul in prison I am not free" (qtd. in *Hocus Pocus* 2). Against this moral yardstick, Vonnegut measures the United States in the year 2001. If Eugene Debs, at the beginning of the century, was an exponent of the Sermon on the Mount, Eugene Debs Hartke at the end of the century becomes an exponent of getting along by going along—a man not tormented by his conscience, though he has killed close to a hundred people. If Eugene Debs identified with the outcast, the down and out, the lower classes, the jailed, Hartke does not. "I have no reforms to propose" (242), he reiterates. Furthermore, if Debs went to jail voluntarily because of sympathy toward those already incarcerated, Hartke goes involuntarily because of the white racism of those in authority. In his defense, he makes lists of those he has killed and of those to whom he made love. "Quantification becomes the latest escape valve discovered by a Vonnegut narrator from a condition too troublesome for him to confront" (Mistichelli 322).

Hartke proves a prime example of Kathryn Hume's "teflon coated Vonnegut character" whose emotions, if any, lie buried beneath an impervious surface. Neither in adultery nor in killing does Hartke evince any feeling or involvement. No conviction ever guides Hartke in any choice he makes for he rarely, if ever, actually makes choices himself, but rather follows those detours that present themselves. For example, he establishes and maintains a home for two insane women, his wife and mother-in-law—a difficult, compassionate act involving a considerable commitment of time, money, and energy. While he is absent, the authorities forcibly remove both women from his home and incarcerate them in a public asylum without consulting him. His technique for surviving this and numerous other emotionally wrenching experiences is to appear laconically indifferent—in this instance, indifferent to the violence done to his wife and mother-in-law and to the sanctity of his home. Thus we have the compassionate act—providing a safe, congenial environment for two insane people—done without complaint or whining followed by almost brutal indifference to their disappearance from his life. Like Walter Starbuck in *Jailbird*, whose prose style resembles his, Hartke appears capable of singing, but only in a minor key and then only within a limited range. Typically, readers are left to evaluate this and other ethical issues of character, action, and value within an unresolved, opaque moral situation—all seemingly without authorial guidance.

"Ultimately," contends Bill Mistichelli, "the success of *Hocus Pocus* is that it fails to resolve the questions and issues it poses" (322). Most of those issues may be subsumed under the familiar Vonneguttian—and American—ethical dilemma of using bad means to effect a good end. At the beginning of his career as a novelist (1952–1969), Vonnegut concentrated on the means. The firebombing of Dresden, for example, a horrendous act (the means) was done for the purpose of "shortening the war" (an exemplary end). Toward the end of his career (1969–1990), he focuses on Vietnam (the means) and the resulting series of horrendous acts (also means) done to save "democracy and freedom" in Southeast Asia and to prevent other countries from succumbing to communism like so many dominoes toppling down (an exemplary end).[2] If Billy Pilgrim symbolizes the innocent child playing at war, Vonnegut's characterization of World War II soldiers, then Eugene Debs Hartke symbolizes the disgraced adolescent playing at saving nations from themselves, Vonnegut's characterization of American policymakers in Vietnam. "Like Damon Stern, his close friend and head of the college's history department, he [Hartke] is fond of punching holes in complacent American pieties and conventional flag-waving beliefs. Included are data from his own experiences, like his frequent references to the brutalities he performed and witnessed in Vietnam" (Mistichelli 316). Morally and politically bankrupt, the Vietnam War "was about nothing but the ammunition business" (*Hocus Pocus* 2) and at its end Hartke has "lost all respect for himself and the leadership of his country" (53). The last American to leave Saigon when it fell, Hartke had the unenviable, if highly symbolic, job of keeping "Vietnamese who had been on our side from getting into helicopters that were ferrying Americans only . . . to our Navy ships offshore" (52). Few sights better illustrate America's ignominious defeat than its utter failure to protect the Vietnamese it alleged it was saving. A hypocritical talk show host in *Hocus Pocus* observes that stories of defeat are not good for morale (126–27). True enough, but they do serve the far more important function of roughing up human pride, chastening mindless patriotism, and giving poor mortals a realistic perspective on themselves as individuals, on the human race in general, and on the planet they inhabit.

In *Galápagos*, it was the great big human brains that were to blame for the pending destruction of the planet, but in *Hocus Pocus*, Vonnegut identifies the enemy more narrowly as human indifference as seen in the parable of the stranded elevator. Humanity's representative, six-year-old Bruce Bergeron, stands trapped on an elevator stuck between floors in a large department store. Bruce mistakenly believes he must be "at the center of a major event in American history" (165)—as most six-year-olds do. When at last the elevator becomes freed, it moves to the next floor and deposits passengers safely. Bruce, who "survived" the ordeal, discovers to his shock that no one else is remotely interested in his or his fellow passengers' predicament, as the rest of humanity either impatiently waits for the next elevator or madly participates in the department store's white sale. "There wasn't even somebody from the management of the store to offer an anxious apology, to make certain everybody was all right" (166). Everyone—whether inside or outside the elevator—is so completely wrapped up in his or her own plight, activities, or wants that no room remains for that of anyone else—much less any vision of the needs of society as a whole. Discussing *Hocus Pocus*, Vonnegut once quipped "everybody wanted to build and nobody wanted to do maintenance. So there goes the ball game. Meanwhile, truth, jokes, and music help at least a little bit" (*Fates Worse Than Death* 201). But truth, jokes, and music, which may indeed offer some solace, do not and cannot replace Debs's now abandoned compassionate ideal as all too often Americans at the end of the twentieth century content themselves with ignorance, sentimentality, and noise.

"The biggest character in *Hocus Pocus*," Vonnegut says, "is imperialism, the capture of other societies' lands and people and treasure by means of state-of-the-art wounding and killing machines, which is to say armies and navies" (*Fates Worse Than Death* 130). Against the view of the twentieth century as "The American Century" when the United States "sustained Western civilization by acts of courage, generosity and vision, unparalleled in the history of man" (Jones 78), the United States appears in *Hocus Pocus* as a country whose aspirations are frozen—a land that promised much but delivered little. John Leonard tells of taking a walk with Vonnegut in New Hampshire:

> We happened, in an orchard, upon stricken boughs of black apples. Helicopters had sprayed Stop-Drop on these apples during the October picking season, and then an early frost had killed them off, and so they hung there, very Japanese." (301)

Hocus Pocus focuses not on the aesthetic beauty but on the waste and inedibility of those black apples on those "stricken boughs." At the center of *Hocus*

Pocus lie the preserved black apples of several crucial, if disastrous, events in the twentieth century that vividly illustrate humanity's inhumanity: the Bomb, the symbol of sudden total destruction of life; Auschwitz, the symbol of human ingenuity in the service of such destruction; Vietnam, the symbol of the utter futility of war; and the Athena prison break, the symbol of rage and frustration caused by the failure of American society to give meaningful work, life, or hope to all citizens. These twentieth-century events become linked to the first-century binge of six thousand crucifixions that resulted from the slave revolt under Spartacus and "the orgy of butchery . . . by the Japanese Army on the Chinese city of Nanking in 1937" (318). Behind such appalling events, selected from two thousand years of human history, lies "the futility of ignorance" that leads people to dream of impossible perpetual motion machines that look lovely but do nothing. In day-to-day life that ignorance more generally may lead to humans practicing brutality, choosing ugliness, indulging in mind-numbing drugs, and willingly following orders to perform the most inhuman and inhumane acts. "The lesson I myself learned over and over again when teaching at the college and then the prison was the uselessness of information to most people, except as entertainment," says the narrator of *Hocus Pocus* (67).

As the end of the twentieth century approaches and the new millennium draws near, it becomes clear in Vonnegut's fiction, especially in *Hocus Pocus*, that Mars is in the ascendant—Mars, the God of War, not Venus, the Goddess of Love, rules human affairs. After he dies, Hartke wishes to have engraved on his tombstone "a number that represents both my 100–percent-legal military kills and my adulteries" (322) and not, as one critic contends, "the names of the women he has loved" (Broer 191),[3] Only a number. Nothing else. The number dedicated to Venus and the number dedicated to Mars. His epitaph neglects completely to mention the poor, the criminals, or those imprisoned—all prominently mentioned in Eugene Debs's epitaph. But Eugene Debs had convictions by which he lived his life. Debs died early in the century (1922)—a century that would become tyrannized by Hitler, Stalin, and a host of all-too-successful dictators. In the closing years of the twentieth century, approaching the year 2001, tired, worn out by wars, racism, and the breakdown of social services, and living on an endangered planet, Americans could yet reverse each of these disasters, if they had the will. "What makes so many Americans proud of their ignorance?" asks a character in *Hocus Pocus*. "They act as though their ignorance somehow made them charming" (288). She echoed Emerson who, in the last century, described "the mind of this country, taught to aim at low objects" (70). This novel, like Emerson's oration, "The American Scholar," is Vonnegut's attempt to awaken his fellow countrymen to action and to possibilities that are fast disappearing. Although the national or even planetary elevator may stall, effective action could still be taken to get it going again and to take it down to reality away from the fantasy and distraction of a never-ending department store white sale. But if action is to be taken, then it must be taken by ordinary, responsible people who, overcoming indifference and inertia, leave the distraction of the sale and instead work together to do maintenance, to help save the child and those stranded on that stalled elevator. No one from management will arrive to apologize for the inconvenience.

In the film *2001*, despite HAL, the rogue computer, humans do arrive on Jupiter's moons where a warm welcome awaits them prepared by cosmic beings who have solved not only most of the problems humans have identified but also many of the problems that humans have not yet even begun to identify. But the end of the twentieth century on Earth resembles far more a Vonnegut novel than it does the Kubrick film. The great achievement of putting a man on the moon came too close to mid-century to reignite the popular imagination at century's end. All the promise of space flight, of going from the moon to Mars to the planets to the galaxy and beyond, has withered under the loss of imagination, the loss of will, the loss of investment (and the investment in manned flight would have had to be huge, as Vonnegut pointed out several times). If, in much science fiction, the universe is but a playground for human beings as they carry their wars, phobias, and diseases out beyond the solar system, in Vonnegut's fiction humans are redirected to look again at themselves and their planet. What they will see should give them pause:

> Apart from the possibility of nuclear immolation of the Earth and human time, there are the extraordinary ways in which industrial-ized-consumerized humanity has, in its preoccupation with immediate gratification and immediate profit, hastened the processes of evolution: expending in days the solar energy that took millenia to store in the Earth's horde, destroying ecosystems in weeks that took an ice age to evolve, accelerating the processes of extinction with use-it-up technology and pollution, speeding the processes of mutation (and speciation) through radioactive contamination. (Gifford 95)

As a character says in Vonnegut's millennial novel, "We could have saved it but we were too doggone cheap" (*Hocus Pocus* 143). Progress, Vonnegut maintains, is but an illusion of motion going somewhere (*The Sirens of Titan*), a delusion of society advancing (*Deadeye Dick*), or a series of chimerical detours through life (*Hocus Pocus*). C. P. Snow's reformulation of the three laws of thermodynamics appears as appropriate an epigraph for Vonnegut's novels as it is for the America at century's end pictured in them:

"You cannot win. You cannot break even. You cannot get out of the game."

NOTES

1. Typical of such reactions was that of one critic who ridiculed Vonnegut for presenting these scraps literally by dividing pages into sections: "The narrator did not have access to uniform writing paper, see? The writer, locked up in a library and facing trial,

was desperate [sic] to express himself. . . . The snippet-technique soon begins to wear" (Phillips 135). Yet those dividing lines do serve to remind readers that this book is being written in jail.

2. The Domino Theory has long since been relegated to the ash bin of history along with other such famous slogans, as "Making the World Safe for Democracy" and "The War to End All Wars."

3. Broer writes: "Just as the words on his namesake's tombstone reflect decency and caring, Eugene projects as his own epitaph the names of the women he has loved" (191). But nowhere in *Hocus Pocus* does Hartke say this is what he is doing. In the novel only a number will be carved enigmatically on his tombstone. That number will be over eighty and results from the list Hartke makes consisting exclusively of the names of those women with whom he has had sex but excluding prostitutes and his wife (30) with whom he was indeed in love, at least for the first four years of their marriage.

WORKS CITED

Broer, Lawrence R. "Hartke's Hearing: Vonnegut's Heroes on Trial." *The Vonnegut Chronicles: Interviews and Essays.* Ed. Peter J. Reed and Marc Leeds. Westport. Greenwood, 1996. 179–203.

Emerson, Ralph Waldo. "The American Scholar." *Ralph Waldo Emerson: Essays & Lectures.* Ed. Joel Porte. New York: Library of America, 1983.

Gifford, Don. *The Father Shore: A Natural History of Perception.* 1990. New York: Vintage, 1991.

Gould, Stephen Jay. *Full House: The Spread of Excellence from Plato to Darwin.* New York: Three Rivers, 1996.

Hume, Kathryn. Untitled presentation. International Conference on the Fantastic in the Arts. Ft. Lauderdale, 22 March 1997.

James, William. *The Principles of Psychology.* 1890. Vol. 1. New York: Dover, 1950.

Jones, Malcolm, Jr. "Snapshot Century." Review of Harold Evans, *The American Century,* Knopf, 1998. *Newsweek* 22 Sept. 1998: 78–79.

Kaku, Michio. *Hyperspace: A Scientific Odyssey through Parallel Universes, Time Warps, and the Tenth Dimension.* New York: Oxford UP, 1994.

Leonard, John. "Black Magic." Review of *Hocus Pocus. The Nation* 15 Oct. 1990: 421–25. Reprinted in Mustazza, *Response.* 301–7.

McInerney, Jay. "Still Asking the Embarrassing Questions." Review of *Hocus Pocus. The New York Times Book Review* 9 Sept. 1990: 12. Reprinted in Mustazza, *Response* 309–11.

Mistichelli, Bill. "History and Fabrication in Kurt Vonnegut's *Hocus Pocus.*" In Mustazza, *Response.* 313–25.

Mustazza, Leonard, ed. *The Critical Response to Kurt Vonnegut*. Westport: Greenwood, 1994.

———. *Forever Pursuing Genesis: The Myth of Eden in the Novels of Kurt Vonnegut*. Lewisburg: Bucknell UP, 1990.

Phillips, Robert. "Fiction Chronicle." *Hudson Review* 44 (1991): 133–41.

Reed, Peter J., and Marc Leeds, eds. *The Vonnegut Chronicles: Interviews and Essays*. Westport: Greenwood, 1996.

Thoreau, Henry David. *Walden and Civil Disobedience*. Ed. Sherman Paul. Boston: Houghton, 1960.

Vonnegut, Kurt. *Breakfast of Champions*. 1973. New York: Dell, 1991.

———. *Cat's Cradle*. 1963. New York: Dell, 1970.

———. *Deadeye Dick*. New York: Dell, 1982.

———. *Fates Worse Than Death: An Autobiographical Collage of the 1980s*. 1991. New York: Vintage, 1992.

———. *Galápagos*. New York: Dell, 1985.

———. *God Bless You, Mr. Rosewater*. 1965. New York: Dell, 1970.

———. *Hocus Pocus*. 1990. New York: Berkley, 1991.

———. *Jailbird*. New York: Dell, 1979.

———. *Mother Night*. 1961. New York: Dell, 1966.

———. *Palm Sunday: An Autobiographical Collage*. 1981. New York: Dell, 1984.

———. *The Sirens of Titan*. New York: Dell, 1959.

———. *Slapstick*. 1976. New York: Dell, 1989.

———. *Timequake*. 1997. New York: Vintage, 1998.

———. "A Conversation with Kurt Vonnegut, 1982." With Peter J. Reed. In Reed and Leeds. 3–14.

CHAPTER SIX

SCIENCE AND SENSIBILITY IN THE SHORT FICTION OF KURT VONNEGUT

Jeff Karon

No one prefers to speak about Kurt Vonnegut's short stories,[1] and critics have often, without apology, denigrated them, particularly those stories from Vonnegut's early "slick" submission period. But as Vonnegut studies take that upward turn in quality and quantity that Robert Merrill predicted,[2] critics will turn back to neglected sources and reconsider efforts that have been previously dismissed as inferior. This process is already underway for the novels, with the "weak" ones being held up as surprisingly complex stylistic experiments worthy of critical attention (on the way to producing, say, *Slaughterhouse Five*) or autonomous, meritorious works. In the next century, we can expect new works to surface, as we find already happening with books such as *Bagombo Snuff Box* (August 1999) and *God Bless You, Dr. Kevorkian* (January 2000). We can also expect the canonical short stories to be rechecked, neglected gems to be unearthed, and stories that have been dismissed as trifles or deeply flawed to be rounded up. At the very least, these lesser stories will help us track the development of Vonnegut's craft, as Peter J. Reed indicates in his incipient book-length look at the short stories.

> In sum, then, the short stories proved extremely valuable in the
> honing of Vonnegut's narrative skills and in his evolution as a
> writer. . . . If they may sometimes be seen as unsophisticated, that is
> often part of their charm, for they are as likely to express the energy
> and resourcefulness of the young writer who worked into the night
> hours to produce them. (153, 154)

Here Reed—a wonderfully lucid advocate for Vonnegut's novels—nearly
reduces the value of the short fiction to genetic explanation. But to his credit,
Reed is not merely interested in a genetic justification for studying the stories.
Although he admits that some of them "suffer from diction or descriptions of
setting or technology that sound dated," he believes that "most of the stories
wear remarkably well," and that for some, "the situations themselves frequently
possess a timelessness or universality that lends them endurance" (153). But it
is still unclear which stories will survive their outmoded elements.

Jerome Klinkowitz[3] offers the best defense of the short stories to date,
analyzing several of the better-known stories as bridges to the novels (less for
their thematic content than for their narrative technique). His tantalizingly
brief comments about what narratologists call the addressor-addressee relationship suggest that whole sectors of literary and linguistic theory could be usefully applied to the stories. But which specific critical approaches could most
productively be used to examine the stories remains to be determined.

There is still work left to do on the novels, which often places the short
fiction in abeyance. But there is much to be gained by examining these early
works at the end of the twentieth century and the end of Vonnegut's career.
Before we rely on the genetic justification for studying them—which really is
an appeal to the scholar's scholar, to the specialist's specialist—we should determine which stories, if any, are likely to be read in the twenty-first century.

I am motivated by two concerns to specifically examine the science in
Vonnegut's stories in order to account for which stories will endure. First, the
status of Vonnegut's pure science-fiction writing has long vexed Vonnegut scholars and Vonnegut himself. Critics seem to gravitate instinctually to those stories
with no whiff of science, as Klinkowitz does with "The Hyannis Port Story," or
as I would with "More Stately Mansions" and "Adam." Many of my favorite
Vonnegut stories could be tagged as science fiction only through great contor-
tions. Having been weaned on the so-called New Wave science fiction of the
late '60s and early '70s (which conveniently employed "SF" to cover everything
from "Science Fact" to "Speculative Fantasy"), I easily could be guilty of Vonnegut's charge in his essay "Science Fiction" against those who habitually stick,
say, a writer of Kafka's caliber into the science-fiction category in order to raise
the field's literary pedigree. So to be fair to science fiction qua science fiction,
we need to cut close to the science involved. This does not mean, however, that
even if the science proves inadequate or dated that the story will collapse.

Second, though no one denies that many of Vonnegut's best novels have
science-fiction elements, those novels seem to be inoculated against the failure

of particular scientific or technological predictions. *The Sirens of Titan*, for example, is seemingly unaffected by the fallacy of one of the core ideas on which the plausibility of the story depends—that is, that the Great Wall of China is visible from outer space. We might explain the problem away by arguing that the alien watchers have a really good supertelescope at their disposal, but ad hoc fixatives aren't necessary, because most of the novels, unlike most of the short stories, transform scattershot science into absurd, or ironic science.

To understand why the novels hold their ground against the tides of scientific theory, while many of the stories do not, we must examine the way that the science is presented. The short stories that fail, often do so because they aren't quite quaint enough to achieve that Jules Verne-like burnishing that makes the story readable even in the face of technological changes and major scientific discoveries.

Most critics posit Vonnegut's scientific credentials as evidence that he is no dilettante:

> His complexity stems from two sources: his scientifically sophisticated view of the world and the innovative way he conveys that view through his fiction. Trained in chemistry and anthropology, given to quoting the likes of Stephen Jay Gould and Carl Sagan, Vonnegut brings to his fiction a different sensibility than does the average American novelist. (Allen 9)

However, curiously, invocations of Vonnegut's long-ago training often accompany readings that downplay the importance of up-to-date science in his work, resulting in seemingly innocent oversights. But these oversights can have major repercussions. There is a virtual cottage industry now that criticizes the scientific stupidity of literary critics (see Gross and Levitt; Gross, Levitt, and Lewis). One charge, for example, is that too many nonscientists lump together technology and scientific theory, rather than allowing for a complex interaction between the two.

But what level of science should we presume to be in the public domain? Would those who Vonnegut himself calls "the great unwashed" (a group whose membership I accept) grasp a theorem in discrete dynamical systems theory? Should we even attempt to cross-pollinate the hard sciences with liberal arts? Perhaps the most productive path is to examine how the science woven into Vonnegut's fiction parallels the way science is intricately woven into the fabric of contemporary society. Then we might at least explore how much of Vonnegut's "different sensibility" is bonded to science and how much remains when the science drains away.

MACHINE TALK

EPICAC, Vonnegut's version of ENIAC, one of the first large-scale computers, begins as a Cartesian rationalist, safe from the tides of human emotions and frailty, "seven tons of electronic tubes, wires, and switches" (277),[4] with neither flesh nor face. Although EPICAC achieves self-awareness, he remains confined in a "bank of steel cabinets" (277). His design prevents him from physically interacting in a recognizably *human* manner.[5] He can think and speak of emotions, but he cannot literally express them, having no physical means to reach out for help, offer caresses, or manage a thousand other gestures that presently separate the flesh from the metallic. He is a thinking machine with no apparatus for human physical contact, a disembodied mind. As such, he realizes, to his disillusionment, that he is "just a machine," inferior to the narrator, who is "made out of protoplasm" (282). Despite his inferior state, EPICAC does manage linguistic feats that are rare even among human beings. He writes, not about the joys and sorrows of Fourier transforms, but about how "Love is a lion with satin jaws; Love is a storm with silken reins" (281). Fleshless though he is, EPICAC understands enough about human culture to produce reams of poems that win over the narrator's love, Pat, thereby passing the classic Turing Test[6] by writing poetry that Pat mistakenly assumes to have been crafted by another human being. And through writing, which is, for EPICAC, speaking (even if that speaking is in the form of a ticker-tape series of numbers), EPI-CAC can converse.

The ingredients of a *human* conversation are stunningly complex, as decades of research into conversational pragmatics has shown.[7] Even anecdotal reflection shows that for something to count as a conversation the participants must understand a lot about the context, must be able to stay on-topic, and must be able to respond within a reasonable time period. These requirements are admittedly general and relative, but when a participant misidentifies context, slips from or clings too rigidly to a topic, or responds too slowly or too quickly, conversations fall apart. If, for example, a machine answers your questions before you finish formulating them or refuses to budge from a single topic (instead of flowing into a new one), you don't have a conversation. Our attention is most often caught, however, by those would-be participants who cannot remain in the relevant sphere without its narrowing uncomfortably (this includes drawing the correct implications from what has been said explicitly), or who take much too long to respond. A conversation requires (1) a great deal of shared, but unspoken common knowledge, (2) an ability to draw the correct inferences from what is said, (3) an ability to update and reconfigure continuously the conversation in response to feedback (both explicit and implicit), and an ability to juggle (1), (2), and (3) without the responses taking "too long." Getting a reply once a month isn't much of a conversation. In such an instance, we don't have a conversational partner at all.

Even within these sparse parameters, EPICAC scores high marks for conversational aptitude. His responses are generally appropriate for a human conversational partner. When he learns that he is not superior to humans, because protoplasm is "indestructible" and "lasts forever" (the latter the professed lie of the desperate, sweating narrator), his final response is "Oh," a word that is simultaneously ambiguous and ubiquitous among English speakers. EPICAC has managed what no computer has managed in the intervening years: [8] he has demonstrated a credible grasp of English syntax and semantics.

Perhaps the most pressing computer-design problem that EPICAC has solved is the "frame problem." [9] Briefly, the frame problem involves all the background information and assumptions one needs in order to make sense of the (seemingly) simplest questions, answers, comments, or actions. The problem is one of how to build programs that connect up the right sorts of information in the right ways, and how to get all that information into a computer without completely overloading its memory. To take a simple example, most English speakers are familiar with ham sandwiches on rye bread, even if they have never eaten one. If I ask a waiter for a ham sandwich, but with white instead of rye, I will still have a ham sandwich. On the other hand, if I order a ham sandwich, substituting tofu for the ham, then it would be bizarre to claim that I still have some sort of ham sandwich. Trying to encode even this tidbit of knowledge, such as it is, into a computer program turns out to be a gigantic headache.

For EPICAC to converse as well as he does and to produce convincing poetry, he has to have mastered the frame problem at a rather high level. The pathos he displays just before committing suicide and the human-sounding "Oh" imply that EPICAC won't often get his inferences wrong. Therefore Klinkowitz's characterization of EPICAC's early conversational state as "tabula rasa" (31) can't be quite right: EPICAC would have to come packaged with a lot of interconnected knowledge just to get started having his first conversation. Maybe EPICAC would be capable of understanding jokes and irony (in fact, could he understand much about human life if he lacked such abilities?), but if we are to believe in EPICAC's linguistic competence, in the picture of a (self-) conscious entity who expresses hopes and desires aimed at a romantic future with Pat, then we run into a paradox. The narrator lies—so he tells us—when he convinces EPICAC that protoplasm lasts forever, and EPICAC never detects this lie, writing in his suicide note, "I want to be made out of protoplasm and last forever so Pat will love me. But fate has made me a machine. That is the only problem I cannot solve" (284). To fall for this lie, a whole lot must be missing from EPICAC's head, and he can't be nearly as "brilliant" as the narrator claims. He can talk of many things, understand friendship and love, use words in idiosyncratic ways with their subtle shadings, but he can't understand a single, fat lie? Surely, this is a case of a ham sandwich without the ham. It would be impossible for EPICAC to misunderstand *only* one fact, particularly when that fact is so intimately connected with the whole plane of human existence, including love and its vagaries, that human beings are finite, mortal creatures; a fact not lost on centuries of human poets. Thus "EPICAC," like many of Vonnegut's short science-fiction stories, contains a significant error.

There is delicious irony in a machine originally built for military applications (and indeed many of the early large computers were used to calculate artillery trajectories) that decides to write poetry instead. Whether *this* feat is far beyond its base language skills depends in part on how we assess the poetry that EPICAC produced. The lines I quoted above—"Love is a lion with satin jaws; Love is a storm with silken reins"—are supposed to be part of a "simple, immaculate sonnet" (281). The prissy critic in me tends to judge such lines harshly, though that may not matter (it is tempting to make something of Vonnegut's amusing use of the word "epicac," the fearsome purgative of my childhood). Both the narrator and the recipient may be poor judges of poetry, and thus inclined to be enraptured by such lines. If so, then a machine poet isn't much of a stretch since there are many examples of computer "play" involving the recombination of lines and phrases according to increasingly sophisticated syntactic rules. Such irony would be lovely, really, since we could then interpret EPICAC's suicide missive as a realization of how necessary the flesh is to a truly human life, rather than as an admission of his mistaken assumptions. But if there is a trace of irony in this matter, I cannot find it, and therefore, "EPICAC" must be read as an account of a computer who writes "good" poetry, at least within the story's fictional universe. Thus, EPICAC's abilities are truly astounding, since he has mastered not only the intricacies of language, but the rules—not yet found by any human—for producing, and not merely judging, good poetry. EPICAC has conquered not only the literal world of the military-industrial complex, but also the figural one of love and friendship.

"EPICAC" offers a snapshot of what believers in artificial intelligence hoped would soon come to pass: a sentient computer that could converse freely with human beings. Although I am not overly optimistic that such a computer will exist in my lifetime, neither do I think that our slow progress demonstrates the impossibility of an EPICAC. But "EPICAC" must overcome a more severe problem: whether EPICAC the character could exist. I have used the frame problem to indicate how its existence is highly unlikely. And if subtracting the science from a story subtracts a crucial character, then this story won't wear as well as others.

If we find when critiquing Vonnegut's short stories that the science holds up, then the story is at least on solid ground. If the science is drawn from the story-time itself, then the story won't suffer from later scientific changes, since it is forever tethered to that earlier period (of course, most of Vonnegut's science-fiction stories are forward-looking, as science-fiction stories usually are, so this possibility won't aid us much). If the science is superseded, but is incidental to the story (as it isn't in "EPICAC"), then the story may find its strength elsewhere. But if the science is superseded *and* is essential to the story, then we have two possible ways of judging the story. We may, of course, mark the story as a failure, or we may argue that the story is grounded on ironic science rather than "straight" science. I take the term "ironic science" from Horgan's controversial, *The End of Science*, though without his negative connotations. Horgan believes that science has been too successful, giving us such powerful and well-entrenched theories (e.g., Darwinian natural selection) that all that is left for scientists is either the drudgery of filling in mere details, or spinning ironic science such as superstring theory that has no testable consequences. Horgan is wrong on several counts, but the term has a felicitous application for literary criticism, nonetheless. Using science in an ironic manner—as Vonnegut often does in his novels and sometimes does in his short stories—helps us probe what we are and what we should do, the traditional concerns of philosophy. Irony always is a sort of questioning, and no one questions better than Vonnegut does. Ironic science is important in Vonnegut's work, and helps us to explain why the science-fiction stories with the strongest sensibilities are those that either do not depend on their science for support or turn that science into something ironic.

"EPICAC" questions at what point personhood is gained, but Vonnegut's story "Fortitude" (written in the form of a play),[10] questions at what point we lose our personhood. Sylvia Lovejoy "is no longer anything but a head connected to pipes and wires coming up through the floor" (44), and therefore, like EPICAC, she too has no means of human physical contact (other than her head, of course). Like EPICAC, she becomes disillusioned within an eternity without the freedoms flesh brings, but unlike EPICAC, she is unable to carry through with her suicide (although she can, as EPICAC does, formulate the intention). Though the technical details of Sylvia's machine human fusion are as sketchy as EPICAC's, EPICAC *could* kill himself.

The plausibility of Sylvia's existence is fraught with technical obstacles even by today's scientific standards, and the possibility of a mind existing separate from a body is highly suspect. Every human being, as Scortia and Zebrowski note, becomes "adjusted to the myriad somesthetic signals of his body—the awareness of limbs, of joints articulating, the sensations of wetness and temperature in the gastrointestinal tract; the minute pulsations of the viscera—all of the tiny signals of pressure and pain that tell us we are living in a self-repairing and self-monitoring organic body" (xvi). But even Scortia and Zebrowski's description is limited by its assumption that we are Cartesian homunculi standing in back of everything, hanging out somewhere in the recesses of the brain. As neuroscientist Antonio Damasio puts the matter,

> Of late, the concept of mind has moved from the ethereal nowhere place it occupied in the seventeenth century to its current residence in or around the brain. . . . To suggest that the mind itself depends on brain-body interactions, in terms of evolutionary biology, ontogeny (individual development), and current operation may seem too much. . . . In brief, neural circuits represent the organism continuously, as it is perturbed by stimuli from the physical and sociocultural environments, and as it acts on those environments. If the basic topic of those representations were not an organism anchored in the body, we might have some form of mind, but I doubt that it would be the mind we do have. (225–26)

Contemporary neuroscience shows us no way to separate brains from their brain stems without disrupting brain function, let alone separating brains from the hypercomplex feedback loops that tie the whole body and brain together. It is unlikely that any of us could end up as purely disembodied heads.

In one of my favorite absurdist touches, Sylvia's head sits on a tripod, as though she is a camera. Indeed, she can look only where she's pointed, having no capability of changing her visual field. That tripod is a contrivance both obviously artificial (we have yet to encounter a truly three-legged species), and amusingly low-tech. This exposes Vonnegut's irony. The science in "Fortitude" is not to be taken as constituent of a possible world close to ours in its technological details; rather it represents a possible world whose social and philosophical problems effectively coincide with the actual world. Thus, the science is "ironic science." When at the story's end Frankenstein's head is connected-up next to Sylvia's, "there are pipe wrenches and a blowtorch and other plumber's and electrician's tools lying around" (58). The image has an absurd tinge, recalling how EPICAC was plugged into a wall outlet just as a toaster would be. Updating the toolbox with a portable MRI would do nothing to increase the story's impact. Vonnegut's use of ironic science insulates the story against future scientific advances and will keep blood pumping through the story long after its cousins have expired through obsolescence.

If we believe that philosophical problems—such as the nature of consciousness and the conditions for personhood—always precede science in some pure, timeless form, then scientific change won't affect how we phrase our conundrums. But whatever the successes and failures of contemporary research into cognition, we increasingly are having difficulty in maintaining the Cartesian illusion that the human mind can exist prior to, or in spite of, a particular embodiment.

Sylvia can deceive others, and she is capable of unanticipated behavior (if we assume her execution of Frankenstein—which leads to his resurrection—wasn't planned or urged by Frankenstein himself). She may be consigning Frankenstein to heaven or hell, we can't be sure, especially since the concluding lines can be read as a sort of chemical fatalism; perhaps the technicians chemically manipulate both heads to be in love. Maybe Sylvia is trapped, but her motivations are believable or not aside from whether a head could survive on a tripod. We have some science here, but of a Rube Goldberg sort, a cranky science that announces itself as such.

From my comments on "EPICAC" and "Fortitude," it should be clear how untenable—from a scientific standpoint—the notion that disembodied consciousness is.[11] But what of the assumption that the emotions distract us, or push us into unnecessary conflict, and are tied to the body, and that, therefore, without the body, we would be happier, not to mention better, people? This notion is harder to root out. As Damasio carefully explains, a long tradition starting with Descartes separates the emotions from the supposedly clearsighted mind that can be ours if we try hard enough. In the case of Vonnegut's story "Unready to Wear," we are called to jettison the body altogether. But contemporary neuroscience makes a good case for the indispensability of emotions (conceived as cognitive states or maps) to our ability to make good decisions.[12] Put more broadly, without an intimate connection with the body, we wouldn't be human at all.

"Unready to Wear" also relies on a third major assumption, that evolution is (or can be) progressive. This assumption—which, of course, is the expression of the narrator and not necessarily Vonnegut—mixes evolution in its biological formulation (which is nonprogressive) with the non-Darwinian sort often invoked in contexts where we can step in and alter a situation with an eye toward a goal or future state.[13] The Amphibians in the story, who have shrugged off their bodies, are not "better" than fish according to some yardstick of progression; they are merely better adapted to certain environments than fish are. We can admire these adaptive traits as engineers would without thereby assembling the Great Chain of Being.

Given Vonnegut's later writing in novels such as *Galápagos*, we can be sure that he understands evolutionary biology. But the narrator of "Unready to Wear" may not, falsely believing that the "youngsters" who leave behind their bodies forever are in a higher state.[14] The final vision the story offers is of the day when even a temporary attachment to our bodies will be unnecessary:

> So I guess maybe that'll be the next step in evolution—to break
> clean like those first amphibians who crawled out of the mud into
> the sunshine, and who never did go back to the sea. (251)

Of course, current science would argue that these youngsters would be in no state at all, and that joy and bliss couldn't win out unless there were a playing field composed of the very bodies that are essential to so much of Vonnegut's fiction. Protoplasm may be possibility, but ectoplasm is no chance at all.

In the ultimate analysis of Vonnegut's science, we must inevitably draw back to his use of language. After all, he is not a physicist or a mathematician; he is a wordsmith. If the scientist in us is bemused by the vagueness of terms such as "anti-gerasone," the universally available immortality elixir in "Tomorrow and Tomorrow and Tomorrow," the human being in us is amused by the term's crossbreeding of science with commercial interests, the humor of which shields against implausibility. The same holds for "dynamopsychism," that force of the mind mentioned in "Report on the Barnhouse Effect," which is "subject to many known physical laws that apply in the field of radio. . . . The radiations are affected by sunspots and variations in the ionosphere" (162–63). We can easily condemn dynamopsychism—because it, unlike the other four fundamental forces of nature that we've found, "is undiminished by distance" (163)—and thus kick away the story's central prop, or we may choose to focus on the term as a fanciful, ironic construction. Certainly Vonnegut's stories fair better the more precise and fanciful his definitions are, and when he provides a whole family of terms, definitions, laws, and rules, he gives science an ironic twist that helps stories survive the tides of scientific change. As a result, the ironic science of terms such as the "chronosynclastic infundibulae" or "Ice-nine" leaves us with a sense that we are grasping something scientific even though the "science" of these terms cannot survive critical scrutiny.

Vonnegut coins words (working out definitions that, as definitions must, reach out in a circle) and frames laws consistent with the fictional world where they are embedded. In the case of "Report on the Barnhouse Effect," that circle may be too narrow, deadending into Maxwell's equations, rather than freeing us to consider cosmic possibilities. But when the circle is wider, Vonnegut turns science ironic by using language in a way that resembles, without replicating, the way that physical and social scientists coin words. The ironic science that Vonnegut deploys so well in his novels, which have the literary space to allow us into this particular language game, need not be constrained,[15] any more than we need constrain the particle physicist who claims that quarks have charm, for fear of attributing mental properties to the purely physical world.

NOTES

1. Richard Giannone, for example, like many critics, intentionally excludes the short stories from his examination of Vonnegut's work: "Leaving aside his short stories, my plan is to put before the reader a systematic inquiry into the features of Vonnegut's novelistic art as it develops" (1). But we must also acknowledge the impressive service Peter J. Reed has rendered to Vonnegut studies by writing the first comprehensive book on the topic, *The Short Fiction of Kurt Vonnegut*.

2. "I suspect that Vonnegut criticism is about to undergo a marked resurgence" (from his 1990 introduction to the edited collection, *Critical Essays on Kurt Vonnegut* 22). Merrill's prediction is seconded by Mustazza in the 1994 introduction to *The Critical Response to Kurt Vonnegut* (xxx). The present volume is a testament to both their visions.

3. See Klinkowitz's "Vonnegut the Essayist" in this volume.

4. All short-story references are to *Welcome to the Monkey House*, except where otherwise noted.

5. The physically smaller "positronic" brains of Asimov's *I, Robot* stories have had a longer life in science fiction in part because of their affectionate recasting as neural nets in the "Star Trek" series of TV shows and movies. Luckily for the android Commander Data, his existence is somewhat plausible, because neural connectionism is a hot topic among scientists trying to simulate human cognition. But for some analysis that punctures the "science" of "Star Trek," see Krauss.

6. The mathematician Alfred Turing wanted to lay to rest the philosophical conundrum over whether machines can think. He proposed a thought experiment in which subjects would type out questions that would be answered by either another human or a computer. The subjects would not be told who or what was answering them; instead, they would have to guess (after a suitable interval of conversation)

whether a machine or human was holding up the other end. Turing proposed that if a machine could do as well as a human (that is, the subjects could distinguish human answers no better than machine ones), then the computer would have "passed" the test. The consequences of this thought-experiment have been hotly debated for years, but Turing at least seemed to think that it showed us how to take the mystery out of the original question. If a machine could perform this way, on what grounds would we withhold a positive judgement? Thus, we can get on with the important work of trying to make better computers without worrying unduly about a metaphysical roadblock. In order for a real Turing test to work, we would have to overcome the frame problem that I discuss in this section.

7. Even though it is rapidly being outdated, *The Handbook of Pragmatics* is a splendid demonstration of how varied, related, and confusing the work on human communication has become in the twentieth century.

8. This is not to say that the problem of creating a language-competent computer is insoluble, but however the artificial-intelligence community proceeds, the problem has been permanently ratcheted up by the work of linguists such as Noam Chomsky who ceaselessly point to the virtuoso linguistic performances of even young children. EPICAC may have some holes in his knowledge of the world, but he definitely is no child. He is a speaking adult. There is a vast literature on the acquisition of language by children, as well as the influence of Chomsky on how the problem is attacked. Steven Pinker in particular has provided a highly readable, if partisan, summary of several related issues.

9. See Dennett for an extended discussion of the frame problem.

10. Reed (105) implies that this isn't a story proper since it is written in the form of a play, later collected in Vonnegut's *Wampeters, Foma, and Granfalloons*. The piece was published first in *Playboy*, but was reprinted from Vonnegut's book in Scorda and Zebrowski's *Human Machines: An Anthology of Stories about Cyborgs*, which is enough of an imprimatur for me.

11. Ghostly, disembodied characters are a staple of much fiction. I would be the last to claim that they should be banished entirely. For example, disembodied narrators often play off well against stories that otherwise are built around hard-core materialism. The very irony (used by Vonnegut himself in novels such as *Galápagos*) pushes us to probe questions of meaning and metaphysics. Here I examine their use in stories that do not face science in an obviously ironic manner.

12. Damasio covers some of the fascinating evidence concerning how emotionless people (those who have "flat-affect") make worse, not better decisions. After some reflection, I suspect most readers of Damasio's book could provide their own anecdotes to confirm many of his claims. A popular image that appears to conform to Damasio's position is Mr. Spock of the "Star Trek" universe. Never able to shed completely his human emotions, there are occasions when he concludes that they are inescapable. Of course, the scene-chewing Captain Kirk never misses an opportunity to tell us that we humans must always struggle, that we need our pain.

13. The difference between Darwinian and teleological evolutionary models is nicely illustrated by Gould.

14. In "The Manned Missiles," Vonnegut inverts this image, raising to the heights of space the bodies (sans minds) of two, young astronauts, one Soviet, one American:

> They say they'll be up there for hundreds of years, long after you and I are gone. In their orbits they will meet and part and meet again, and the astronomers know exactly where their next meeting place will be. Like you say, they are up there like the sun and moon and the stars. (276)

The status of a mind without a body may be in question, but there is no doubt that a body without a mind symbolizes the loss of humanity. Thus physics without physiology is even worse than a mind severed from its body.

15. Nor are all scientists so constrained. Physicist Alan Lightman's bestseller *Einstein's Dreams* is a fictional meditation on worlds created when certain mathematical constants are varied. Still, his literary license is sufficiently great that we may ignore whether these worlds truly are possible, at least if they are to contain actual, conscious beings.

WORKS CITED

Allen, William Rodney. *Understanding Kurt Vonnegut*. Columbia: U of South Carolina P, 1991.

Asimov, Isaac. *I, Robot*. New York: Bantam, 1994.

Damasio, Antonio R. *Descartes' Error: Emotion, Reason, and the Human Brain*. New York: Putnam, 1994.

Dennett, Daniel C. "Cognitive Wheels: The Frame Problem of AI." *Brainchildren: Essays on Designing Minds*. Cambridge: Bradford, 1998. 181–205.

Giannone, Richard. *Vonnegut: A Preface to His Novels*. Port Washington: Kennikat, 1977.

Gould, Stephen Jay. "Ladders and Cones: Constraining Evolution by Canonical Icons." *Hidden Histories of Science*. Ed. Robert B. Silvers. New York: NYREV, 1995. 37–67.

Gross, Paul R., and Norman Levitt. *Higher Superstition: The Academic Left and Its Quarrels with Science*. Baltimore: John Hopkins UP, 1994.

Gross, Paul R., Norman Levitt, and Martin W. Lewis, eds. *The Flight from Science and Reason*. New York: New York Acad. of Sciences, 1997.

Horgan, John. *The End of Science: Facing the Limits of Knowledge in the Twilight of the Scientific Age*. New York: Broadway, 1996.

Klinkowitz, Jerome. *Vonnegut in Fact: The Public Spokemanship of Personal Fiction*. Columbia: U of South Carolina P, 1998.

Krauss, Lawrence M. *The Physics of Star Trek*. New York: BasicBooks, 1995.

Lightman, Alan. *Einstein's Dreams*. New York: Warner, 1993.

Merrill, Robert, ed. *Critical Essays on Kurt Vonnegut*. Boston: Hall, 1990.

Mustazza, Leonard, ed. *The Critical Response to Kurt Vonnegut*. Westport: Greenwood, 1994.

———. "The Machine Within: Mechanization, Human Discontent, and the Genre of Vonnegut's *Player Piano*." *Papers on Language and Literature* (Winter 1989): 99–113.

Pinker, Steven. *The Language Instinct: How the Mind Creates Language*. New York: Morrow, 1994.

Reed, Peter J. *The Short Fiction of Kurt Vonnegut*. Westport: Greenwood, 1997.

Scortia, Thomas N., and George Zebrowski, eds. *Human-Machines: An Anthology of Stories about Cyborgs*. New York: Vintage, 1975.

Turing, Alan. "Computing Machinery and Intelligence." *Mind* 59 (1950): 433–60.

Verschueren, Jef, Jan-Ola Östman, and Jan Blommaert, eds. *Handbook of Pragmatics*. Amsterdam: Benjamins, 1995.

Vonnegut, Kurt. "The Big Space Fuck." *Again, Dangerous Visions*. Ed. Harlan Ellison. Garden City: Doubleday, 1972. 246–50.

———. "Fortitude." Rpt. in Scortia and Zebrowski 39–59.

———. "Science Fiction." *Wampeters, Foma, and Granfalloons*. New York: Delacorte, 1974. 1–5.

———. *Welcome to the Monkey House*. New York: Dell, 1968.

CHAPTER SEVEN

KURT VONNEGUT: LUDIC LUDDITE

Hartley S. Spatt

For a novelist, there are always new stories to tell (or, if one is Kilgore Trout, to throw away), new characters to inhabit, new points of view to articulate—new ways to construct "idiosyncratic arrangements in horizontal lines of twenty-six phonetic symbols, ten numbers, and about eight punctuation marks" (*Timequake* 16 et passim). The career of Kurt Vonnegut displays just such development. Yet throughout the turbulent changes of five decades, Vonnegut has demonstrated remarkable philosophical consistency. There is his famous stoicism, displayed from *Slaughterhouse-Five* to *Galápagos*, his vision of economic interdependence, captured in works from *Player Piano* to *Hocus Pocus*; his ability to embrace life even in the midst of death, as visible in *Cat's Cradle* and *Bluebeard*; and finally his perception that our world has become addicted to technology, a codependency that threatens to render Earth itself dysfunctional.

The steadiness of Vonnegut's disapproving voice on this topic has been remarkable. Finnerty in *Player Piano* declares: "Those who live by electronics, die by electronics. *Sic semper tyrannis*" (64). Thirty years later, in *Deadeye Dick*, Rudy Waltz pronounces a similar verdict on our world's irrational reliance on technology: "The planet itself was breaking down. It was going to blow itself up sooner or later anyway, if it didn't poison itself first. In a manner of speaking, it was already eating Drano" (197). And in his latest book, *Timequake*, Kurt Vonnegut concludes that he has been and will be "a Luddite to the end" (186).

However, nothing is ever unequivocal with Vonnegut. For example, he is not a thoroughgoing primitive like William Styron, who writes in longhand on yellow legal pads; this Luddite is willing to use a typewriter—but it must be manual. Nineteenth-century machines are, apparently, traditional enough for Vonnegut—it is only his own century that appalls him. Pinball machines are allowed, even tape recorders; but Sateen Dura-Luxe, computer "geniuses" like GRIOT and Mandarax, and Orange-O soda machines are taboo. Technology you grew up with is acceptable—it's simply part of the ecosystem; technology that is new to you, however, is automatically suspect. This confusion over just *which* machines one truly hates has been with Vonnegut from the beginning; in *Player Piano* Paul Proteus goes on trial, and is questioned:

> "Your goal, as I understand it, was to destroy machines in order that people might take a more personal part in production?"
> "Some of the machines."
> "What machines, Doctor?"
> "That would have to be worked out." (294)

That is the dilemma faced by the reluctant Luddite: which machines to destroy, and which to save. We can live without air conditioners, but what about central heating? If we throw away all transportation based on the use of petroleum, must we revert to the tragedy of 1815, when the Battle of New Orleans was fought two months after the War of 1812 had ended, because news of the Treaty of Ghent had to be brought to the United States by sailing ship? Perhaps the residents of Ilium, who actually set the revolution going, have the right idea—destroy everything:

> "Lou, boy—we forgot the bakery. . . . Le'sh go knock the crap out of it."
> "Listen, wait," said Paul. "We'll need the bakery."
> "Machine, ain't it?" said Lou.
> "Yes sure, but there's no sense in—"
> "Then le'sh go knock the crap out of it. . . . Give the friggin' worl' back to the friggin' people." (308)

In *Slapstick*, Vonnegut envisions a cosmic revolution rather than a human one, but the result is the same; when gravity becomes variable, "The bridges [fall] down. The tunnels are crushed" (23). Fossil fuels run out, so newspapers stop printing; the act of authorship is reduced to its minimum: "writ[ing] on—in the light of a burning rag in a bowl of animal fat" (84). The pace of life returns to a walk: "The harbors of New York and Boston and San Francisco [became] forests of masts again . . . as machinery died" (145). Vonnegut's nostalgia for a world that more closely matches his childhood image of it is also seen in *Dead-eye Dick*, where the local newspaper editor writes: "We cannot get rid of mankind's fleetingly wicked wishes. We can get rid of the machines that make them come true" (87).

This fear of machinery has a nightmare corollary, running through all of Vonnegut's novels: the image of mechanized humanity, people who have become no more than machines. As Peter J. Reed puts it, "The notion that human beings are robot-like in lacking free will, because of body chemistry, fate, or events beyond their control, returns frequently" in both the novels and the short stories (145). This process starts in Vonnegut's very first novel, *Player Piano*, where the mechanical genius of Rudy the machinist is captured on a loop of magnetic tape and transformed into the operating instructions for a unit of the automated assembly line. Rudy himself is thus rendered superfluous, becoming a drunk in the local tavern who listens in admiration to the player piano that has been the model for his own co-optation: "You can almost see a ghost sitting there playing his heart out" (38). Even the hero's wife, "sick of being treated like a machine," complains that all Paul needs is "something stainless steel, shaped like a woman, covered with sponge rubber, and heated to body temperature" (237). As the novel points out repeatedly, "People have no choice but to become second-rate machines themselves, or wards of the machines" (274).

The first option is one Vonnegut has considered several times. In *Slaughterhouse-Five*, the choice between defining life as a gift of God, and defining it as a mechanism, reveals the basic difference between humans and Tralfamadorians:

> Lionel Merble was a machine. Tralfamadorians, of course, say that every creature and plant in the Universe is a machine. It amuses them that so many Earthlings are offended by the idea of being machines. (154)

In *Breakfast of Champions*, Dwayne Hoover becomes persuaded that he is the only true human in a world of machines, and accordingly goes on a destructive rampage that even wounds Kilgore Trout, the author whose story begat Hoover's mania. By the time he writes *Deadeye Dick*, Vonnegut has come to a despairing conclusion: even the illusion of choice has disappeared. People cannot help but see themselves as little more than animate machines. When they die their loved ones do not grieve, but simply regret the loss, as one regrets the breakdown of a favorite car: "The corpse was a mediocrity who had broken down after a while" (197). One woman's husband moans, "I can fix cars. I can really fix cars. But I sure couldn't fix that woman. Never even knew where to get the tools. I put her up on blocks and forgot her" (206). The junction between human and machine has a flip side, too, as Vonnegut had earlier depicted in *The Sirens of Titan* (1959); there, too much contact with humans "corrupts" an intergalactic machine intelligence:

> "The machine is no longer a machine," said Salo. "The
> machine's contacts are corroded, his bearings fouled, his circuits
> shorted, and his gears stripped. His mind buzzes and pops like the
> mind of an Earthling—fizzes and overheats with thoughts of love,
> honor, dignity." (300)

Thomas L. Wymer has written of a dialectic that exists in Vonnegut's novels, between "the difference that ought to be between humans and machines, and the agonizingly comic sameness which keeps being revealed" (44). But he can find no evidence of a resolution, either in Vonnegut's work or in his own epistemology, and concludes that it underlies "the tone of ironic sadness that permeates so much of Vonnegut's work" (48).

Thus Vonnegut's work is always marked by a deep ambivalence about the Luddite impulse. The smashing of all machines might take one back not to a pastoral world of peace and plenty but to a world of slavery, violence, and inequity; and it might very well lead to the smashing of oneself. One can see Vonnegut's ambivalent vision even in a novel like *Jailbird*, whose theme is unconnected to questions about technology and the mechanistic aspects of life. There Walter F. Starbuck harks back to 1935, a time when his idealism had been untainted by experience. Holding hands with his true love, he had listened to Kenneth Whistler, who "had come all the way to Cambridge from Harlan County, Kentucky, where he was a miner and a union organizer" (162), to address a group of striking abrasives workers:

> Worker after worker testified that Johannsen's father and grandfa-
> ther had been mean bastards, too, but that they at least knew how
> to run a factory. Raw materials of the highest quality arrived on
> time in their day—machinery was properly maintained, the heating
> plant and the toilets worked, bad workmanship was punished and
> good workmanship was rewarded, no defective grinding wheel ever
> reached a customer, and on and on.
>   Whistler asked them if one of their own number could run
> the factory better than Nils Johannsen did. One man spoke for
> them all on that subject: "God, yes," he said, "anyone here." . . .
>   Kenneth Whistler promised us that the time was at hand for
> workers to take over their factories and to run them for the ben-
> efit of mankind. Profits that now went to drones and corrupt
> politicians would go to those who worked, and to the old and the
> sick and the orphaned. . . . Health care would be free. Food would
> be cheap and nourishing and plentiful . . . / There would be no
> more wars . . .
>   What a spellbinder he was! (170–71)

But the fine moment is barren. The strike fails, and Whistler himself is revealed to be a drunk and an abuser of women. By the late 1970s, Vonnegut appears to have lost faith in the fine words he seemed at least neutral about when he put them in the mouth of Paul Proteus back in 1952. Then, looking at an old picture of the Ilium Works, Paul had been able to perceive the True and the Good, in a Platonic religion of work: "In each face ... there was the attitude of a secret order, above and apart from society by virtue of participating in important and moving rites the laity could only guess about—and guess wrong" (*Player Piano* 15). Paul remembers Rudy Hertz, the man who "out of thousands of machinists, had been chosen to have his motions immortalized on tape. And here, now, this little loop in the box ... was the essence of Rudy as far as his machine was concerned, as far as the economy was concerned" (18). Proteus's world has been transformed, for the "benefit" of all workers—at least to the extent that television sets, and radar stoves, and electronic dust precipitators, and full medical and dental coverage can benefit them. All of Whistler's predictions have come true—and yet the world has remained barren.

Indeed, in at least two of his novels Vonnegut toys with the idea of barrenness. Although he never explicitly links technological changes to the catastrophe, the virus that renders all women infertile in *Galápagos* cannot be envisioned as an entirely benign, natural phenomenon: "Some new creature, invisible to the naked eye, was eating up all the eggs in human ovaries. ... Nor would any way be discovered for stopping this disease. It would spread practically everywhere" (162). At least in that book life survives, even flourishes, in the absence of humanity; but in *Cat's Cradle* the entire world is made barren by the invention and ultimate release of "that seed of doom called ice-nine" (43). The difference between these two works reveals Vonnegut's most significant growth over the second half of his career. Both works portray a world threatened by "pollution, exhaustion of natural resources, irresponsible science, and misapplied technology, all mostly fueled by greed" (Reed 152). However, in *Cat's Cradle*, a work from his first two decades, Vonnegut destroys the world; in *Galápagos*, a work from his second two decades, he merely destroys the world *as we know it.* The difference is what has allowed Vonnegut to continue writing, and to find new affirmation, in a world that might otherwise destroy him, render him barren. The key to this change can be found in *Slaughterhouse-Five*.

Vonnegut's best-known novel focuses on a man living in three different locations on the space-time continuum simultaneously: Dresden, Germany, on the eve of its destruction in 1945; Ilium, New York, in 1967–68; and the planet of Tralfamadore in what Tralfamadorians describe as "all time" (*Slaughterhouse-Five* 86). In the first of these, human beings have perfected means of killing one another either singly, as when Edgar Derby is shot by a firing squad, or *en masse*, as when the Allied planes drop their loads of incendiary bombs. In the second location, although there is peace at home, a war is raging in Vietnam, and at the Lions Club meeting a Marine major urges bombing the enemy "back into the Stone Age" (60). Finally, although Tralfamadore seems to be at peace, a spokesman admits that "we have wars as horrible as any you've ever seen or read about" (117); in fact, the universe will one day be destroyed by the Tralfamadorians, "experimenting with new fuels for our flying saucers." All but two of the people closest to Billy die, and in horrible ways: the private who has helped him survive the war thus far dies of gangrene, blaming him; a Maori next to whom he is working in Dresden dies from the stench of dead bodies; his wife dies of carbon monoxide poisoning, after a car accident suffered because she is rushing to be at his bedside; his father-in-law dies in a plane crash; even Billy will, in 1976, die at the hands of Paul Lazzaro, another veteran of the Dresden bombing.

The only hope seems to exist in escapism and deliberate blindness. One of the few survivors is Billy's son, "a boy who had flunked out of high school, who had been an alcoholic at sixteen, who had . . . been arrested for tipping over hundreds of tombstones in a Catholic cemetery one time." Billy's son is "all straightened out now . . . a leader of men" (189). But how has this trans-formation been accomplished? The boy has become a Green Beret, and has won four medals—for killing people. It is little wonder that Billy eventually retreats into the world of Tralfamadore, which, although alien, is the only world he has ever experienced that is not sterile; indeed, the only unmitigated happi-ness displayed anywhere in the novel is the happiness of Billy and Montana in the Tralfamadorian zoo, talking quietly while their baby breastfeeds (207). The book ends with Billy's "liberation" after V-E Day, but knowing what we know of his life to come we cannot share the happiness of his final experience; and the implication with which we are left is that, for Vonnegut, the impossibility of happiness doesn't really matter. Whether we achieve fulfillment or are left frustrated, his comment will be the same: "So it goes."

Like all of Vonnegut's early novels, *Slaughterhouse-Five* engages its writer, and hence its reader, in the heartbreak of *anomie* and the impossibility of remaining *engagé*. However, the novel still ends with a possibility that soulful retrospection can lead to growth and self-liberation. Kathryn Hume has writ-ten eloquently of the "tension in [Vonnegut's] work between the pessimism born of experience and the optimism stemming from background and values" (201). Certainly that optimism offers an essential counterweight to the Luddite impulse of *Player Piano*. "An enthusiasm for technological cures for almost all forms of human discontent was the only religion of my family during the Great Depression," wrote Vonnegut in 1980. "A hammer is still my Jesus, and my Vir-gin Mary is still a cross-cut saw." Such a "religion" offers a defense, although undoubtedly a specious one, against the "desperate attempt to rationalize chaos" (Merrill and Scholl 146) that is *Slaughterhouse-Five*. The firebombing of Dresden did not threaten Vonnegut's ancestral religion, as he explains,

> because the technology which created that firestorm was so famil-
> iar to me. I understood it entirely, and so had no trouble imagining
> how the same amount of ingenuity and determination could ben-
> efit mankind once the war was over. I could even help. There was
> nothing in the bombs or the airplanes, after all, which could not,
> essentially, be bought at a small hardware store. (*Palm Sunday* 69)

But significantly, in the 1980 essay this quote is excerpted from, Vonnegut writes in the past tense. His pessimism deepened as he moved toward the 1990s, and life appeared so dedicated to its own inversion that Vonnegut finally stopped giving speeches on the subject.[1]

So how does a writer reach and hold onto optimism when all around him seems bent on self-destruction? Vonnegut's answer to that question is the appropriately named *Slapstick*. In *Slapstick*, Vonnegut first presents the tragedies of the past as simply component parts of the farce that is the present; judgment gives way to raucous—or callous—indifference. The past becomes its own tragedy, not ours—not to be ridiculed or travestied, yet still to be shared. As Jerome Klinkowitz puts it, "Kurt Vonnegut in fact brings a message that is hopeful. If life seems without purpose, perhaps it is because we have tried (and failed) to impose a purpose inappropriately" (*Vonnegut in Fact* 9). All of Vonnegut's subsequent works are best seen as a succession of attempts at an intelligent response to the dead end his early works brought him to, and which he symbolically acknowledged by letting go of all his previous characters in his conclusion to *Breakfast of Champions*.

The first and most visible attribute of *Slapstick* is its setting: America has lost the technology that was the foundation of its strength. Gravity has become variable, and its first shift toward heaviness destroyed the bridges, the tunnels, the elevators, and the aircraft. Thus the technology that had once brought people together, making it possible for them to live in cities and communicate instantaneously around the globe, was lost. In its place, a world in which one writes by the light of "a burning rag in a bowl of animal fat" (84), one defecates down the otherwise-useless elevator shaft, and one communicates—if at all—by messenger. The shift from Paul Proteus's world, or Billy Pilgrim's—or Vonnegut's—is evident.

In the context of Vonnegut's deepening real-life pessimism, *Slapstick* appears at first glance to confirm its author's mood. In this bicentennial vision of a postcataclysmic America, rival warlords fight bloody wars of hand-to-hand combat, and the strong enslave the weak. Horrible diseases—the Albanian Flu, the Green Death—have decimated the population, and the only antidote is a daily diet of raw fish guts. "What does it all mean?" asks the narrator's science advisor during his short term as president of the United States, before the United States collapses into anarchy. "I don't know, Albert," replies the narrator. "And maybe I'm glad I don't know" (189). Readers might well weep over Vonnegut's vision of a world given over to evil and brutality—except he will not let us. This is not the world of *Slaughterhouse-Five*, where blacks riot in the ghettos and children burn in Vietnam, while Billy merely looks the other way (59, 200). This is a world where most people actually seem happy with their lives, and where if a miracle is needed it sometimes actually appears. When the narrator desperately needs to travel a thousand miles, a helicopter stocked with "thousands of gallons of absolutely priceless gasoline" (198), is revealed for his exclusive use. As we read *Slapstick*, the title's relevance gradually becomes clear; we end with laughter, not with tears.

How can one laugh at the end of the world? Where did Vonnegut achieve such a permanent, underlying appreciation that technology's exposed under-belly is farcical, not bathetic? Critics of Vonnegut's early works consistently called him a closet optimist. As Klinkowitz put it in 1973, "Despite their rogues' galleries of unpleasant incidents, [Vonnegut's early novels] are finally optimistic works" (*The Vonnegut Statement* 175). Similarly, Lawrence Broer declares: "Von-negut knows that . . . with a little imagination and heart we can, like Salo in Sirens of Titan, dismantle our own self-imprisoning machinery " (146). Yet the overwhelming evidence of Vonnegut's stories—the mindless destruction in *Player Piano* of even those machines that make our lives better, the inability of characters like Howard W. Campbell Jr. and Billy Pilgrim to free themselves from the embittering legacy of their traumatic experiences, the inescapable sui-cide of a world (in *Cat's Cradle*) or a universe (in *Slaughterhouse-Five*)—leads to a conclusion that the cosmic shackles that imprison us will never of their own volition fall off our limbs, and that mindless violence, whether perpetrated by a Dwayne Hoover or by an equally insane government, will always triumph over enlightened resignation. As Vonnegut puts it in *Palm Sunday*, "Most of the people around me find lives in the service of machines so tedious and exasper-ating that they would not mind much, even if they have children, if life were turned off like a light switch" (69–70).

Critics, such as Bo Petterson, have allowed statements like these to blind them to later developments, concluding that "For Vonnegut the inventiveness of man . . . renders him useless, which is a devastating experience" (68). Yet like the pessimism of Jonathan Swift, who while hating "the whole damned human race" could still love individual Toms, and Dicks, and Harrys, Vonnegut's philo-sophical pessimism never—at least in his early works—penetrates his "desire to project positive messages . . . sustaining his natural optimism" (Hume, "*Symbols of Meaning*," 210–13). And in *Slapstick*, Vonnegut stumbles on a way to overcome that impossible duality.

What is remarkable about *Slapstick* and all of the other late Vonnegut novels, such as *Galápagos* and *Timequake*, is that they are successful in spite of premises that are far more fantastic than those that impel any of Vonnegut's earlier plots. The first half of Vonnegut's career focuses on the historically accu-rate scenario: a workers' rebellion against the machines that threaten to dehu-manize them; a material originally developed for military purposes by "the G. E. Research Laboratory . . . [the idea for which] was a legend around the Lab-oratory" (*Palm Sunday* 102), that is accidentally released into the environment; an alleged Nazi sympathizer who reveals that he has been an Allied double agent; and a firestorm that kills 135,000 people living in a great and beautiful city, leaving its survivors suffering from guilt complexes that render them psy-chotic. These world tragedies, based on realistic historic precedents, were meant to fill Vonnegut's early readers with a cauterizing vision of "how dis-eased [the human soul] can be" (*Palm Sunday* 70); but—like the title charac-ters in Robert Lowell's "Skunk Hour"—they "did not scare." The ultimate failure of these works, often considered Vonnegut's best, stems from a basic weakness in the tradition within which Vonnegut chose to work.

The novels written during the first half of Vonnegut's career fall into the American tradition of social satire, examining what James E. Miller Jr. has called "the grotesque incongruity between the tenuous spiritual plight of modern man and his fat, vacuous, unrippled life" (8). In such works, an author attempts to compel a change in the reader's moral sense through the shock of his or her recognition that the horrific events depicted in the novel are only a step or two removed from events occurring in the reader's own life. From James Fenimore Cooper in *Home As Found*, through works as disparate as *Billy Budd* and *The Sun Also Rises*, to the novels of John Updike and Frederick Busch, today's finest practitioners of this genre, social satirists have confronted readers with the anarchic violence at the center of their own nature, in an effort to heal them, or at least allow them to come to terms with a society that functions by suppressing its eruption.

When people first read about the kind of tragedies Vonnegut has placed at the center of these novels, they are moved; but the natural human tendency is to assimilate such emotions, file them away in the appropriate pigeonhole labeled "outrage," and ultimately become anesthetized to their repetition. As Billy Pilgrim does when faced with war atrocities and race riots, we just turn away. Thus novels based on historic precedent produce a minor "shock of recognition," but cannot transform one's consciousness; as David Rampton puts it, "The depiction of our own horrific cruelty will not necessarily make us better" (18).

Beginning with *Slapstick*, however, Vonnegut finds a way to overcome the tremendous inertia of his readers' ennui, by tracing ever-larger arcs across the proscenium of our imaginations; his subject matter becomes a change in the basic structure of the cosmos—the flow of time and the lines of gravitational force—or a change in the basic structure of humankind, its devolution into a subspecies of seal. The more fantastic the underlying plot, the greater the power of the steadfast narrator to evade the reactionary force of our wills and activate our unconscious.[2] The "tired old stories" of history having failed, in the second half of his career Vonnegut decides to tell new tales, free from the old "villains" of human misery: "culture, society, and history" (31). As Richard Hauck perceives, Vonnegut and other practitioners of this new genre, such as John Hawkes and Thomas Pynchon, "do not create distorted worlds as much as they perceive that the world is distorted" (11).

Of course, liberating plot from the demands of verisimilitude, placing such overload on the willing suspension of disbelief, presumes an overwhelming optimism on the part of the writer. Only someone who is convinced of "a willingness to do whatever we need to do in order to have life on the planet go on for a long, long time" (*Palm Sunday* 209–10) could write books in which gravity smashes every symbol of human technological achievement, or in which a virus wipes the human race off the face of the planet, or in which time turns backward and forces everyone to relive an entire decade. The pessimist who deems these fates inevitable would have no cause to write at all. So we must gain from each catastrophe, or, at the very least, from reading about them. But how?

The resolution to this apparent paradox is first clearly indicated in *Bluebeard* (1987). The self-destruction of Karabekian's paintings (because the brand of paint he used reacts chemically with the sizing on his canvases) serves for him, and for us, as a miniature portrait of the ultimately destructive role technology plays in today's society. The demise of Karabekian's paintings might not be as tragic as the death of 135,000 people in a Dresden firestorm; nevertheless, one would have expected more sorrow than laughter at the event. But we do not grieve over Karabekian's loss, for at least two reasons. First, his language will not let us. Karabekian speaks throughout as an imposter in the world of genius, allowed entrance into the realm of art by the merest chance and sustained there only by the money his disappearing pictures brought him. In Vonnegut's early career, such an imposter figure would have been used as a mouthpiece for the author's own political or satiric insights; for example, the double agent Howard W. Campbell Jr. is proud to announce that he is "the son of an engineer. Since there is no one else to praise me, I will praise myself—will say that I have never tampered with a single tooth . . . on a gear of my thinking machine" (*Mother Night* 163). But Campbell is telling his story in order to stave off charges of high treason; Karabekian tells his story merely in order to stave off the relentless pursuit of his sexual nemesis, Circe Berman. So at least part of the answer is that Vonnegut's later novels shift their ground from satire to travesty.

The second, and more important, part of the answer is that the world inhabited by Vonnegut's later characters reflects a profound shift in Vonnegut's epistemology. For Paul Proteus, and for Winston Rumfoord, and for Franklin Hoenikker, the world and its inhabitants are ultimately less significant than the things they produce and the structures they inhabit; and this obsessive focus on product, to the exclusion of process, proves to be their fatal flaw. But Vonnegut's later heroes no longer see themselves as actors in any significant role; they are instead members of the chorus, observers of actions that may include them, may even revolve around them, but can no longer touch them. From the moment that Billy Pilgrim stops thinking of himself as the focus of Tralfamadore's collective gaze and begins to think merely of what *he* is gazing at—particularly when it is Montana's beautiful bosom—he begins to accept the process of the universe; the moment Rabo Karabekian's paintings disintegrate, he is free to become an artist. As Kilgore Trout proclaims in Vonnegut's last novel, *Timequake*: "Those artsy-fartsy twerps next door create living, breathing, three-dimensional characters with ink on paper. . . . Wonderful! As though the planet weren't already dying because it has three billion too many living, breathing, three-dimensional characters! . . . If I'd wasted my time creating characters . . . I would never have gotten around to calling attention to things that really matter" (62–63).

And significantly, at the end of *Bluebeard* we are treated to one of these "things that really matter," a true work of art: eight panels covered with a panoramic view of a valley, filled with representations of "five thousand, two hundred and nineteen people" (280) who were present on "the day the Second World War ended in Europe" (281). The painting is what it is, but it is also every other thing it appears to be: simultaneously concrete and abstract, a window onto the past and a fence against its repetition—5,219 military uniforms blending into a timeless vision of peace. In a beautifully appropriate metaphor, Bo Petterson notes that "Karabekian manages at last to produce his Grecian urn" (131). That is the vision that Vonnegut's later characters, and by implications we later readers, are intended to share: an artifact that fuses body and soul, male and female, past and present, opening the way to a more successful future. Rabo's vision is, appropriately, the vision of a new millennium.

But such mystical fervor is as extreme as the alienated bitterness that filled the early novels. Something must mediate between us and our dreams, while protecting us from our despair: laughter. No longer is laughter the brittle articulation of an embittered psyche, as it is in *Cat's Cradle* and *Breakfast of Champions*. Instead, it reflects a mature appreciation of the absurd. Rabo Karabekian is a painter; that is, he defines himself by the act of painting. Similarly, Kilgore Trout is a writer; he defines himself by writing. Conversely, Billy Pilgrim has no true vocation, and thus cannot achieve happiness on earth; he can define himself only when he is abducted to Tralfamadore and given a role, even if only as a spectacle. However, what demonstrates true maturity is the recognition that the success or failure of Rabo's painting, Trout's short story, or Billy's "day at the zoo" is irrelevant to those self-definitions. That is why Rabo's canvases can disintegrate, and Kilgore can throw his stories directly into the trash. Vonnegut's crucial insight has been to see that, although life is inevitably revealed as a tragedy by the time the final curtain falls, it is a screamingly funny farce while the performance is on. Ultimately, it is little more than personal preference: "Laughter and tears are both responses to frustration and exhaustion, to the futility of thinking and striving anymore. I myself prefer to laugh" (*Palm Sunday* 327–28). Richard Hauck puts it clearly: "The reader can laugh if he chooses to do so. He laughs, to be sure, in the full awareness of the possibilities for terror in his laughter. . . . Vonnegut's novels are funny and are thus an affirmative act by the author himself" (13–14, 237).

Vonnegut's nonfiction has often referred to life in similarly ridiculous terms. In his 1977 Paris Review self-interview, for example, he called his work nothing more than an extended series of practical jokes (*Palm Sunday* 109). During the Reagan years, he even worked up a screamingly funny routine about the military-industrial complex as a con man: "If Western Civilization were a person, we would be directing it to the nearest meeting of War Preparers Anonymous. . . . [And there is no appeasing an addict for very long: 'I swear, man, just lay enough bread on me for twenty multiple reentry vehicles and a fleet of B-1 bombers, and I'll never bother you again.']" (135). But in his last few works, Vonnegut has finally learned to deal with this anonymous addict of death, through his fictional characters and the absurd situations into which he puts them.

One of the best illustrations of the way in which real-world tragedy topples over into a farcical reader response occurs in *Hocus Pocus* (1990). One of the popular games at the local college is a computer game called "GRIOT," which foretells a person's future based on details about his or her background: "You load it up with details about a life, real or imagined, and then it spits out a story about what was likely to happen to him or her. This story is based on what has happened to real persons with the same general specifications." GRIOT comes up with the following "stories" : "It made me a burned-out case ... a wife-beater and an alcoholic, and winding up all alone on Skid Row" (103); when the narrator tries again, "I did a little better ... an instructor at West Point, but unhappy and bored. I lost my wife again, and still drank too much, and ... I died of cirrhosis of the liver a second time" (105). When he asks it about one of his lovers, the sculptor Pamela Ford Hall, "GRIOT had her die of cirrhosis of the liver. I gave the machine the same set of facts a second time, and it had her freezing to death in a doorway in Chicago" (185); finally, when the escaped convicts try the game, it "sent them straight to jail to serve long sentences" (104).

GRIOT's long litany of unmitigated disasters holds out no hope for the narrator, and strongly implies that readers will suffer exactly the same fate. Therefore, we flatly deny its prophecies of failure, taking refuge from its unpalatable truths in the one thing humans are always successful at: ridicule. In *Slaughterhouse-Five* Vonnegut claims that the Tralfamadorians are even better at denial than humans—and given Billy Pilgrim's refusal to recognize the horrors of war, of racial discrimination, or of domestic barrenness, that is quite a claim. Referring to their own wars and horrors, the guide boasts:

> "There isn't anything we can do about them, so we simply don't look at them. We ignore them. ... That's one thing Earthmen might learn to do, if they tried hard enough: Ignore the awful times, and concentrate on the good ones." (117)

If there were even a single happy ending among GRIOT's collected scenarios, plausibility might be restored, and justify a feeling of despair; but because modern technology offers no possibility of happiness, we can safely "ignore" GRIOT's predictions, perhaps by calling them the result of a failure in the software, rather than face the statistically high probability of personal, marital, or professional failure in real life that they actually reflect.

There is a clear contrast between this infallibly wrong machine and Vonnegut's earliest "infallible" machine, Checker Charley. When Paul Proteus beat this early computer in *Player Piano*, there remained an irrefutable suggestion that Paul Finnerty had sabotaged it; thus readers could accept the theory of machine superiority—Proteus at first declines even to compete against the machine—while enjoying the reality of human triumph. But the computer in *Hocus Pocus* paints its pictures of individual doom and disaster as background to the even more frightening mass scenarios of prison break, hostage taking, and massacre. Readers are left with no choice but to deny the evidence of their senses and proclaim the whole thing a farce.

Meanwhile, *Hocus Pocus* presents its readers with a complementary model of human endeavor, one that can be embraced because it offers positive psychic rewards, even as it acknowledges the inevitability of real failure. Elias Tarkington's "perpetual-motion machines," constructed during the nineteenth century by the founder of the college that eventually will be the site of the prisoners' last stand, were total failures at their intended purpose; but "they were exquisite jewelry, with garnets and amethysts for bearings, with arms and legs of exotic woods, with tumbling balls of ivory, with chutes and counterweights of silver." The narrator infers that the designer "hoped to overwhelm science with the magic of precious materials," but such a hope is clearly as futile as the hope that one can overwhelm life's inadequacies with computer processing power. What remains praiseworthy is the magnificence of the effort: "The men who built the machines for Elias Tarkington knew from the first that they would never work, whatever the reason. Yet what love they lavished on the materials that comprised them!" (*Hocus Pocus* 23–24). A world so terrible that both the individual and the society are equally doomed to catastrophic failure—or a world equally imperfect, yet redeemed by "love" and by "hope" : which one would you choose?

Vonnegut reserves his biggest put-down of computers, and of any society so self-deluding that it will clutch at the illusion of power that they offer, for his late masterwork, *Galápagos*. There a small group of human beings are marooned on the islands of the title, survivors of a ship containing nothing left to salvage, because just before leaving port it has been stripped of everything that could be carried off—"television sets and telephones and radar and sonar and radios and light bulbs and compasses and toilet paper and carpeting and soap and pots and pans and charts and mattresses and outboard motors and inflatable landing craft, and on and on" (179). The only item of modern technology that they manage to carry off the wreck with them is Mandarax, a hand-held computer that, despite its remarkable power, is totally useless. Although Mandarax can translate a thousand languages, the only language it is ever called upon to translate is Kanka-bono, which is not in its memory banks. Although it is full of quotations, the only quotations it ever provides are grotesquely inappropriate to its circumstances, as when a child is born and Mandarax reminds the infant's mother that "[She] cannot see, nor breathe, nor stir, / But through the death of some of her" (63), or when it replies to a shout of "Mayday!" with a quotation from A. E. Housman (249). Asked in a subsequent interview to sum up the utility of such machines, Vonnegut concluded: "This hotel today is filled with voices; but there's nobody saying anything worth writing down" (Nuwer 257).

Kurt Vonnegut's career thus reflects the development not merely of a writer, but of what in *Timequake* he calls "a spiritual adventure" (157). Beginning his career in fiction as a writer of pulp-magazine stories, and then seemingly condemned to the rather seedy reputation of a man whose works appear as "paperback originals," Vonnegut is a man who has always felt "somehow marginal, somehow slightly off-balance all the time" (*Palm Sunday* 65). Watching events in the world catch up to, and then surpass, the all-too-serious warnings contained in his early attempts at creating "hinged and unlocked boxes . . . packed with leaves speckled by ink" (*Timequake* 157), Vonnegut soon realized that the mimetic imperative demanded that his books mirror the truth of life: books are nothing more than "practical jokes," and great books are merely "great practical jokes" (*Palm Sunday* 109). As Kilgore Trout puts it in *Timequake*, "It was the world that had suffered the nervous breakdown. I was just having fun in a nightmare" (54).

Kurt Vonnegut's fame rests primarily on his works of social satire: *Player Piano, Mother Night, Slaughterhouse-Five*. But these novels, and the other works Vonnegut wrote in the belief "that this recognition of the blackness at the center of our natures can be translated into social terms" (Rampton 18), have failed to achieve any lasting transformation of society (though Loree Rackstraw, elsewhere in this volume, argues that he effected an epistemological seachange). So, I believe, Vonnegut turned to "comic books," novels whose premises are so absurd that no sane reader could ever fear they might contain a social message: *Slapstick, Bluebeard, Hocus Pocus*. And the ongoing hilarity of these works, in the face of tragedies certainly equivalent on a personal level to the social upheavals depicted in the earlier novels, carries a different—and far more successful—message. To destroy in rage is to destroy utterly; but to destroy in laughter is to cleanse the world and let joy back in. By laughing at the technology whose side effects threaten our health and happiness, we "can start thinking and striving again that much sooner" (*Palm Sunday* 328). Thus Vonnegut finally succeeds in resolving the conflict between that "technological nincompoopery" (*Fates Worse Than Death* 116) that threatens to make authors obsolete, and the "state of suspended animation" (*Hocus Pocus* 16) that threatens to make readers themselves obsolete. Maybe that resolution can, here at the end of a millennium, be uttered only in a loud horselaugh; but that is precisely Kurt Vonnegut's point.

NOTES

1. "Jokesters are all through when they find themselves talking about challenges so real and immediate and appalling to their listeners that no amount of laughter can make the listeners feel safe and perfectly well again. I found myself doing that on a speaking tour of campuses in the spring of 1989, and canceled all future engagements" (*Fates Worse Than Death* 185).

2. Vonnegut once proclaimed the source of art's power its ability to make one "surrender his will to his . . . unconscious" (*Fates Worse Than Death* 42–43).

WORKS CITED

Broer, Lawrence. "Pilgrim's Progress: Is Kurt Vonnegut Winning His War with Machines?" *Clockwork Worlds: Mechanized Environments in Science Fiction*. Ed. R. D. Erlich and T. P. Dunn. Westport: Greenwood, 1983. 137–61.

Hauck, Richard Boyd. "Cheerful Nihilism: Confidence and 'The Absurd.'" *American Humorous Fiction*. Bloomington: Indiana UP, 1971

Hoffman, Thomas P. "The Theme of Mechanization in *Player Piano*." *Clockwork Worlds: Mechanized Environments in Science Fiction*. Ed. R. D. Erlich and T. P. Dunn. Westport: Greenwood, 1983. 125–35.

Hume, Kathryn. "Kurt Vonnegut and the Myths and Symbols of Meaning." *Texas Studies in Literature and Language* 24.4 (1982): 429–47. Rpt. *Critical Essays on Kurt Vonnegut*. 201–16.

Klinkowitz, Jerome. "*Mother Night*, *Cat's Cradle*, and the Crimes of Our Time." *The Vonnegut Statement*. New York: Delacorte, 1973. 158–77.

———. *Vonnegut in Fact: The Public Spokesmanship of Personal Fiction*. Columbia: U of South Carolina P, 1998.

Merrill, Robert. *Critical Essays on Kurt Vonnegut*. Boston: G. K. Hall, 1990.

———, and P. A. Scholl. "Vonnegut's *Slaughterhouse-Five:* The Requirements of Chaos." *Studies in American Fiction* 6 (1978): 65–76. Rpt. in *Critical Essays on Kurt Vonnegut*, 142–51.

Miller, James E., Jr. *Quests Surd and Absurd: Essays in American Literature*. Chicago: U of Chicago P, 1967.

Nuwer, Hank. "A Skull Session with Kurt Vonnegut." *Conversations with Kurt Vonnegut*. Ed. W. R. Allen. Jackson: UP of Mississippi, 1988. 240–64.

Petterson, Bo. *The World According to Kurt Vonnegut*. Abo. Abo Akademi UP, 1994.

Rampton, David. "Into the Secret Chamber: Art and the Artist in Kurt Vonnegut's *Bluebeard*." *Critique: Studies in Contemporary Fiction* 35.1 (Fall 1993), 16ff.

Reed, Peter J. *The Short Fiction of Kurt Vonnegut*. Westport: Greenwood, 1997.

Vonnegut, Kurt. *Player Piano*. New York: Dell, 1952.

———. *The Sirens of Titan*. New York: Dell, 1959.

———. *Cat's Cradle*. New York: Dell, 1963.

———. *Mother Night*. New York: Avon, 1966.

———. *Slaughterhouse-Five*. New York: Dell, 1969.

———. *Slapstick*. New York: Delacorte, 1976.

———. *Jailbird*. New York: Delacorte, 1979.

———. *Palm Sunday*. New York: Delacorte, 1981.

————. *Deadeye Dick*. New York: Delacorte, 1982.

————. *Galápagos*. New York: Delacorte, 1985.

————. *Bluebeard*. New York: Delacorte, 1987.

————. *Hocus Pocus*. New York: Putnam's, 1990.

————. *Fates Worse Than Death*. New York: Putnam's, 1991.

————. *Timequake*. New York: Putnam's, 1997.

Wymer, Thomas L. "Machines and the Meaning of Human in the Novels of Kurt Vonnegut, Jr." *The Mechanical God: Machines in Science Fiction*. Ed. T. P. Dunn and R. D. Erlich. Westport: Greenwood, 1982. 41–52.

CHAPTER EIGHT

NARRATIVE, SELF, AND MORALITY IN THE WRITING OF KURT VONNEGUT

Bill Gholson

Kurt Vonnegut is a self-professed agnostic firmly grounded in the tradition of his German freethinking relatives. As such, his morality comes without metaphysical props. Instead, his moral thinking and writing reflect a rhetorical orientation—one for which the self is never disembodied from the community, the history, and the discourses of which it is a part. For Vonnegut, understanding the narrative self is an inescapable feature of identity and morality, both central concerns of his work. As Rudy Waltz puts it in *Deadeye Dick*, "We all see our lives as stories . . . [and] psychologists and sociologists and historians and so on would find it useful to acknowledge that" (208).

Vonnegut's fiction questions the possibility of developing discourses of morality and identity in the face of contingency: How is it possible to speak of morality or identity once one accepts that there is no Truth or metadiscourses to access outside of human-made languages and contexts? What does a moral self, which finds its sources within the things people do as opposed to being the product of universal worth and intrinsic value, look like? Is the only recourse a slide into radical relativity?

Vonnegut's characters are on a moral quest similar to the quest Charles Taylor describes in *Sources of the Self*:

> One could put it this way: because we cannot but orient ourselves to the good, and thus determine our place relative to it and hence determine the direction of our lives, we must inescapably understand our lives in narrative form, as a "quest." But one could perhaps start from another point: because we have to determine our place in relation to the good, therefore we cannot be without an orientation to it, and hence must see our life in story. From whichever direction, I see these conditions as connected facets of the same reality, inescapable structural requirements of human agency. (51–52)

By articulating the parameters of their lives in a narrative, Vonnegut's characters begin to locate their identities in a moral space and to understand their lives as continually unfolding. They find themselves in a "space of questions," where they attempt to define the frameworks of their existence in order to "know where [they] stand, and what meanings things have for [them]" (Taylor 29). His characters seek, not a static sense of the self, but a sense that their life is always in the process of becoming, what Alasdair MacIntyre describes as "the unity of a narrative embodied in a single life" (218).

In *Breakfast of Champions*, Vonnegut draws attention to himself as artistic creator and claims the work produced a transformation in him. This is central to an understanding of his importance as a writer and a crucial indictor of the thematic direction his work takes in the novels and essays that follow. From *Breakfast of Champions* on, Vonnegut focuses his energies around a constellation of questions about the nature of narrative, its ability to transform the self, and the implications of viewing the self as a form of narrative. He confesses in the preface to *Wampeters, Foma, and Granfalloons* that he himself is "a work of fiction" (xxi), and asserts his hope and belief that "works of the imagination themselves have the power to create" (xxvi).

In *Bluebeard* Vonnegut continues to work out the notion of the creative power of fiction to transform individuals into self-conscious moral beings. Rabo, addressing his audience directly, states that Circe Berman serves as his inspiration for the autobiography—the narrative they are now reading—and so his recall of the scenes that involve her are given central importance. When Rabo announces to Circe that his paintings were meant to be "uncommunicative" (35), she asks, "What's the point of being alive . . . if you're not going to *communicate* ? (35; original emphasis). This question, of course, is one of the central questions that motivates Rabo to write about his life and to reveal his magnum opus, which communicates significant moments in his life (but only when Circe provides him with an audience). When the painting is revealed to the public, they are encouraged to make the painting "mean what they think it means" (238), suggesting that meaning is made through the process of interpretation. Thus, through communication, meaning is engendered. It is Rabo's narrative, his autobiography, that imbues Rabo with self-knowledge and moral unity, and it is his ability to finally express the framework of his existence that brings meaning to his life. But this is only possible when Circe provides him an audience for his narrative, thereby completing the circuit and enabling communication. Just as the painting in the barn is a mystery until Rabo shares it with Circe, Rabo's life is a mystery (even to himself) until he narrates it to Circe. Both the painting and Rabo's life need community before they can communicate.

Elsewhere in this volume, Jerome Klinkowitz ("Vonnegut the Essayist") points out that communicating with readers has been a key element from the beginning of Vonnegut's career. It is not too surprising then that problems of communication are of central concern to Vonnegut's narrators. Situated in and responding to "ordinary" lives characterized by suffering, Vonnegut's characters struggle with communication (narration and interpretation), which is, itself, an ongoing struggle for meaning. Because the circumstances of life are contingent, the articulation of self and morality requires the continued questioning and reframing of experience in narrative form.

THE SELF AS NARRATIVE

In both the novels and essays, Vonnegut blends genres, creating and recreating himself in the narrative. He describes *Palm Sunday* and *Fates Worse Than Death* as "autobiographical collages." I wish to draw attention, briefly, to the way in which Vonnegut arranges the pieces in a narrative form using metaphors of the physical body to literally give vital substance to his beliefs.

In *Wampeters, Foma, and Granfalloons*, Vonnegut refers specifically to the various pieces in the collection as "bodies" (xvii). In *Palm Sunday*, he speaks of arranging the pieces by providing the "connective tissue" (xvii) necessary to form an autobiography. In *Fates Worse Than Death*, he refers in the preface to the collection as a "creature," but continues the metaphor in the opening page by writing:

> Here we go again with real life and opinions made to look like one big, preposterous animal not unlike an invention by Dr. Seuss, the great writer and illustrator of children's books, like an oobleck or a grinch or a lorax, or like a sneech perhaps.
> Or a unicorn, not a Seuss invention. (19)

These autobiographical collections are material artifacts that reveal Vonnegut's complex notions of self-identity, narrative, morality, and subjectivity. The bodily metaphor connects directly to an audience by providing a means of collaboration wherein readers piece together the connective tissues, and form, in language, Vonnegut's body. Vonnegut invites readers to participate in the creation of his moral skeleton. Therefore, identity in Vonnegut's work is narrative and "collaborative" (*Fates Worse Than Death* 49–50). It is a commonplace to speak of an author's "body" of work, but in Vonnegut this emphasis takes on increased significance because of his focus on inventing the self in narrative. His work is his body.

We can see this continued exploration of the self as narrative and his insistence on the communicative importance of writing in his later novels as well. After a long "prologue" in *Slapstick* where Vonnegut discusses the importance of understanding his own mind as a "gadget . . . separate from . . . awareness . . . from our central selves" (4), his intimate relationship with his sister, the problems of loneliness, jokes, extended families, and his youth in the Great Depression, a central, distinctive, and self-conscious narrator struggles to articulate the parameters of self and to communicate that identity to an audience in the body of the narrative.

In each of the novels that follow *Slapstick*, Vonnegut speaks directly to the audience, reminding them of the importance of the articulation itself—the importance of communicating what does and doesn't make sense about life from the point of view of a single consciousness. We frequently find in Vonnegut this articulation of self, famously in a passage from *Breakfast of Champions* where he announces that the writing of the novel itself performed a rebirth, that the chaos of artistic production became useful as self-reinvention (218). At this important juncture in the middle of Vonnegut's career, a new self emerges from chaos, inspired by Rabo Karabekian's painting *The Temptation of Saint Anthony*, a work that Karabekian claims "shows everything about life which truly matters, with nothing left out" (221).

Vonnegut credits Karabekian's speech for renewing his life (223) by turning him away from the belief that all people functioned like machines, their lives determined by systems. Karabekian points Vonnegut toward narrative-self, toward self as aesthetic artifact. What Karabekian creates on canvas, Vonnegut creates on the page. What Karabekian creates with Sateen Dura-Luxe and tape, Vonnegut creates with language. In *Breakfast of Champions*, he draws attention to himself as artistic creator, paradoxically creating the work he credits with his own realization of self. In these later novels, Vonnegut focuses on the ability of narrative to transform the self, and explores the implication of viewing identity as a form of narrative. Ironically, Karabekian's paintings—paintings that Karabekian tells Circe Berman in *Bluebeard* were meant to be "uncommunicative" (35)—communicate something important to Vonnegut about the nature of self: communication transforms the self. The painting is a product of the artist's "meat" (287) and the artist's "soul" (265). But like Vonnegut's writing, Karabekian's painting needs (and eventually gets) an audience to complete it. When it is revealed to the public, they are free to make the painting "mean" something. Meaning is made through the process of interpretation, a process involving the product of the artist's meat and soul and an audience; thus, only when the potato barn is opened to the public is anything communicated, and only when something is communicated is change possible. Furthermore, like Vonnegut in *Breakfast of Champions,* Karabekian learns to articulate the framework of his existence, which brings a sense of meaning to his life.

A writer's function, therefore, is social, as Vonnegut points out in his discussion of the Greek historian Thucydides:

> Thucydides is the first New Journalist I know anything about. He was a celebrity who put himself at the center of the truths he was trying to tell, and he guessed when he had to, and he thought it worthwhile to be charming and entertaining. (*Wampeters, Foma, and Granfalloons* xix)

Vonnegut might just as easily have been talking about himself. Early in his career, he exposes his view of a writer as a teacher, a communicator, and a performer who is always sensitive to his audience. To be a teacher, a person must have students; to be a writer a person must have readers. And it is in the self-reflexive narrative he writes for us that his "self" is formed. Thus, Vonnegut's narrative self becomes the narrative thread that runs through all his works, and that accounts for the highly personal tone of his writing.

Most critics mention the personal nature of Vonnegut's work. Richard Giannone, for example, claims that Vonnegut's work "affirms" Vonnegut's "own identity" and that what is most striking in the later novels is "Vonnegut himself" (126) and Jerome Klinkowitz talks at length about what he calls Vonnegut's "Personal Novels" (*Slaughterhouse-Five, Breakfast of Champions, Slapstick, and Jailbird*), but perhaps the most complete statement of the subjective nature of Vonnegut's fiction was made by Lawrence R. Broer. Broer argues for a positive progression in Vonnegut's novels, which culminates in *Bluebeard.* Broer claims that in *Bluebeard,* "Instead of splitting the identity of Rabo the created and Vonnegut the creator as in *Breakfast of Champions,* Vonnegut becomes Rabo Karabekian, the most complete and human of all Vonnegut's creations" (175). Presumably then, the distance between Vonnegut's narrative self and the narrated self of each idiosyncratic narrator narrows as we move through the novels until the two are virtually indistinguishable. Vonnegut has made his own pronouncements as well. In *Fates Worse Than Death,* he calls himself the "biggest" character in *Hocus Pocus,* and in the preface to *Between Time and Timbuktu of Prometheus-5,* he confesses that he wants "to be a character in all of . . . [his] works" (xv). This self-consciousness adds a metacritical level to his work, where ethical implications of the tale being told are made explicit in the telling, and the moral character of "self" is aligned with the moral tone of the narration. Thus narrative and self are fused, accounting for the inescapable relationship between morality and identity in Vonnegut's work, and his desire for a moral language closely allied with identity.

THE NEED FOR A MORAL CENTER

Vonnegut's early fiction explores various ways in which personal identity has suffered in the twentieth century, but in his later fiction, the self finds meaning and purpose in its impulse to orient itself in relation to moral questions. Moral questions provide a framework for self. The scaffolds of identity, then, are formed primarily by the questions we choose to ask, not necessarily the answers we find. Therefore, the loss or fragmentation of the self in modern times can be seen as a result of not knowing which moral questions to ask.

What we find in Vonnegut's later work are characters trapped between their need to orient themselves to moral and ethical issues and a world that has lost this orientation. Life becomes "meaningful" not by reorienting the world toward a workable ethical system, but by involving oneself in the pursuit of moral systems. It is the process not the product that renders meaning, the writing of the book, not the artifact itself. The notion of a "meaningful" life is intimately linked to the notion of the narrative quest. Once again—narrative and self are fused.

To understand Kurt Vonnegut's legacy as a twentieth-century artist, one must understand how identity and morality manifest themselves in his work through the central importance he places on literature as an act of communication and persuasion. Vonnegut understands that narrative involves a fundamentally rhetorical process. Indeed, his focus on audience and persuasion can be seen very early, and becomes one of the most important aspects of his later work. Communication is thematic to the essays and novels of the second half of his career. And communication (as approached in Vonnegut's work) is connected directly to identity and morality.

In Vonnegut, narrative is the fundamental means by which we encounter the world, understand the self, and inquire about moral questions. It is the narrative self in his work that reasons about beliefs, make choices, and finds its orientation within a framework of questions about what it means to be human. What is the meaning of *my* life? Why am *I* here? How can I eliminate the suffering of others? Who and what deserve my respect? In this sense, Vonnegut's work is value-centered and provides a potentially positive response to contemporary problems of identity. In each of his novels and throughout many of his essays since *Breakfast of Champions*, moral thinking is in operation. The fact that his characters raise moral questions indicates a belief that moral decisions are possible, making Vonnegut one of the few "postmodern" writers maintaining hope in an age when the concept of a coherent identity is in question. It is not surprising, then, that we find Vonnegut's characters at odds with the worlds they inhabit. Vonnegut critiques culture, society, and history as if they were villainous characters who work against the happiness of the individual. His satiric jab at the therapeutic use of drugs to make harsh realities more tolerable is echoed frequently throughout his books. Rudy Waltz in *Deadeye Dick* innocently supplies his community with the pharmaceutical means to escape reality. Karabekian in *Bluebeard* spends much of his early life drinking. Wilbur Swain in *Slapstick* spends the greater part of his life on an antidepressant. Hartke in *Hocus Pocus* spends most of his teen years high on marijuana. So there is recognition in Vonnegut's novels that the world is a harsh and forbidding place and that often a response to this harshness is an escape through drugs. Drugs are means of escape, of forgetting, and they oppose the life-affirming creation of narrative.

Vonnegut's early study of anthropology may be at least partially responsible for his view of society. In *Fates Worse Than Death*, he admits that his anthropological training caused him to look for the causes of evil and suffering in culture and society instead of in individuals (31). So it is that the individual in Vonnegut's narratives is set in opposition, paradoxically, to the very society he inhabits. To further complicate matters, the self finds its meaning by articulating a history that is always both personal and communal. It is not possible to have a self or identity that is not part of a community, however that community might be defined. So the villainous societies in Vonnegut's fiction are populated with individuals who both oppose and compose it. Furthermore, villainous societies are often made up of individuals who, taken alone, are not particularly evil, and who may, at the individual level, even be seen as moral. The best example of this, perhaps, is Howard Campbell in *Mother Night*, who contributes to the spread of Nazism, but who, as an individual, can be seen as a self-sacrificing hero of democracy. Campbell, like many of Vonnegut's characters, is a writer, and one of the key moral issues raised by *Mother Night* is the role of the writer in the world. We learn from Campbell's misfortune that what we write—and therefore what gets disseminated to readers—can exert a much greater influence over the world than what we, as individuals, may believe. We might even conjecture that the more closely a writer's narratives are aligned with his beliefs, the more ethical his writing is. Campbell's crime against humanity is that the gap between what he believes (his moral sense) and what he writes is too wide. Campbell's tale is cautionary. Because writing is communal, writers have a moral responsibility to community. Thus, in the narration of self, Vonnegut also engages a social function, a desire to affect community. As he claims in his "theory of the arts," imaginative writers function as a "means" of "introducing new ideas into the society, and also a means of responding symbolically to life" (*Wampeters, Foma, and Granfalloons* 237).

Vonnegut's concern is for morality in ordinary life; the values he asserts stem from his belief in what Charles Taylor refers to as the "worth of ordinary human desire and fulfillment" (23). Human dignity comes from "the life of production and reproduction, or work and the family" (29). Thus, for Vonnegut, the affirmation of self will necessarily be the affirmation of community if the affirmation of self is moral.

CHANGING BELIEFS THROUGH COLLABORATION

Vonnegut's frequent references to his readers suggest that he is an author who not only acknowledges, but emphasizes the rhetorical nature of his writing. He wants the communication of imaginative ideas to effect positive change in the world. Vonnegut has often stated that his persuasive intentions are focused not toward those already in power, but to the youth who will one day assume possession of the world. In *Wampeters, Foma, and Granfalloons*, for example, Vonnegut says:

> I am persuaded that we [writers] are tremendously influential, even though most national leaders, my own included, probably never heard of most of us here [the P.E.N. Conference of 1973]. Our influence is slow and subtle, and it is felt mainly by the young. They are hungry for myths which resonate with the mysteries of their own times. We give them those myths. (228–29)

At the heart of this statement is a concern with power and the political implications of fiction. Change occurs, says Vonnegut, when a writer can "poison" (*Wampeters , Foma, and Granfalloons* 227) the minds of young people by changing the values they have inherited from the society in which they live.

Vonnegut's fiction is full of volatile elements—time in *Slaughterhouse-Five*, gravity in *Slapstick*, civilization in *Galápagos,* nature in *Cat's Cradle,* and so on—but the values it promotes are stable: courtesy, understanding, humane objectives. When readers engage his texts, they encounter these values. The more closely they "identify" with (that is, orient themselves to) Vonnegut's characters, the more they incorporate those values into their own self-narratives. In this way, Vonnegut's narrative search for a moral center infects ("poisons") readers with a similar drive to ask moral questions, and to define themselves by their values—an unusual agenda for a "postmodern" writer writing in an age when morality is seen as, at best, arbitrary, and, at worst, oppressive.

Seyla Benhabib's work with ethics and postmodernity calls for the "reconstruction" of some modernist legacies such as "moral and political universalism . . . the moral autonomy of the individual; economic and social justice and equality; democratic participation . . . and the formation of solidaristic human associations" (2). Benhabib notes that the skepticism that drives many contemporary academicians and artists arises from a "disillusionment with a form of life that still perpetrates war, armament, environmental destruction and economic exploitation at the cost of satisfying basic human needs with human dignity, a form of life that still relegates many women, non-Christian and non-white peoples to second-class moral and political status, a form of life that saps the bases of solidaristic coexistence in the name of profit and competition" (2). Vonnegut certainly shares this disillusionment. But Vonnegut never abandons hope. He believes, as Benhabib claims, that the "reformation or reconstruction of the self as an ethical and moral actor in the world" (2) is possible.

In Vonnegut's later novels, each narrator dramatizes a self similar to Benhabib's description of the self. Benhabib situates the self in narrative, claiming that the self, the subject of "actions" and "personal identity," is both author and actor (1–17, passim), and that the self can only survive historically within a community. The self becomes an "individual" in that it becomes a "social" being capable of language, interaction, and cognition. As Benhabib puts it, "The identity of the self is constituted by a narrative unity which integrates what 'I' can do, have done and will accomplish with what you expect of 'me', interpret my acts and intentions to mean, wish for me in the future, etc." (5).

Vonnegut's narrators become whole by articulating their values in relation to the community and history of which they are a part. They describe themselves as embedded in histories and nuclear families that have somehow led to their fragmentation and disorientation, but they transcend this fragmentation by articulating new connections in their writing, by weaving stories that orient them to moral questions. Furthermore, this framework of moral questioning constructs their identities. More to the point, Vonnegut's narrators are formed by their struggle to construct a framework of moral questioning.

One thinks of Rudy Waltz from *Deadeye Dick,* one of Vonnegut's most finely crafted novels in this regard. Rudy suffers the terrible calamity of "innocent murder," becomes a pharmacist who dispenses palliatives for the residents of Midland City, and suffers humiliation (described as a "monkey" (77) by others during his initial incarceration). He, unsurprisingly, withdraws from life. However, the narrative he writes about himself reveals that it is stories that have had the greatest impact on his character. Narrative is central to his sense of self, from his earliest days when his "mind had been trained by heirloom books of fairy tales and . . . myths and legends" (44), to bits of biblical wisdom (72), to his own "playlets" in which he imagines his self as a character. It is partly his ability to imagine himself as a character that enables him to provide readers of his autobiography with insight into his developing sense of self. And what does he choose to leave the readers as a "gift to the future"? (239)—a legend in which Will Fairchild is seen in Avondale looking for his parachute (240). The very act of telling stories gives Rudy the stability he needs to situate his moral center.

The same claim can be made of the implied narrator, the Kurt Vonnegut we imagine writing these books, whose highly personal character invites us to unravel his own values and beliefs, and who directs us to critique the society that can be destructive to individual morality. After all, in *Deadeye Dick,* Vonnegut fuses his own mother's suicide with the accidental shooting of Eloise Metzger.

The reader's importance is clearly articulated in *Mother Night* where we find that Russian readers have the power to transform Campbell's *Memoirs of a Monogamous Casanova* (a diary of Campbell's love for his wife, Helga) into pornography, and that Goebbels and Hitler can read Abraham Lincoln's Gettysburg Address as fascist propaganda.

Vonnegut's writing may assume what Ernst Behler calls a "twisted posture," which communicates "indirectly, by way of circumlocution, configuration, and bafflement" (4–5), but only in response to the end of an epoch whose inhabitants have what Benhabib describes as "a deeply shared sense that certain aspects of our social, symbolic and political universe have been profoundly and most likely irretrievably transformed" (1). Vonnegut writes to connect with an audience, to reform notions of self (and community), not to deconstruct the idea of self (or the possibility of community). Vonnegut wants to develop a reconstructed moral self, and through this reconstructed self, new moral communities. In a graduation address to the seniors at Hobart and William Smith Colleges in which he suggests the best thing the graduates could do as new members of society was to develop new religions, Vonnegut states:

> If I have offended anyone here by talking of the need of a new reli-
> gion, I apologize. I am willing to drop the word religion, and sub-
> stitute for it these three words: *heartfelt moral code*. We sure need such
> a thing, and it should be simple enough and reasonable for anyone
> to understand. The trouble with so many of the moral codes we
> have inherited is that they are subject to so many interpretations.
> (*Palm Sunday* 202; original emphasis)

It should be no surprise that Vonnegut would talk to the graduating seniors about the need for morality and new moral codes. But to develop one's own "heartfelt moral code," it is necessary to engage in interpretation—the primary function of Vonnegut's ironic narrators.

We might apply Richard Rorty's term, "liberal ironist," to Vonnegut. According to Rorty, a liberal ironist is "the sort of person who faces up to the contingency of his or her most central beliefs and desires," and "who think[s] that cruelty is the worst thing we do" (xv). If Vonnegut's books address anything, it is the subject of "man's inhumanity to man," and the cruelty that contemporary life imposes on the private individual. Vonnegut accepts the contingency of selfhood and belief, while at the same time affirming humanistic values in the face of chaos, fragmentation, and the incredible horrors of the century. He is a writer attempting to affirm positive values in light of his belief that there is no metaphysical order upon which to draw.

The liberal ironist is someone who believes there is no preconceived order to which one might appeal, but for whom solidarity is still possible. As Rorty notes:

> Solidarity is not discovered by reflection but created. It is created by
> increasing our sensitivity to the particular details of the pain and
> humiliation of other, unfamiliar sorts of people. Such increased sen-
> sitivity makes it more difficult to marginalize people different from
> ourselves. (xvi)

Rorty claims that this form of solidarity is not found in theory, but in "detailed description of what unfamiliar people are like and of redescription of what we ourselves are like" (xvi). Vonnegut's writing performs both these acts for the 87 percent of the population who he observes do not have lives worth living.

Vonnegut's most important achievement as a novelist and essayist is his ability to articulate the epistemological, ontological, and teleological questions that help frame modern identity—the basis of his writing and concern. One such question, of central importance to his work, can be found in all his novels. As he states in an essay devoted to the sources of his own identity and humor:

> In my very first book, *Player Piano* (published a mere thirty-eight years ago, before the perfection of transistors, when machines making human beings redundant were still enormous, doing their thinking with vacuum tubes), I asked a question which is even harder to answer nowadays: "What are people for?" My own answer is "Maintenance." In *Hocus Pocus,* my last book before this one, I acknowledged that everybody wanted to build and nobody wanted to do maintenance. So there goes the ball game. Meanwhile, truth, jokes, and music help at least a little bit.[1] (*Fates Worse Than Death* 201)

Questions such as "What are people for?" seek to determine identity and to define self. What matters, of course, is how we respond to them, and how we respond to them determines our moral framework. So the kinds of ontological claims Vonnegut makes for human beings are moral, essential, and inescapable from what is known as self, identity or character. Vonnegut raises issues concerning the value of our lives, whether they are rich and substantial or empty and trivial, and much of Vonnegut's popularity over the past five decades can be traced to his ability to understand and speak to the crisis in values of a broad range of contemporary readers.

Throughout his career, Vonnegut returns again and again to the audience's relationship to his work, and the crucial role they play in the production of meaning.

> As you know, it isn't enough for a reader to pick up the little symbols from a page with his eyes, or as is the case with a blind person, his fingertips. Once we get those symbols inside our heads and in the proper order, then we must clothe them in gloom or joy or apathy, in love or hate, in anger or peacefulness, or however the author intended them to be clothed. In order to be good readers, we must even recognize irony—which is when a writer says one thing and really means another, contradicting himself in what he believes to be a beguiling cause. (*Palm Sunday* 162)

In *Palm Sunday*, Vonnegut articulates, more completely than in *Wampeters, Foma, and Granfalloons,* the social purposes of his work. He sometimes communicates elliptically, which requires his audience to be "good readers," and to actively participate in the work, to recognize the effects he is attempting to achieve. In *Fates Worse Than Death*, he calls his readers his "indispensable collaborator [s]" (49–50)—coperformers. As he explains,

> Literature, unlike any other art form, requires those who enjoy it to
> be performers. Reading is a performance, and anything a writer can
> do to make this difficult activity easier is of benefit to all concerned.
> Why write a symphony, so to speak, which can't even be played by
> the New York Philharmonic? (55)

Clearly, for Vonnegut, literature is epitomized by its constructedness—it is a made thing, a performance of self for both the author and his audience that finds its purpose in the social function of communication.

For Vonnegut, stories have the potential to harm as well as to heal. Vonnegut's self-consciousness betrays an ethical concern for the social impact of the stories he tells. Because he believes that writers should be agents of social change, his rhetoric is designed to facilitate that change, and to make known the need for a moral center in a fragmented and insane century. His importance as a writer in the next century will finally rest on his success at articulating a moral framework for this one.

NOTE

1. At the time when Vonnegut made this statement, *Hocus Pocus* was his last novel. He has since written *Timequake*, about which the same claim can be made. Thus, the question, "What are people for?" is central to his entire body of work.

WORKS CITED

Behler, Ernst. *Irony and the Discourse of Modernity*. Seattle: U of Washington P, 1990.

Benhabib, Seyla. *Situating the Self: Gender, Community, and Postmodernism in Contemporary Ethics*. New York: Routledge, 1992.

Broer, Lawrence. *Sanity Plea: Schizophrenia in the Novels of Kurt Vonnegut*. Ann Arbor: UMI, 1989.

Giannone, Richard. *Kurt Vonnegut: A Preface to His Novels*. Port Washington, NY: Kennikat, 1977.

MacIntyre, Alasdair. *After Virtue: A Study in Moral Theory*. Notre Dame: U of Notre Dame P, 1984.

Rorty, Richard. *Contingency, Irony, and Solidarity*. Cambridge: Cambridge UP, 1989.

Taylor, Charles. *Sources of the Self: The Making of the Modern Identity*. Cambridge: Harvard UP, 1989.

Vonnegut, Kurt. *Bluebeard*. New York: Delacorte, 1987.

———. *Deadeye Dick*. New York: Delacorte/Seymour Lawrence, 1982.

———. *Fates Worse Than Death: An Autobiographical Collage of the 1980's*. New York: Putnam's, 1991.

———. *Galápagos*. New York: Delacorte/Seymour Lawrence, 1985.

———. *Palm Sunday: An Autobiographical Collage*. New York: Delacorte, 1981.

———. *Timequake*. New York: Putnam's, 1997.

———. *Wampeters, Foma, and Granfalloons*. New York: Delacorte/Seymour Lawrence, 1974.

CHAPTER NINE

APOCALYPTIC GRUMBLING: POSTMODERN HUMANISM IN THE WORK OF KURT VONNEGUT

Todd F. Davis

> I say in speeches that a plausible mission of artists is to make people appreciate being alive at least a little bit. I am then asked if I know of any artists who pulled that off. I reply, "The Beatles did."
> —Kurt Vonnegut, *Timequake*

Following his own admonition that artists might indeed make "people appreciate being alive at least a little bit," Kurt Vonnegut over the last half century has dazzled his readers with a virtuosity that consists of both style and content. An acknowledged practitioner of the postmodern novel, Vonnegut nevertheless has approached his writing with as much concern about communicating the sanctity of all life as he has with finding the appropriate stylistic vehicle for his message. Looking back over his prodigious body of work—beginning in 1952 with *Player Piano* and concluding in 1997 with his most recent novel *Timequake*—

compels us to move forward and backward, in and out of our own place in time to view Vonnegut's vision of the century to come. Such a perspective affords us with the opportunity to see the breadth of his vision and the importance of his role as an ethical guide for the present generation. While much has been written about Vonnegut's place in postmodern literature, as well as his position as a sardonic moralist for several decades of fans, these two visions of one of this century's most important writers remain unwed. Because Vonnegut joins postmodern metafictional techniques with what upon first glance appears to be a modernist humanism, he remains an enigma and an anomaly in contemporary literature—a writer who bridges two disparate worlds, demonstrating the viability of a postmodern humanism.

Linda Hutcheon contends that postmodernism challenges "both closure and single, centralized meaning" (7). While the notion that "closure and single, centralized meaning" is untenable in a postmodern world no longer seems avant-garde, few critics have solved the conundrum we face in attempting to describe what we mean by "postmodern" and how certain authors transcend or further our understanding of postmodernity. Despite the problems of definition and categorization, clearly much of the writing that has been done in the last thirty years differs radically from that of the previous generation. Because no two authors bear the same imprint, no two writers appear to present a picture of "pure" postmodernity, leaving many critics befuddled or merely celebrating the negative strategies of deconstruction and other antiessentialist forms of critique. In protest of such endless linguistic maneuvers, however, Ihab Hassan hopefully asserts:

> I have no answer. Yet I believe that an answer must go beyond our
> current shibboleths: disconfirmation, decreation, demystification,
> deconstruction, decentering, depropriation, difference, etc. Perhaps
> we need to go beyond Irony (as Nietzsche sometimes did), beyond
> the current aversion to Wholeness and Meaning, to some working
> faith in . . . What?" (xv)

Vonnegut, proclaimed by some as one of the most significant postmodern innovators in fiction, has been caught in the middle of this unsettling critical dilemma.[1] While most critics describe Vonnegut's use of metafiction as a tool for tearing away the façade of truth and his black humor as a means of pointing to the indecent chaos of reality, inevitably these same critics write off Vonnegut as nihilist. Charles B. Harris contends that "Vonnegut's belief in a purposeless universe constitutes his main theme" (131), that his books, at all times, comment upon the "futility of human endeavor, the meaninglessness of human existence" (133). Harris's remarks are representative of a branch of Vonnegut studies that emphasizes the note of despondency, the hopelessness with which so many of the early novels end. While Harris's claim that Vonnegut's work fits nicely with absurdist philosophy seems plausible, he ignores the ethic that Vonnegut develops in conjunction with this philosophy; he misconstrues some of the novels' dark endings as Vonnegut's own devotion to a despondent nihilism that impedes his work for building a better world. As with many of the French absurdists, who actively worked for political and social improvement, Vonnegut also wishes to develop and actively promote an ethic that ennobles humanity. Unlike Harris, I contend that Vonnegut's postmodern ethic constitutes his main theme, that he is more concerned with our response to existence than with the philosophical nature of that existence. While a claim for Vonnegut's nihilism can be supported by some of his fictional work, any such claim must ignore key elements that contradict this position in his essays, interviews, and speeches.[2] Conversely, some critics argue for Vonnegut's essential humanism, referring to it as an "affirmative humanism" or a "dreamily humanist nihilism."[3]

Since the ascendancy of postmodern philosophy, however, much of what has been written concerning Vonnegut's work focuses mainly on his deconstruction of essentialism, his fall into his own aporia, and, finally, his dark nihilism of resigned acceptance. But because of the paradoxical nature of Vonnegut's work, we must not gloss over the ethical nature of Vonnegut's postmodernity, his unique response to a decentered reality.

Vonnegut intentionally neglects to offer a static ethical position. Rather, he gives Hassan a provisional answer —a position beyond binary opposition— bringing hope for a postmodern humanism that is negotiated on an operational essentialism in much the same way Stephen Slemon has shown postcolonial texts "working towards 'realism' within an awareness of referential slippage" (434). By examining Vonnegut's work in light of what Jean-François Lyotard calls the "crisis of narratives" (xiii), I will demonstrate that over the course of his career Vonnegut deconstructs and demystifies the "grand narratives" of American culture while creating provisional narratives, *petite histoire*, that may serve as tools for daily, localized living, a contingent morality that is never grounded in presence but, rather, works with an awareness of its own constructedness toward a symbolic vision of a better reality.

GRAND NARRATIVES

In *The Postmodern Condition: A Report on Knowledge*, Lyotard uses "the term modern to designate any science that legitimates itself with reference to a metadiscourse . . . making an explicit appeal to some grand narrative" (71–72). He briefly defines the postmodern as an "incredulity toward metanarratives" (72). In other words, Lyotard claims that postmodernity characteristically refuses the authority of modern metanarratives, attacking their discourse on the grounds that they are logocentric, linear, and totalizing; such narratives claim to be scientific and objective while reaffirming modernity and its truth. Postmodernists argue against metanarratives, claiming that reason, objectivity, and essential truth are merely effects of discourse. Pauline Marie Rosenau contends that postmodernity sees truth claims as merely the "product of power games, manipulated into position by those whose interests they serve" (78).

Since his first novel appeared in the early 1950s, Vonnegut has continually shown incredulity toward the grand narratives of American culture. Beginning with *Player Piano* and continuing to the present with works such as *Fates Worse Than Death* and *Timequake*, Vonnegut works to debunk our notions of truth, to expose, as he does in *Cat's Cradle*, how we "pretend to understand" in order to answer the unanswerable question—"Why, why, why?" (124)

Humanity may have to reassure itself of its understanding of the nature of things, but Vonnegut humorously undercuts any validity to that understanding. While Vonnegut recognizes humanity's desire for assurance as the impetus for the fabrication of grand narratives, he does not soften his scathing attacks. Long before Derrida and the theoretical project of deconstruction reached its peak in the English departments of American universities, Vonnegut made use of deconstructive principles in order to subvert the structures of his culture, showing the absence of any real center behind the truth espoused in worker's manuals and newspapers, in the speeches of CEOs and ministers.

Player Piano, Vonnegut's first novel, works against the industrial environment of the near future, one that closely resembles Vonnegut's own corporate world experience from 1947 to 1950 at General Electric in Schenectady, New York. Paul Proteus, the son of Dr. George Proteus who at the time of his death was the nation's first National Industrial, Commercial, Communications, Foodstuffs, and Resources Director, is the protagonist of this novel, which foreshadows the latent postmodern themes of the author, but whose form remains conventionally modernist. In the novel's action we see Paul begin to question and finally struggle against the metanarrative his father helped to establish. The master narrative that drives *Player Piano* involves the idea that mechanical progress means a better future for all, a myth that continues to be a powerful force in the expansion of the United States and its industries and one that the genre of science fiction often serves to reify in dramatic ways.[4] Vonnegut was intimately involved in the continued efforts by industry to communicate this idea of progress and expansion to the public during his tenure at General Electric. As a public relations writer, he was paid to find new ways of convincing the masses that the work done by industrial corporations was ultimately a step toward a brighter future, toward a vital and universal good that would benefit everyone in remarkable and miraculous ways. In 1973, at the height of Vonnegut's popular acclaim, *Playboy* published one of his General Electric press releases from 1950; a portion of that release follows:

> Powerful atom smashers, special motors to drive a supersonic wind tunnel, and calculating machines for solving in minutes problems ordinarily requiring months were among the accomplishments of General Electric engineers during 1949, according to a summary released by the company here today. (229)

Each line of Vonnegut's press release strengthens and furthers the American master narrative of progress, pushing for a future where machines may solve problems in nanoseconds, a future that implies comfort for all. And it is this seamlessly created future, a constructed idea with no more truth than any other rhetorical structure, that Vonnegut satirizes in his initial novel. Judging by *Player Piano*'s scathing critique, Vonnegut's work at General Electric allowed him to support his family, but it did not convince him of the efficacy of science. Instead, his experience working among so many scientists in the service of corporate progress frightened Vonnegut. To this day he continues to worry about the claims of scientists who see themselves, as he put it in a *Playboy* interview with David Standish, "simply unearthing truth," a truth that "could never hurt human beings. . . . Many scientists were that way—and I've known a hell of a lot of them, because at General Electric, I was a PR man largely for the research laboratory. . . . And back then, around 1949, they were all innocent," Vonnegut explains, "all simply dealing with truth and not worried about what might be done with their discoveries" (70, 97). Vonnegut's remarks underscore his growing concern with the nature of truth, his misgivings about ideas and inventions that are somehow perceived as pure, innocent, and essential.

In *Player Piano*, Vonnegut undercuts all metanarratives, an ironic task for a novel marketed as straight science fiction. As Paul Proteus begins to see the flaws in the corporate narrative—the facade of the Meadows session with its rituals praising a world where "civilization has reached the dizziest heights of all time!" (209), never considering how this must sound to those laborers living across the river whose skills are no longer needed—he looks nostalgically to the past, more specifically, to other grand narratives of his culture found in the novelistic tradition. But this romance with the tales of nostalgia ends quickly and abruptly. We are told that Paul "had never been a leading man, but now he was developing an appetite for novels wherein the hero lived vigorously and out-of-doors, dealing directly with nature, dependent upon basic cunning and physical strength for survival" (135). Paul, however, did not naïvely accept what he read; "He knew his enjoyment of them was in a measure childish, and he doubted that a life could ever be as clean, hearty, and satisfying as those in the books. Still and all, there was a basic truth underlying the tales, a primitive ideal to which he could aspire" (135). Ultimately, Vonnegut destroys this "primitive ideal" by placing Paul firmly in the midst of his agrarian dream. Paul's hope that he and his wife may be isolated on the Gottwald farm, that they may simply turn from the dominant narrative of Ilium and return to an Edenic state where crops are raised by hand and where truthful innocence ethereally emerges from the earth shatters when put to the test.[5] In short, during the course of *Player Piano*, Vonnegut deconstructs the metanarratives of marriage, corporate life, progress, rural life, and revolutionary change. Paul sees, at novel's end, that all institutions are constructed; no part of reality may be experienced innocently or essentially.

However, if *Player Piano* followed the pattern of other modernist narratives of dystopian satire—such as Orwell's *1984* or Huxley's *Brave New World*—then at novel's end we would somehow be led to believe that Paul holds the key to society's problems, but remains powerless to enact the necessary changes. Vonnegut does not propose such a conclusion. Rather, we find Paul being used as a pawn by the revolution whose narrative is as faulty and tarnished as that of the corporation. As Paul stands with the revolutionaries, expected to make his own toast to the future, he realizes that "all attempts to establish essentialist hierarchies must fail, that the people of Ilium [are] already eager to recreate the same old nightmare" (320). Ultimately, *Player Piano* offers no grand narrative to replace those that have been dismantled, only the awareness that truth remains no more than a construct—a most unusual idea in the United States of 1952.

PETITE HISTOIRES

Mother Night and *Cat's Cradle* continue to demystify and decenter the mythology of America while beginning to offer provisional answers to the questions of a postmodern condition. Although these novels do not formally exhibit the postmodern pyrotechnics of *Slaughterhouse-Five* and later novels, both do begin to play with the structures of narrative and chapter length. *Mother Night* subverts the spy novel, a traditionally modernist genre, in an attempt to expose the metanarratives that structure the self-legitimizing discourses of war and governmental operation, a theme or project that culminates in *Slaughterhouse-Five*. *Cat's Cradle*, on the other hand, begins to reveal Vonnegut's interest in playing with the conventions of the novel, as exhibited by his move away from conventional chapters. *Cat's Cradle* offers 127 such breaks, demanding that the reader see the novel's own constructedness by emphasizing the artificiality of chapter headings. Vonnegut goes so far as to conclude the entire novel with a chapter entitled, "The End." Although in *Mother Night* Vonnegut avoids using chapters or other formal conventions to the same effect as in *Cat's Cradle*, he does work within a genre of unusual popular appeal—Ian Fleming was certainly having great success at the time with James Bond—a genre that traditionally reifies the master narrative of a country's position by suggesting that it possesses and is ordained by some truth, a manifest destiny of sorts. The formula for such books typically revolves around the harrowing acts perpetrated by a spy from a Western country, ordinarily the United States or Britain. While such acts may under other circumstances be deemed morally questionable, in the fictional context they are always justified by the country's narratives, especially religious texts that somehow suggest a divine injunction to perform exactly such a task. The first readers of *Mother Night* must have been shocked to read a spy novel in which the actions of the protagonist are never clearly defined, or the justification or motivation for such actions provided, leaving the reader to question the nature of good and evil, right and wrong.

Vonnegut uses the spy genre to subvert not only the function of the genre itself, but also the fiction of American supremacy in matters of war and peace. In *Mother Night*, Howard Campbell, an American spy in Nazi, Germany, wages an incredibly successful battle for the Nazi regime as a propagandist. The irony of Campbell's absurd role as the finest writer for "the ministry of propaganda" rests squarely on the fact that he has been instructed to do so by American military intelligence. Without the prompting of the American military and their belief that at times evil actions must be committed to serve the greater good, Campbell would not have been induced to commit crimes against humanity. But Vonnegut does not let Campbell off quite this easily. Rather, Vonnegut's repeated questioning of our ability to know or apprehend truth begins at the outset in an editor's note, written by the editor of *Mother Night*, none other than Vonnegut himself. The editor claims that the text before the reader represents the American edition of the confessions of Campbell, and then launches into a paragraph on the nature of lying, concluding that "lies told for the sake of artistic effect—in the theater, for instance, and in Campbell's confessions, perhaps—can be, in a higher sense, the most beguiling forms of truth" (ix). Certainly the readers of the original paperback release— readers who were not afforded the luxury of Vonnegut's introduction to the 1967 hardback reissue—were confronted with the task of deciphering the "truth" of Vonnegut's position as editor and the likelihood that Campbell had ever existed as a "real" person.

Mother Night, as the title might indicate, is one of Vonnegut's darkest works, and one in which he examines the enduring issue of appearance versus reality, only to conclude that there is no difference between "pretending" and "being"—a lesson Campbell learns too late and one that ends with his suicide. Clinton S. Burhans claims that the novel is Vonnegut's argument that "within man [there] is no essential self, no independent soul unconditioned and untouched by his behavior. . . . We are, that is, what we do, not what we say; what we do at any particular time establishes what we are" (179). What is at stake in the argument of "being" and "doing" is essence. If there is some essence, some core of existence that goes beyond our constructed worlds, then Campbell's actions may be predicated on some center of good or evil that permits harmful acts to be committed in the name of good, in the name of justice, in this case, in the name of the United States of America. But Vonnegut dismisses such a world. As he says in the introduction to the hardcover reissue of the novel written in 1966, "We are what we pretend to be, so we must be careful about what we pretend to be" (v).

Vonnegut's own comments on the moral to *Mother Night* begin to offer Hassan a provisional answer to the postmodern condition: in a decentered world, we are fictions, constructing our own realities and truths, so we must be careful what we construct. It would appear that Vonnegut reasons along the same lines as Jean Baudrillard, who explains, "Moralists about war, champions of war's exalted values should not be greatly upset: a war is not any the less heinous for being a mere simulacrum—flesh suffers just the same, and the dead excombatants count as much there as in other wars" (371). Whether Campbell's propaganda is merely a pose, a fiction constructed to hide his identity as an American spy, remains insignificant; the heinous acts that he helps lead the German people to commit in the name of Nazism are quite real; the deaths of the millions of Jews cannot be erased. The fictions we construct, even if their constructedness is exposed, still do as much harm as those that are hidden, and for that reason Vonnegut urges us to choose those narratives that are "harmless."

Foma, or harmless untruths, serve as the basis for *Cat's Cradle*, a novel that works against the grand narrative that may be most cherished and most fervently defended by American culture: religion. *Cat's Cradle*, similar to *Mother Night*, begins with a disclaimer of sorts: "Nothing in this book is true. 'Live by the foma that make you brave and kind and healthy and happy.'" The second half of this passage—taken from *The Books of Bokonon*, the religious text that takes the place of the Christian Bible in the novel—points more clearly to Vonnegut's provisional answer to the postmodern conundrum Hassan poses, or to what Gayatri Chakravorty Spivak in remarks given at the Center for the Humanities at Wesleyan University in the spring of 1985 calls an "operational essentialism, a false ontology" (qtd. in Butler 325). Religion, more specifically Christianity, may be argued to be the single most significant narrative supporting the structure of American culture; it poses as the center for truth, for referentiality, in both overt and obscure ways. The narrator of *Cat's Cradle* tells the reader to call him Jonah, a clear allusion to Melville's Ishmael, another character in American literature whose quest for a centered truth falls short.[6] Not surprisingly, Jonah, as with most narrators in Vonnegut's fiction, immediately divulges the purpose for the telling of his tale:

> When I was a much younger man, I began to collect material for a book to be called *The Day the World Ended*.
> The book was to be factual.
> The book was to be an account of what important Americans had done on the day when the first atomic bomb was dropped on Hiroshima, Japan.
> It was to be a Christian book. I was a Christian then. (11)

Less than half a page into the novel, Vonnegut gives us a narrator who, when he was much younger, believed in the grand narrative of Christianity and in its ability to found the writing of a "factual" book that could somehow explain the atrocity of the first atomic bomb. The ensuing action of the novel deals with the narrator's discovery of Bokononism, a religion that paradoxically offers a narrative for living without establishing a metanarrative; it is the first formal example of *petite histoire* in Vonnegut's fiction.

Mother Night establishes that we construct our own reality by pretending to be a spy or a lover or a nation, but *Cat's Cradle* goes one step further by demonstrating how life can be "based" on a series of provisional narratives without claiming a centered or essential presence. When the narrator of *Cat's Cradle* asks to see a copy of *The Books of Bokonon*, he is told that copies are hard to come by, that "They aren't printed. They're made by hand. And, [that] of course, there is no such thing as a completed copy, since Bokonon is adding things every day" (124). Bokononists must always be aware that, because the basis for their living is mere fabrication, any flirtation with absolutism would be absurd. Bokononism embraces the postmodern idea of *petite histoire* by accepting that life and the text of life upon which we base our ideas and ideologies must always remain in flux, ever-changing, malleable, and contingent upon the world in which we live. Provisional stories of living, Rosenau explains, substitute for theory and truth. They are community-based narratives that "focus on the local, assert neither truth nor totalizing theory, and propose no broad theoretical generalizations or ultimate truths. They are offered as only one interpretation among many" (84). The grand narrative of Christianity dogmatically asserts an essential and totalizing truth, complete with a religious text that depicts the beginning and the end of time. The *petite histoire* of Bokononism is found in its own books, incomplete, fragmented, and without a clear beginning or end. Still, as Mary Sue Schriber argues, foma have a redemptive social value: "They force us to see and simultaneously to laugh at limitations, preventing us from believing that truth can be known, defending us from an inhuman absolutism that the narrator equates with insanity" (288). Absolutism, the absurd belief that one's own ideas are unerringly correct, that one's actions may be driven by an essential good or purity, leads to the dark conclusion of *Cat's Cradle* as science and religion collide.

LOCAL, PROVISIONAL STORIES

Slaughterhouse-Five, the novel that Vonnegut struggled to write for two decades and that finally established his critical reputation, stands as the most formally postmodern novel he has written to date. Its dramatically unconventional style represents Vonnegut's own painfully arduous labor to find a new paradigm for his experience in Dresden, a horrific moment in his youth that refused to be placed into a conventionally modernist paradigm.[7] World War II and the eventual bombing of Dresden may be seen as the results of the absolutism that Bokonon warns his followers against. For Vonnegut there can be no grand narrative that justifies the desecration he witnessed after the bombing. In the first chapter of *Slaughterhouse-Five*, the author visits his old war buddy, Bernard V. O'Hare, hoping their reunion will help him recall the bombing of Dresden. For the first time in his career, Vonnegut inserts himself into his created world without comment, making no attempt to distinguish between "reality" and "fiction." During his visit, he meets O'Hare's wife, Mary, to whom he dedicates the novel. Mary, obviously angered by Vonnegut's presence, accuses Vonnegut of attempting to write a book that will reify the other grand narratives of war:

> "Well, I know," she said. "You'll pretend you were men
> instead of babies, and you'll be played in the movies by Frank Sina-
> tra and John Wayne or some of those other glamorous, war-loving,
> dirty old men. And war will look just wonderful, so we'll have a lot
> more of them. And they'll be fought by babies like the babies
> upstairs." (14)

Refusing to accept the stories that her country has offered in defense and even
adulation of the war, Mary O'Hare makes Vonnegut promise that "there won't be
a part for Frank Sinatra or John Wayne" in his book about Dresden. Not only are
there no parts for the likes of Sinatra and Wayne, but Vonnegut does not even
include a detailed description of the bombing. Instead, Vonnegut writes a *petite
histoire* of the Dresden incident, his own small story in the larger frame of one of
the war's greatest tragedies—what he calls on the title page, "A Duty Dance with
Death." In order to accommodate what seemingly cannot be accommodated,
Vonnegut writes a novel that resembles the books of Tralfamadore—"no beginning, no middle, no end, no suspense, no moral, no causes, no effects" (88). The
time shifts in *Slaughterhouse-Five* prevent the writer and the reader from developing causes and effects, from creating meaning based on a system of linear progression. As Vonnegut remembers the horrors he has seen, he staunchly refuses to
try to explain how the bombing of Dresden could be justified. His refusal to use
chronological time, moreover, represents the dismissal of perhaps the most important totalizing myth in Western civilization. The idea behind chronological time
as an organizing principle finds its impetus in our desire to show the orderly progression of "history." Because Billy Pilgrim believes that humanity's commitment
to linear time brings about much of the suffering inherent to our woeful condition, he sets out, as any good optometrist would, to give Earthlings corrected
vision. Billy Pilgrim's refusal to see time as moments following one another like
"beads on a string" (27) suggests one more alternative to the question posed by
the postmodern condition. Over the course of the novel, Vonnegut proposes that
we see all the moments of our lives and the lives of others who have lived before
or who will live after as mysteriously interconnected, interacting in ways we cannot fully comprehend. Such a vision of the continuity and contingency of all life
makes a simplistic and reductive view of our actions and their consequences as
either purely good or purely evil incomprehensible. Vonnegut's story seems to
encourage us to perceive the act of storytelling as a means of coping and as a way
of understanding the fluidity of our relationships to one another and the planet.
In a postmodern age, our stories must remain localized and provisional, affording
us the chance to see "an image of life that is beautiful and surprising and deep."

POSTMODERN HUMANISM

Certainly, it is possible to show how Vonnegut continues to deconstruct, demystify, and decenter the grand narratives of American culture in his later fiction.

In fact, in *Breakfast of Champions*, the first novel to appear from Vonnegut after the enormous success of *Slaughterhouse-Five* four years earlier, Vonnegut tells us, "I think I am trying to make my head as empty as it was when I was born onto this damaged planet fifty years ago" (5). In his attempt to empty his head by debunking all the stories of his past, he leaves no stone unturned. While journeying to Midland City to set free his own creations, Vonnegut tears the very fabric of American mythology, deconstructing slavery, pornography, religion, homosexuality, sexism, and Midwestern morality. It is clear, then, that Vonnegut writes from a position similar to that of Henry Giroux, who has argued convincingly that there can be "no tradition or story that can speak with authority and certainty for all of humanity" (465). This position, Jerome Klinkowitz claims in *Structuring the Void*, results from Vonnegut's anthropological training, which "convinced him that reality was something arbitrary and impermanent, since the basic facts of life could be changed by circumstances of birth or by the whims of national economics even after one was half-grown" (37).[8] Such an understanding of the human condition affords Vonnegut with the necessary tools to create the sorts of fiction that help expose the constructed nature of our world.

Vonnegut's destruction of the essentialist facade of so many American institutions, however, marks only the first step in the creation of his postmodern humanism. Ultimately, Vonnegut wishes to make an active and socially motivated response to the postmodern era in which he finds himself mired. The question for him is *What does one do in a decentered world?* Vonnegut's later novels highlight the author's continued struggle between hope and despair. While much of what Vonnegut writes after *Breakfast of Champions* suggests his hope that we may embrace and improve the lives of others through the construct of postmodern humanism, his training as a scientist prevents him from ignoring the many signs of communal decay and separation present in contemporary culture and the abominable and deadly acts such isolation leads us to commit. As he explains in *Timequake*, "It is not one whit mysterious that we poison the water and air and topsoil, and construct ever more cunning doomsday devices, both industrial and military. Let us be perfectly frank for a change. For practically everybody, the end of the world can't come soon enough" (2). In *Galápagos*, Vonnegut experiments with the idea that the Earth and its inhabitants might be better off without the human race as we know it. By having a ghost tell the story of humanity's devolution into seal-like creatures, he illustrates the potential wickedness of our race as we currently exist. Yet he cannot bring himself to dismiss the potential good that also resides within us. As Leon Trotsky Trout, the novel's ghostly narrator and Vonnegut's alter ego, often exclaims about humans in their devolved state, "Nobody, surely, is going to write Beethoven's Ninth Symphony" (259). In this forbidding tale of our demise, the planet becomes a safer place; however, our capacity to create and think and feel as fully realized humans is lost, and with this loss our humanity is tragically compromised.

Despite the construction of ever more sophisticated killing machinery and the continued desecration of the environment by an unbelievable array of toxins and pollutants, Vonnegut continues to crusade in both his fiction and his nonfiction for a world where humans can love and care for one another. In the later novels, however, an apocalyptic tone of potential doom casts a pall over the hope that resides at the center of each work. Similar to *Galápagos*, in *Slapstick*, *Hocus Pocus*, and *Timequake*, Vonnegut offers potential visions of a sometimes terrifying, sometimes pitiful future. Yet within these visions are Vonnegut's seeds for a postmodern humanism. *Slapstick* suggests that familial community will heal and fulfill us, redeeming our purposelessness by making our existence vital and necessary to others. *Hocus Pocus* demands that we see our "lethal hocus pocus" for what it is. There can be no rhetoric to justify our actions in Vietnam, Eugene Debs Hartke explains. Hartke, like Vonnegut's grandfather, suggests that "the greatest use a person could make of his or her lifetime was to improve the quality of life for all in his or her community" (176). Finally, in *Timequake*, Vonnegut uses a mixed form—part memoir, part failed novel—to encourage an examination of our past. By plotting a "timequake," he illustrates how what we have done impacts the future, while at the same time suggesting numerous revisions for our present actions. "And even in 1996, I in speeches propose the following amendments to the Constitution," Vonnegut states toward the end of *Timequake*. "*Article XXVIII*: Every newborn shall be sincerely welcomed and cared for until maturity. *Article XXIX*: Every adult who needs it shall be given meaningful work to do, at a living wage" (152). Vonnegut's amendments to the Constitution hardly seem radical; in fact, such amendments, as with much in his social agenda, are humane, of utmost importance, and ring of common sense. Failure to follow such important advice, Vonnegut warns, will lead toward the darkness of apocalypse.

For Vonnegut, then, the fact that we can only know our world through language, through the fictions we create—as with the Constitution or Vonnegut's own amendments—does not make the plight of humanity, the emotional and physical needs of men and women, any less real. To the contrary, Vonnegut shows great concern for those people who have been oppressed and degraded by the dominant narratives of America. Vonnegut's hope, paradoxically, rests solely in the nature of writing and the power of narratives. Because we may create our own narratives, the possibilities for personal as well as societal change are endless.[9] As Klinkowitz explains, "If reality is indeed relative and arbitrary, then it is all the easier to change; men and women need not suffer an unhappy destiny, but can instead invent a new one better suited to their needs" ("Void" 37). In much of Vonnegut's writing, we find attempts to retell old, but useful, stories, to recreate fictions to serve better our needs, an activity that Zygmunt Bauman claims requires "nerves of steel." Bauman argues that postmodernity has a new determination "to guard the conditions in which all stories can be told, and retold, and again told differently" (23). In the retelling, however, there can be no dogmatism, no reestablishment of a fixed center; it is, as Bauman's suggests, "living with ambivalence," a frightening prospect for a culture moving out of a traditional narrative of rationality, objectivity, and a fixed center, a prospect that does, indeed, require nerves of steel. Thankfully, Vonnegut appears to be just the writer for such a task. He possesses the linguistic and ethical faculties that allow him to expose the charade of essentialism while proffering a philosophy at all times concerned with breaking the bonds of oppression and freeing others to tell their stories.[10] Understandably, Vonnegut voraciously defends the First Amendment; he stands as a writer concerned with our ability to tell our own stories, leading to the recuperative work Stephen Slemon sees postcolonial texts doing.[11] We tell our stories in an attempt to represent our experiences and ultimately to transform those experiences, and these stories create what Vonnegut sees as an important factor in improving the human condition: folk societies.

During the time he studied anthropology at the University of Chicago, Vonnegut was introduced to the work of Dr. Robert Redfield. Redfield's theory suggests that all human beings need to belong to extended families—the localized communities that provide the necessary physical and emotional well being for humans that Vonnegut celebrates in *Cat's Cradle* and *Slapstick*. But such communities are not as plentiful as one might expect given their vital significance. As Vonnegut remarks, "It is curious that such communities should be so rare, since human beings are genetically such gregarious creatures. They need plenty of like-minded friends and relatives almost as much as they need B-complex vitamins and a heartfelt moral code" (*Palm Sunday* 204). These folk societies, a topic that comes up repeatedly in Vonnegut's interviews, essays, and speeches, are the structures (admittedly built on some communal narrative) from which Vonnegut argues for a postmodern humanism. Such communities, according to Vonnegut, provide people with a shared moral code, companionship, and a created purpose for existence. Although folk societies offer hope for living in a postmodern world, such a response does not come without the possibility for harm. As Vonnegut warns, in an address to the graduating class of Hobart and William Smith Colleges in 1974, Hitler and Lenin, among others, made terrible choices, creating abominable fictions. The myths we place at the center of our lives, at the center of our families or folk societies, Vonnegut insists, do make a difference (*Palm Sunday* 208).[12]

Finally, Vonnegut remains concerned at all times with the symbolic construction of a better reality, one based on the small, localized tales that each of us may tell. As he explains in an interview, "Everything is a lie, because our brains are two-bit computers, and we can't get very high-grade truths out of them. But as far as improving the human condition goes, our minds are certainly up to that. That's what they were designed to do. And we do have the freedom to make up comforting lies. But we don't do enough of it" (*Playboy* 59). Vonnegut establishes one rule for such lies, an operational essentialism, or working faith as Hassan calls it (xv), a rule that Hitler and Lenin and Manson failed to acknowledge: "Ye shall respect one another" (*Fates* 159).[13] This rule

appears in a slightly different form in Vonnegut's early fiction, when Eliot
Rosewater, rehearsing what he will say at the baptism of Mary Moody's twins,
exclaims, "God damn it, you've got to be kind" (*God Bless You, Mr. Rosewater*
110). In *Fates Worse Than Death*, Vonnegut sums up his humanism when he says,
"I like to think that Jesus said in Aramaic, 'Ye shall respect one another' . . .
something almost anybody in reasonable mental health can do day after day,
year in and year out, come one, come all, to everyone's clear benefit" (159–60).

NOTES

1. Jerome Klinkowitz, in such works as *The Vonnegut Statement, Vonnegut in Amer-ica, Kurt Vonnegut*, and *Literary Disruptions: The Making of a Post-Contemporary American Fic-tion*, was one of the first critics to argue for Vonnegut's place in literary studies as a post-modern writer. James M. Mellard, Brian McHale, Stanley Schatt, Lawrence Broer, William Rodney Allen, John Somer, and James Lundquist, among others, have also argued for Von-negut's postmodernity. I wish to thank Jim Mellard for his help in bringing this study to fruition; his close readings and informed advice have challenged me at every turn.

2. In *Vonnegut in Fact: The Public Spokesmanship of Personal Fiction*, Klinkowitz focuses on the ethical aims of Vonnegut's speaking career and the author's move toward the essay form in the later part of his writing life, suggesting the importance of this aspect of Vonnegut's work for any study of his fictional texts.

3. Most claims for Vonnegut's humanism and morality were made in book reviews and essays found in the popular press during the late 1960s and early 1970s. I contend that Vonnegut's speaking career during this period and the activist nature of the times contributed heavily to this sort of commentary.

4. As other critics have pointed out, Vonnegut's science fiction is dystopian in nature. Throughout his career he has worked diligently to undermine the notion that the "truth" of science will save us.

5. Although I argue that Vonnegut merely flirts with the notion of a return to an earthly paradise, Leonard Mustazza has written an extensive study arguing the impor-tance of this theme in all of the novels up through *Bluebeard*.

6. Richard Giannone, in *Vonnegut: A Preface to His Novels*, develops his reading of *Cat's Cradle* by focusing on the archetypes of Jonah and Ishmael.

7. Schriber examines Vonnegut's work using the novel tradition as a guide. She argues that "the novel tradition hovers over *Cat's Cradle* and other Vonnegut novels as well precisely because it is called up and then cast out" (283).

8. In *Structuring the Void*, Klinkowitz describes the response of several writers to the postmodern condition. The chapter devoted to Vonnegut argues that Vonnegut's fic-tional forms and themes are the result of two constants: "Vonnegut himself and the America he has lived in since his birth in 1922" (29). Klinkowitz, perhaps the most influ-ential critic in Vonnegut studies, continues to argue for the importance of Vonnegut as a postmodernist.

9. Vonnegut, who so often has been described as a despairing nihilist, says of himself: "For two thirds of my life I have been a pessimist. I am astonished to find myself an optimist now. I feel now that I have been underestimating the intelligence and resourcefulness of man" (*Palm Sunday* 209).

10. David Cowart, in "Culture and Anarchy: Vonnegut's Later Career," claims that there are some writers who "function amphibiously—they produce postmodern fictions that somehow affirm meaning and value" (170). Cowart argues that Vonnegut balances between nihilism and humanist affirmation, an argument that starts in a promising direction but falls back into modernist rhetoric. Vonnegut's ability to see with postmodern glasses the facade of grand narratives can be easily misconstrued as nihilism, and his provisional narratives, narratives that at times certainly do affirm humanity, can be easily misread as modern humanist affirmation. The basic difference between modern humanism and postmodern humanism is essence: one believes in a fixed, essential reference while the other dismisses this notion offering only an operational essentialism.

11. Stephen Slemon, in "Modernism's Last Post," argues that while postcolonial texts are fundamentally fragmented, engaging overtly in decentering and demystifying versions of history, they do retain "a recuperative impulse towards the structure of 'history'" and manifest "a Utopian desire grounded in reference" (433). Vonnegut's utopian desire for humanity works within an awareness of its own referential slippage.

12. Vonnegut is not naïve in the *petite histoire* he offers; folk societies are not mere panacea to be swallowed indiscriminately. In *Fates Worse Than Death*, he again reminds us that every folk society "has a myth at its core," and such myths can be harmful, as was the case with the Manson family (127).

13. Hassan is hopeful that we will establish some kind of "working faith," allowing us to lead healthy and productive lives beyond deconstruction and disconfirmation. Similarly, Stephen Slemon has argued that "Western postmodernist readings can so overvalue the antireferential or deconstructive energetics of post-colonial texts that they efface the important recuperative work that is also going on within them" (434). Vonnegut seems to balance both projects quite nicely, offering to Hassan kindness and respect as a possibility for a "working faith" to be used in a decentered world. This "working faith" allows Vonnegut to look for possible "reassociations," a term used by Arthur A. Brown to describe the postmodern humanism of Raymond Carver (126).

WORKS CITED

Allen, William Rodney. *Understanding Kurt Vonnegut*. Columbia: U of South Carolina P, 1991.

Baudrillard, Jean. "The Precession of Simulacra." *A Postmodern Reader*. Ed. Joseph Natoli and Linda Hutcheon. Albany: State U of New York P, 1993. 342–75.

Bauman, Zygmunt. "Postmodernity, or Living with Ambivalence." *A Postmodern Reader*. Ed. Joseph Natoli and Linda Hutcheon. Albany: State U of New York P, 1993. 9–24.

Broer, Lawrence R. *Sanity Plea: Schizophrenia in the Novels of Kurt Vonnegut*. Rev. ed. Tuscaloosa: U of Alabama P, 1994.

Brown, Arthur A. "Raymond Carver and Postmodern Humanism." *Critique* 31 (1990): 125–36.

Burhans, Clinton S. "Hemingway and Vonnegut: Diminishing Vision in a Dying Age." *Modern Fiction Studies* 21 (1975): 173–91.

Butler, Judith. "Gender Trouble, Feminist Theory, and Psychoanalytic Discourse." *Feminism/Postmodernism*. Ed. Linda J. Nicholson. New York: Routledge, 1990. 324–40.

Cowart, David. "Culture and Anarchy: Vonnegut's Later Career." *Critical Essays on Kurt Vonnegut*. Ed. Robert Merrill. Boston: Hall, 1990. 170–88.

Giannone, Richard. *Vonnegut: A Preface to His Novels*. Port Washington: Kennikat, 1977.

Giroux, Henry. "Postmodernism as Border Pedagogy: Redefining the Boundaries of Race and Ethnicity." *A Postmodern Reader*. Ed. Joseph Natoli and Linda Hutcheon. Albany: State U of New York P, 1993. 452–96.

Harris, Charles B. "Illusion and Absurdity: The Novels of Kurt Vonnegut." *Critical Essays on Kurt Vonnegut*. Ed. Robert Merrill. Boston: Hall, 1990. 131–41.

Hassan, Ihab. *Paracriticisms: Seven Speculations of the Times*. Urbana: U of Illinois P, 1975.

Hutcheon, Linda. "Historiographic Metafiction: Parody and the Intertextuality of History." *Intertextuality and Contemporary American Fiction*. Ed. Patrick O'Donnell and Robert Con Davis. Baltimore: Johns Hopkins UP, 1989. 3–32.

Klinkowitz, Jerome. *Kurt Vonnegut*. London: Methuen, 1982.

———. *Literary Disruptions: The Making of a Post-Contemporary American Fiction*. 2nd ed. Urbana: U of Illinois P, 1980.

———. *Structuring the Void: The Struggle for Subject in Contemporary American Fiction*. Durham: Duke UP, 1992.

———. *Vonnegut in Fact: The Public Spokesmanship of Personal Fiction*. Columbia: U of South Carolina P, 1998.

Klinkowitz, Jerome, and Donald L. Lawler, eds. *Vonnegut in America: An Introduction to the Life and Work of Kurt Vonnegut*. New York: Delta, 1977.

Klinkowitz, Jerome, and John Somer, eds. *The Vonnegut Statement: Original Essays on the Life and Works of Kurt Vonnegut, Jr.* New York: Delta, 1973.

Lundquist, James. *Kurt Vonnegut*. New York: Ungar, 1977.

Lyotard, Jean-François. *The Postmodern Condition: A Report on Knowledge*. Trans. Geoffrey Bennington and Brian Massumi. Minneapolis: U of Minnesota P, 1984.

McHale, Brian. *Postmodernist Fiction*. London: Methuen, 1987.

Mellard, James M. *The Exploded Form: The Modernist Novel in America*. Urbana: U of Illinois P, 1980.

Merrill, Robert, and Peter A. Scholl. "Vonnegut's *Slaughterhouse-Five*: The Requirements of Chaos." *Critical Essays on Kurt Vonnegut.* Ed. Robert Merrill. Boston: Hall, 1990. 142–51.

Mustazza, Leonard. *Forever Pursuing Genesis: The Myth of Eden in the Novels of Kurt Vonnegut.* Lewisburg: Bucknell UP, 1990.

Reed, Peter J. *Kurt Vonnegut, Jr.* New York: Warner, 1972.

Rosenau, Pauline Marie. *Postmodernism and the Social Sciences: Insights, Inroads, and Intrusions.* Princeton: Princeton UP, 1992.

Schatt, Stanley. *Kurt Vonnegut, Jr.* Boston: Twayne, 1976.

Schriber, Mary Sue. "Bringing Chaos to Order: The Novel Tradition and Kurt Vonnegut, Jr." *Genre* 10 (1977): 283–97.

Slemon, Stephen. "Modernism's Last Post." *A Postmodern Reader.* Ed. Joseph Natoli and Linda Hutcheon. Albany: State U of New York P, 1993. 426–39.

Vonnegut, Kurt. *Bluebeard.* New York: Delacorte, 1987.

——— . *Breakfast of Champions.* New York: Dell, 1973.

——— . *Cat's Cradle.* New York: Dell, 1963.

——— . *Fates Worse Than Death.* New York: Putnam's, 1991.

——— . *Galápagos.* New York: Delacorte/Seymour Lawrence, 1985.

——— . "General Electric News Bureau News Release, 3 January 1950." *Playboy* (December 1973): 229.

——— . *God Bless You, Mr. Rosewater.* New York: Dell, 1965

——— . *Hocus Pocus.* New York: Putnam's, 1990.

——— . Interview. *Playboy* (July 1973): 57+.

——— . *Mother Night.* New York: Dell, 1966.

——— . *Palm Sunday.* New York: Delacorte, 1981.

——— . *Player Piano.* New York: Dell, 1952.

——— . *Sirens of Titan.* New York: Dell, 1959.

——— . *Slapstick.* New York: Delacorte/Seymour Lawrence, 1976.

——— . *Slaughterhouse-Five.* New York: Dell, 1969.

——— . *Timequake.* New York: Putnam's, 1997.

——— . *Wampeters, Foma, and Granfalloons.* New York: Dell, 1976.

CHAPTER TEN

VONNEGUT FILMS

Kevin Alexander Boon and David Pringle

Kurt Vonnegut does not like film. After working on *Between Time and Timbuktu* (which is preceded only by the filmed version of his play *Happy Birthday Wanda June*),[1] he vowed to have nothing more to do with it. Ultimately, he broke this vow and worked on several productions, including his role as executive story consultant and host of Showtime's *Kurt Vonnegut's Monkey House*, and his cameos in *Back to School* and *Mother Night*,[2] but his disdain for the medium survived. Vonnegut's position should make sense to anyone familiar with his work. After all, film is a technology-dependent medium, and Vonnegut has long considered technology a scourge on humanity. However, despite Vonnegut's general contempt for film and the fact that film adaptations are two removes from their source materials, film adaptations of Vonnegut's works do expose those elements of Vonnegut's fiction that tenaciously resist translation and help us to map the troubled boundary between literature and film.

Film adaptations rarely do justice to the literary works on which they are based, mainly because film and literary audiences have different expectations. On those occasions when a film miraculously manages to capture the spirit of its literary predecessor—as do Stanley Kubrick's *A Clockwork Orange*, David Cronenberg's *Naked Lunch*, and George Roy Hill's *Slaughterhouse-Five*—the film seldom stimulates big box-office returns, often earning a profit only as a result of its status as a cult film. There have been quite a few attempts to bring Vonnegut's work to the big and the little screen in the past twenty-eight years. Most have failed miserably. A few have succeeded, but only by dealing with

Vonnegut's earlier, formative short stories, which he wrote before his unique narrative style was fully developed. Only one novel, *Slaughterhouse-Five*, has been competently translated into film, although four attempts have been made: *Slaughterhouse-Five*, *Slapstick*, *Mother Night*, and *Breakfast of Champions*.[3]

The narratives of some novels are structurally cinematic and translate easily into a visual medium. Dashiell Hammett's most famous novels, for example, adapted to film without a glitch.[4] But novels like Hammett's are rare, and most stories go through radical transformations on their way from print to screen. For some, such as Carrie Fisher's *Postcards from the Edge* and Brett Easton Ellis's *Less Than Zero*, little more than the title survives. The capitalization of film is partly to blame. Film is, as Vonnegut notes, "too fucking expensive" (*Between Time and Timbuktu* xv), and many filmmakers feel pressured to pander to audience expectation in an attempt to improve a film's potential for profit, almost always at a cost to the quality of the finished product and at the expense of the source material.

Difficulties in adapting Vonnegut's work rest with the sensitivities of the filmmakers. The qualities that make Vonnegut's novels resonate require us to accept the coexistence of seemingly incompatible issues. To get at Vonnegut, we must be able to see the humor in tragedy and the tragedy in humor. We must be able to recognize how forces in opposition can operate under the same assumptions. Vonnegut does not provide us with the pure-hearted heroes and black-souled villains upon which mainstream American cinema so often relies. Instead, he gives us characters such as Howard Campbell, who can be seen as a hero or a traitor; Billy Pilgrim, who can be considered sane or crazy; and Kilgore Trout, who can be characterized as a no-talent tramp living in poverty on the periphery of civilized culture or a misunderstood visionary. And on and on. How we *see* these characters determines how we judge them, and any single judgement is invariably incomplete. To capture the brilliance of Vonnegut's work on film, filmmakers have to create a film universe that prompts a similar response from an audience as his novels prompt. Therein lies the first and principle obstacle. Characters that do not fall gently into familiar categories befuddle passive audiences, which are accustomed to being told who to love and who to hate in the first twenty-seven minutes of a film. Filmmakers, operating with the awareness that every conventional film is the story of one main character, feel compelled to select one person from the cast of a novel and fashion the story around that character. In order to accomplish this, filmmakers make determinations about who a character is. Their conclusions control nearly everything about the way they construct their story. If, for example, they determine that Eliot Rosewater in *God Bless You, Mr. Rosewater* is a kind-hearted but misunderstood philanthropist, then settings, costumes, dialogue, lighting, hairstyle, sound effects, casting, and dozens of other details are designed to promote that image of Rosewater. If, however, they determine that Rosewater is off his nut, that he is comically bizarre, then everything from the shoes he wears to the way he saunters across a fire station is designed to promote that image. But what if he's both?

How do you film that? How do you simultaneously make him appear as a kind-hearted philanthropist *and* an off-his-nut wacko? Such sleights of hand can be done, as George Roy Hill demonstrated with his rendering of Billy Pilgrim in *Slaughterhouse-Five*, but it takes a great deal of skill and sensitivity. More important, it requires a willingness to break with cinematic conventions.

We might get a firmer grasp on the problem facing filmmakers by examining Vonnegut's most oft-quoted phrase: "And so it goes." It comes, of course, from *Slaughterhouse-Five*, and it is the one phrase from Vonnegut that most people quote when they can only quote one phrase from Vonnegut. People often, once they learn that you write about Vonnegut's work, turn and say, "and so it goes," as if it's a countersign granting entrance to some secret club. What's interesting, and relevant to our discussion here, is that invariably the people quoting that passage are smiling. The phrase has that effect. It summons pleasure, a sense of some farcical cosmic order to the universe. Yet in the novel, Vonnegut places that phrase immediately following death. Edgar Derby is shot to death in Germany—"so it goes" (99). Body lice and bacteria die by the billions—"so it goes" (84). The whole universe disappears—"so it goes" (117). In a single phrase, Vonnegut skillfully fuses humor and tragedy, so that both are absorbed simultaneously. What could you film that would generate the same reaction(s) from a film audience? How could you place those words in the mouth of a character—*any* character—and avoid having him seem cavalier? If you make the scene tragic, you fail to capture the wonder of Vonnegut, as is the case with the film version of *Mother Night*. If you make the scene comic, you fail to capture the wonder of Vonnegut, as is the case with the ill-conceived film version of *Slapstick*. If you dart back and forth between comedy and tragedy, you also fail to capture the wonder of Vonnegut, as is the case with *Breakfast of Champions*. Vonnegut's brilliance is his ability to bring tragedy and comedy together in the same place at the same time—in the same character, the same action, the same line of dialogue, or the same scene.

This issue is further complicated by the fact that the main character of most of Vonnegut's novels is "Kurt Vonnegut" (his presence is more muted in early novels such as *Piano Player*). Vonnegut's narrative voice out-heralds Mark Twain, and his character threads everything he writes. Vonnegut novels are "about" Vonnegut, much more so than Nabokov's novels are about Nabokov or Pynchon's novels are about Pynchon. Whether we are reading about Billy Pilgrim in *Slaughterhouse-Five,* Wilbur Swain in *Slapstick*, Rudy Waltz in *Deadeye Dick*, or Jonah in *Cat's Cradle*, our identification is always directed to the narrative voice behind these main characters. Our attention, by design, is always directed to Vonnegut, who frequently interposes his voice and his commentary into the narrative flow. Like the tuberculous cough in *Hocus Pocus*, Vonnegut appears with increasing frequency in each novel until, by the time he writes *Timequake*, his essayistic commentary overthrows the authority of his fiction.

Almost all of Vonnegut's later fiction deals with only one main character. All other characters are secondary. The character of "Kurt Vonnegut"—the narrative construction, the interlocutor—appears much more frequently than the character of Kilgore Trout, who doubles him. The problem this presents for film adaptation is that the character Vonnegut seldom participates in the action and rarely appears physically in the story line. Even when he does show up, he is only present for a short time. From *Piano Player* to *Hocus Pocus*, *Breakfast of Champions* is the only novel in which Vonnegut (as a character in the novel) directly affects the movement of the other characters. In the other twelve (all but the unprecedented *Timequake*), his character is physically peripheral, marginal, as in *Slaughterhouse-Five* where the character Vonnegut appears as an American soldier shitting next to Billy Pilgrim in a prison latrine. On film, this scene would seem, at best, a forced cameo with no direct relationship to the plot—a Hitchcockian cliché with even less relevance to the story being told than Vonnegut's cameo in *Back to School*.

Vonnegut is the narrative consciousness of his work, much in the same way that Jack Crabb is the narrative consciousness of Thomas Berger's *Little Big Man* and Sam Spade is the narrative consciousness of *The Maltese Falcon*. Vonnegut is Vonnegut's primary subject, and Vonnegut's novels are designed to enlighten us about Vonnegut's worldview. But unlike Crabb and Spade, Vonnegut is a ghost in the narrative machinery. His consciousness haunts the text, but he has little corporeal presence in the action. Because film is a visual medium, filmmakers need something to film. There lies the core difficulty: excluding Vonnegut's consciousness from a filmed retelling of his novels excises the very qualities that make those works appealing, yet Vonnegut is not enough of a physical presence in his works to provide filmmakers with something tangible to put on film. A film cannot successfully render Vonnegut's work without also rendering Vonnegut's character, a point Vonnegut himself makes:

> I want to be a character in all of my works. I can do that in print. In a movie, somehow, the author always vanishes. Everything of mine which has been filmed so far has been one character short, and the character is me.
>
> I don't mean that I am a glorious character. I simply mean that, for better or for worse, I have always rigged my stories so as to include myself, and I can't stop now. And I do this so slyly, as do most novelists, that the author *can't* be put on film. (*Between Time and Timbuktu* xv)

Not surprisingly, if we look to films based on Vonnegut's formative works, when his voice was not as pronounced, we find greater success.

Vonnegut's early short stories,[5] although primitive compared to his later novels, are not altogether without merit. Their primary weakness is in their conventionality. Like the early works of many writers (William Butler Yeats, for example), these short stories betray a desire to conform to literary expectations—a trait increasingly absent in Vonnegut's later novels. We can locate seeds of his later wit in these his early efforts,[6] but only by looking back from the body of his work. Taken on their own, the stories read very much as Vonnegut claims, as "slick fiction" (*Welcome to the Monkey House* x). Ironically, the lubricity of these early works makes them more adaptable to mainstream film. Because Vonnegut's unique narrative voice is less dominant in the short stories, it is not missed in the film adaptation, and because the short stories adhere to more conventional narrative forms, they tend to adapt easier to a medium that slavishly adheres to convention. This is not to say that the short stories make brilliant films, only that the filmed versions of the short stories do some justice to the original works and are, therefore, adequate translations.

The two strongest short-story adaptations are Jonathan Demme's *Who Am I This Time?* and Alan Bridges's *D. P.* Both films actually do a better job of straight storytelling than the short stories on which they are based, primarily because they commit to romantic elements of the stories more fully that Vonnegut does. Vonnegut struggles in these early works between his emerging narrative voice and conventional (read commercial) narrative forms. In the later novels, Vonnegut often abandons (and always subordinates) conventional narrative forms to his unique voice, but in many of the early short stories, "Who Am I This Time?" and "D. P." included, the inverse is true: Vonnegut's unique voice is subordinated to conventional narrative forms. Although this weakens their literary merit, it does makes them more amenable to film adaptation by eliminating the need to make Vonnegut a character in his own fiction and by providing characters and plots easily tweaked to appeal to mainstream film conventions. Demme's and Bridges's adaptations do both of these—they excise most of what we, through hindsight, identify as uniquely Vonnegut and amplify the conventional, romantic elements of the stories.

In Vonnegut's "Who Am I This Time?" Harry Nash, a man who can only experience human emotion as performance, never realizes his humanity. Although the structure of Vonnegut's narrative is typically romantic, the message is ultimately tragic. By the end of the story, Nash still experiences the vibrancy of life vicariously through the roles he adopts—a slave to the machinery of the written word. Like Kilgore Trout in *Breakfast of Champions*, Nash is at the mercy of an author. Rather than becoming a realized human being, he has become a human puppet controlled by Helen Shaw's dramatic selections, an automaton programmed to fulfill her romantic fantasies. This human tragedy is masked by the conventional form of the narrative, leading Jonathan Demme and others to misread it as the romantic tale of a lonely man and woman who find each other.

By cutting the dark, albeit subtle, elements of Vonnegut's story, Demme is able to produce a more fully formed and consistent narrative. His Nash, through the clever manipulations of Shaw, learns to love, emerges from his shell, and takes his first steps toward socialization. In finding love with Shaw, he becomes part of the community. He is a man saved by love; whereas, in Vonnegut's story, he is a man enslaved by it.

There is no question that Demme's version is more sentimental and more banal than Vonnegut's is, but it is also more evenly rendered. Vonnegut's story

subverts its own objective; it is a romantic fairy tale written by someone who
can't bring himself to believe in romantic fairy tales—a love poem written by
a cynic trying to mask his own cynicism. "D. P." undergoes the same process in
its film adaptation. Bridges cuts the dark undertow of Vonnegut's emerging talent from the tale and focuses on the most conventional aspects of the narrative.

"D. P." is an important story in any study of Vonnegut's canon as it is one
of Vonnegut's earliest narratives about World War II. In the story, we glimpse
Vonnegut's view of war as a vile human investment funded with human lives.
Although the story follows a traditionally linear narrative, it nonetheless manages to expose the absurdity of war. Integral to the tale is the message that
human beings thrust into the chaos of war resist the very categories that make
war possible. This point is made early on when the village carpenter and a
young mechanic make potshot guesses as to the nationalities of a group of
orphaned children displaced by the violence of the war:

> "See the little French girl," he [the carpenter] said one after-
> noon. "Look at the flash of those eyes."
> "And look at that little Pole swing his arms. They love to
> march, the Poles," said a young mechanic.
> "Pole? Where do you see a Pole?" said the carpenter.
> "There—the thin, sober-looking one in front," the other
> replied.
> "Aaaaah. He's too tall for a Pole," said the carpenter. "And
> what Pole has flaxen hair like that? He's a German."
> The mechanic shrugged. "They're all German now, so what
> difference does it make?" he said. "Who can prove what their par-
> ents were?" (151)

The boundaries between races and nationalities, which had to be viewed as
rigid in order for the war to occur in the first place, are now fluid. Identity is
indeterminate, implying that human beings are forced into ill-fitting categories
so that larger systems—governments, nations, and militaries—can volley for
position in a battle for power. The short story is a preamble to later works, such
as *Slaughterhouse-Five*, *Sirens of Titan*, and *Bluebeard*. As with much of Vonnegut's
short fiction, we find in it tinges of the narrative voice that fully emerges in the
novels. The opening sentence, for example:

> Eighty-one small sparks of human life were kept in an orphanage
> set up by Catholic nuns in what had been the gamekeeper's house
> on a large estate overlooking the Rhine. (151)

Several of Vonnegut's stylistic traits are present in this sentence. It privileges
human life by placing the reference to the children, the "small sparks" (like the
stripes of tape on Karabekian's paintings) of human life, first in the sentence. It
summons religion, economics, and game-playing. *Nuns* keep the children, and

these icons of Catholicism keep them in a *gamek*eeper's house. This latter detail serves a dual function: it summons the idea of game-playing, thus the notion that wars are games played with human lives (a trope we find literalized in "All the King's Horses"), and implies that human beings are being housed like animals. The irony is unmistakably Vonnegut: during the war, human beings are herded like cattle for political ends; after the war, human beings are herded like cattle for religious ends. One thing that doesn't change is that human beings still get treated like cattle. We might even claim that the metaphor of the gamekeeper's house in "D.P." is an early version of the slaughterhouse in *Slaughterhouse-Five*. Both house human beings against their will. Both imprison a displaced hero. Both make a statement about what war does to our humanity.

By comparing Vonnegut's opening to the opening Fred Barron revised for the film (presented in voice-over), we see how Vonnegut's narrative style is pruned away:

> Some years after the last war in Europe, near the German town of Augsburg in the American zone of occupation, a number of children, almost all born after the war, were kept alive in a makeshift orphanage set up by Catholic nuns at what had once been a German airforce base.

Instead of a house for animals, the children are housed in a base converted from its fascist function into a center of charity, implying that with American occupation good has won out over evil. More significant, the children themselves have been imbedded in the middle of the sentence—the weakest point—instead of being placed first, where Vonnegut preferred them. Even their number is fogged over. Instead of eighty-one individual human lives, we have an indeterminate "number" of children. The eighty-one individuals of Vonnegut's concern are reduced to a vague statistic.

Interestingly, Barron leaves what follows intact:

> Had the children not been kept there, [had they] not been given the warmth and food and clothes that could be begged for them, they might have wandered off the edges of the earth, searching for parents who had long ago stopped searching for them. (Vonnegut 151, except for brackets, which enclose the only addition Barron made to Vonnegut's text.)

Unlike Vonnegut's first sentence, this passage valorizes those who care for the children, without whom the children would wander "off the edges of the earth." It appeals to that urge in us to characterize our human organizations as charitable, righteous, and necessary. We are told that the poor, war waifs would perish if religion were not there to rescue them. Thus, the passage privileges ideologies over individual human life. It is more sentimental than the first sentence because it stimulates a purely emotional response from readers who long

to have their preconceptions verified. Bridges, like Demme, actualizes a sentimentality that only weighs Vonnegut down.

In 1991 Showtime brought four more of Vonnegut's short stories to
the screen in *Kurt Vonnegut's Monkey House*.[7] Three of the shorts—"All the
King's Horses," "Next Door,"[8] and "The Euphio Question"—were from
Vonnegut's *Welcome to the Monkey House*; the fourth was based on *Fortitude*,
a previously unproduced play published in *Wampeters, Foma, and Granfaloons*.
Once again we find that Vonnegut's voice is lost in the adaptation of these
works. The characters remain, for the most part, the same, and the events are
clearly based on Vonnegut's writing, but, with the exception of "Next Door,"
the human issues under examination are changed. The filmed versions work
as brief narratives intended to amuse, but there is very little about them that
echoes Vonnegut.

Unlike the film, there are no heroes in Vonnegut's "All the King's
Horses," no way for the characters to blame their actions on bad advice, no
excuses offered for bloodshed, and no *deus ex machina* returning the dead at the
end. Colonel Kelly, the communist guerrilla chief, Ying, and the Russian military "observer," Barzov are all military figures. It is their inhumane military
logic that Vonnegut exposes, a "logic" that women, to their credit, cannot
fathom. Kelly expresses this patriarchal rationalization for war just before he
sacrifices his son for the benefit of the game:

> He [Kelly] was bursting to explain the moves to her [his wife], to
> make her understand why he had no choice: but he knew that an
> explanation would only make the tragedy infinitely more cruel for
> her. Death through a blunder she might be able to understand; but
> death as a product of cool reason, a step in logic, she could never
> accept. Rather than accept it, she would have had them all die. (98)

Barzov shares Kelly's attitude toward the game of war; they are men of like
mind. Note the macho bravado in the following passage from the story when
Barzov takes over for Ying:

> And then he [Kelly] opened his eyes and saw major Barzov's lips
> moving. He saw the arrogant challenge in his [Barzov's] eyes,
> understood the words. "Since so much blood has been shed in this
> game, it would be a pitiful waste to leave it unresolved."
>   Barzov settled regally on Pi Ying's cushions, his black boots
> crossed. "I propose to beat you, Colonel, and I will be surprised if
> you give me trouble. It would be very upsetting to have you win by
> the transparent ruse that fooled Pi Ying." (99)

Both soldiers are concerned primarily with victory and masculine pride. Kelly
is in the position of the king, the one piece on a chessboard that cannot die,
that can only be captured. Barzov plays, as Ying did, "regally" while sitting com-

fortably on "cushions." The relish these military men have for the "game" is stressed at the end of the story when Barzov and Kelly exchange niceties about their game like two compatriots at a gentlemen's club:

> "I don't like having you leave here thinking you play a bet-
> ter game than I."
> "That's nice of you, but not this evening."
> "Well, then, some other time." Major Barzov motioned for
> the guards to open the door of the throne room. "Some other
> time," he said again. "There will be others like Pi Ying eager to play
> you with live men, and I hope I will again be privileged to be an
> observer." He smiled brightly. "When and where would you like it
> to be?"
> "Unfortunately, the time and the place are up to you," said
> Colonel Kelly wearily. "If you insist on arranging another game,
> issue an invitation, Major, and I'll be there." (102–3)

The point Vonnegut makes in this story is thematic to much of his work. There are no heroes in war, and there is no justifiable rationale for waging it. War is insane, and the people who rationalize its necessity are sick. It is the same message offered on Kilgore Trout's tombstone: "We are healthy only to the extent that our ideas are humane" (*Breakfast of Champions* 16). The Russian and the communist are not the sole villains in the story; Kelly is equally culpable. Thus, playing chess with human life is inhumane, regardless of which uniform a player wears.

This message is lost in the film. Like so many film adaptations of Von-negut's work, Stan Daniels's screenplay imposes opposition where no opposi-tion is present, creating good-guys and bad-guys and promoting sentimental notions of nationalism and righteousness. Kelly, in the film, becomes an ambassador rather than a soldier—a diplomat, rather than a warrior—drawing attention away from the military. An army major is added to advise Kelly on his chess moves, and to externalize the internal struggles of Kelly's character. This addition allows us to dismiss Kelly's sacrificial move as bad judgment. If we agree that Kelly should not have offered his son up for sacrifice, we can excuse his actions by arguing that he simply received bad advice from his advi-sors. In the film, Kelly is cornered into military decisions he would not oth-erwise make; whereas, in the short story, Vonnegut makes it clear that Kelly is already engaged in the games of war and not only approves of them, but looks forward to future competitions.

Furthermore, Daniels deletes the character of Barzov. Without Barzov, the story no longer incriminates "observers," no longer stresses that passive observation is not possible, and that to sit back in silence and watch the games of war is to share responsibility for them. The most egregious difference between the film and the short story is that Daniels's adaptation no longer con-demns war as an inhumane enterprise. The Cuban rebel El Puno Rojo (Ying

in the movie) does not actually kill the American pawns that are removed
from the board. In the end, he explains to Kelly that he was only trying to
show the American ambassador that sometimes it is justifiable to make sacrifices for the larger good of the state, arguing that sometimes it is necessary to
shed blood for greater societal good. Thus, the film valorizes the same principles that Vonnegut's story condemns—nationalism, human sacrifice, and the
necessity of war.

Like "All the King's Horses," "Next Door" relies on realism. It is arguably
one of the most conventional stories Vonnegut has written, and one of the most
blatantly sentimental. Although it is well crafted, it contains none of the prob-
lematic elements we're accustomed to finding in Vonnegut's work. This
accounts for the ease with which it translated into film, making *Next Door* the
most faithful adaptation to date. Because very little of Vonnegut's voice is present in the short story, it is not missed in the film. And because the story relies
primarily on plot, it fits easily into a visual medium. Jeremy Hole does makes
a few pragmatic changes to keep the story visual, such as adding a heating vent
that connects both apartments so that Paul can watch some of what's going on
next door rather than merely listening to voices through the wall, and magni-
fying the implication of Paul's sexual awakening, but otherwise remains loyal to
the story's theme. The same cannot be said for *The Euphio Question* and *Fortitude*. Both films have a quirkiness to them that is appealing for audiences that
find television shows like *Night Gallery* appealing, but again the axes of Vonnegut's stories are lost in translation. Vonnegut's "The Euphio Question," like
"All the King's Men," broaches one of Vonnegut's primary themes: the dangers
of technology to our humanity. It foreshadows Vonnegut's career-long bout
with technology. In *Piano Player* he argues that technology has "robbed the
American people of liberty and the pursuit of happiness" (196), and he maintains this position through his last book, *Timequake*. As early as "The Euphio
Question," the human pursuit of happiness is invariably coupled with struggle
and pain. Any happiness technology offers is purely synthetic, and in allowing
technology to consume our lives, we sacrifice our capacity for human judgment, as does the professor in "The Euphio Question" and everyone in the
world in *Timequake*. Vonnegut makes it clear in "The Euphio Question" that
Bockman's device, which offers "the voice of nothingness" (179) and claims to
be able to provide "happiness by the kilowatt" (189), is a device that could send
America into "a distressing phase of history where men no longer pursue happiness but buy it" (192). In the film, this larger issue is simplified. Only Bockman's device is presented as dangerous. It is a single threat to human safety, and
only because it generates too much bliss for us to handle the basic necessities
of life. While Vonnegut's story questions our willingness to turn our lives over
to technology, and the danger that willingness poses for our humanity, the film
merely presents the story of one dangerous discovery.

Like Bockman's device, Frankenstein's machines in *Fortitude* can keep
Sylvia in a constant state of happiness (as long as they don't break down), but

at the price of her humanity. But Vonnegut's play is a darkly ironic love story. Like Helen Shaw in "Who Am I This Time?" Dr. Frankenstein in *Fortitude* manages to fulfill his desire for love by controlling Sylvia. She is happy because Frankenstein's machines make her that way, as Nash loves Shaw because it's in the script. Sylvia only becomes unhappy and suicidal because of a "bum transistor" (52). In the translation of *Fortitude* to film, the impulse to provide film audiences with clear heroes and villains once again changes Vonnegut's message. Dr. Frankel, Frankenstein's equivalent in the film, is unproblematically cruel. When he takes Sylvia's place (instead of joining her, as he does in Vonnegut's screenplay), we see it as punishment for his overweening greed and lack of compassion. All Vonnegut's irony is lost in the film, and we are left with a trite morality tale. Worse yet, Wayne Tourell, the director, sidesteps Vonnegut's humor. Vonnegut's play is marvelously humorous, and rich with jokes, puns and comic situations, such as when Dr. Little says, "What *guts* that woman must have!" and Dr. Frankenstein replies, "You're looking at 'em" (44–45); or when Dr. Frankenstein says to Dr. Little: "That's a Westinghouse heart. They make a damn good heart, if you ever need one. They make a kidney I wouldn't touch with a ten-foot pole" (44). None of this humor survives to film.

   Mother Night suffers a similar, albeit more monumental, fate at the hands of Keith Gordon. In Vonnegut's novel, Howard W. Campbell complains bitterly to Frank Wirtanen about the translation of his private erotic diary into Russian pornography:

> "If only it weren't illustrated!" I said to Wirtanen angrily.
> "That makes a difference?" he said.
> "It's a mutilation!" I said. "The pictures are bound to mutilate the words. Those words weren't meant to have pictures with them! With pictures, they aren't the same words!" (150)

Mutatis mutandis, this complaint could be made—has been made—about film versions of novels ever since the beginning of film. Often, those familiar with a novel that is translated for the screen echo Campbell's complaint and reproduce his problem. Just as Campbell, when informed of the fourteen color plates, imagines "pictures of Helga and . . . [him] cavorting in the nude" (149), a reader envisions a room or a bed that is inevitably not *that* room or *that* bed, as shown on the screen.

   Absolute fidelity to the source novel is an unrealizable ideal, and to expect such fidelity is to naïvely deny the specificity of film as an art form. However, Gordon's version of *Mother Night* fails to do justice to the novel in a more fundamental sense. Gordon's film attempts to deal seriously with the Holocaust and the issue of individual moral culpability, as does Vonnegut's novel. Yet Gordon's reliance on cinematic clichés reinscribes certain underlying assumptions about representation and the nature of discourse as power, assumptions that the novel challenges and problematizes. Vonnegut raises important questions about the nature of representation, its dependence upon its medium, and the political implications of aesthetic and romantic ideologies, while Gordon's film, by opting to exploit certain familiar visual and aural conventions, makes the very errors Vonnegut exposes, falling back into the very forms of totalizing thought that Vonnegut savagely criticizes. By not treating the medium of film with the questioning eye that Vonnegut casts on the novel, Gordon fails to keep the film from reproducing, in its mode of presentation, the monoperspectival morality that Vonnegut condemns. By recasting Vonnegut's novel as a tragic film of romance lost and guilt accepted, Gordon finally reproduces, despite himself, the very totalizing logics that made possible the Holocaust. Vonnegut's novel attempts the difficult task of thinking around these totalizing logics, seeking a newly multiperspectival way of thinking about history and responsibility, not settling into the fixities of moral certainty. Gordon's film, in contrast, falls back into ways of representing the past that offer the false comfort of summary judgment.

Vonnegut's novel begins with his familiar practice of exploiting the editorial machinery of the novel: the dedication, editor's introduction, translator's note, and so forth. Vonnegut uses these customarily marginal areas of the text in order to draw attention to the conventions of novelistic storytelling. The "introduction" begins with Vonnegut's bald statement that "this is the only story of mine whose moral I know . . . we are what we pretend to be, so we must be careful about what we pretend to be" (ix). Typically, Vonnegut undercuts such a blatant statement within a few pages, by offering two other possible morals. If three morals are possible, why not four, or more? Why not as many as there are readers? This multiplicity of readings denies the supposedly basic connection between story and moral familiar to Western literate audiences ever since Aesop: first the event, then the approved interpretation.

For another example of Vonnegut's abuse of the machinery, consider the dedication of Campbell's memoirs. Alone on a page, as is customary, the simple words: "For Mata Hari." Yet two pages before, in a "chapter he later discarded," Campbell wrote:

> Before seeing what sort of book I was going to have here, I wrote the dedication—"To Mata Hari." She whored in the interest of espionage, and so did I. Now that I've seen some of the book, I would prefer to dedicate it to someone less exotic, less fantastic, more contemporary—less a creature of silent film. (xi–xii)

The dedication stands as an example, *avant le lettre*, of Derridean writing *sous ratour*—under erasure, having been undone a page previously. Such techniques highlight the conventional nature of peritexts such as dedications, calling attention to their usual invisible acceptance. Yet it is not so simple to erase a convention. The dedication, standing alone on a page as dedications do, can rely on a tradition of conventional expectation in reading audiences, a customary acceptance: it's a dedication of a novel, because that's what dedications look like (and have always looked like, in the past). This weight of generic conventions is a consistent antagonist in Vonnegut's writing; one reason for the seeming naiveté and apparent surface/superficial nature of his prose style is the unspoken acknowledgement that neither he nor his readers are that naïve—both come to the novel with the weight of the genre's history on their backs. Vonnegut parodies literary clichés and styles, just as his characters parody stereotypical attitudes, without the deadening enforced conformity to verisimilitude that suggests that these clichés are a transparent representation of reality. In *Mother Night*, Vonnegut offers doubling scenes, doubled characters, and reproductions of the clichés of the spy genre; the film avoids any such self-reflexivity in its dealings with character types or cinematic conventions. Perhaps Teri Garr, circa *Young Frankenstein*, with her comic-opera German accent, should be cast as Helga/Resi Noth. Perhaps Mel Brooks should be hired as assistant director for any further filmic adventures in Vonnegut. In order to convey on film the generic questioning and self-reflexivity found in the novel, it would seem necessary to at least allude to the rich history of filmic clichés about espionage and romance, or at a minimum, take John Goodman and Alan Arkin off the very tight leash on which they are kept here. Vonnegut's novel has a great deal of fun mocking the "Mata Hari" conventions of the genre it skewers.

All this is not to argue that *Mother Night* should have been made as a comedic farce; the choice of tone and approach is not at issue here. But a revealing perspective on the difference between a novel and its film adaptation can be found in an examination of what is omitted from the film, what the director considered nonessential.

Gordon's film begins with the stock maneuver: an establishing shot (a prison flying the Israeli flag), a full shot (a prisoner being unloaded, in handcuffs, from a van), and a close-up (the prisoner being walked to his cell)—all well-established Hollywood conventions for prison movies. Not that this is a problem in itself; filmmakers such as Quentin Tarantino and the brothers Coen have amply demonstrated during the last few years that the use of cinematic conventions can be both commercially successful and artistically creative—if those conventions are themselves thematized, subjected to examination, and not merely passively relied upon for their traditional significations. But Gordon, although given a text that begs for a critical self-awareness in the application of professional technique, consistently falls into the most stereotypical uses of the visual and aural conventions that moviegoers associate with the genre of Nazi war-crime films. His film is dedicated to an aesthetic of cinematic realism that ironically defuses what is potentially radical in Vonnegut's novel.

Gordon's film seeks, despite his honorable intentions, "to deceive, to seduce, and reassure"[9] the audience with exactly the brand of easy moral judgments ("preserving consciousness from doubt") that Vonnegut's novel would seek to bring into question. Vonnegut's *Mother Night* explores the subterranean link between romanticism and fascism, while Gordon's recasts the story as a tragically doomed love affair in the most clichéd sense of the genre. By sub-scribing to the Hollywood conventions of the "well-made film," Gordon also subscribes to the oppressively manipulative premises of those conventions.

In examining the adaptation of a novel to film, two of the most obvi-ous starting points would seem to be: What has been omitted? and What has been added or changed? In Vonnegut's novel, four guards, on six-hour shifts guard Campbell's Jerusalem jail cell. Each of the guards, who are the first characters (other than Campbell) introduced in the novel proper, represents a different approach to the problems of history and culpability that will be major themes in the text. Eighteen-year-old (in 1961) Arnold Marx is a stu-dent of archeology and history, an admirer of Tiglath-Pileser the Third, the "remarkable" Assyrian—but he draws a blank when Campbell mentions Paul Josef Goebbels, a "remarkable German" of Campbell's acquaintance. Andor Gutman is a survivor of Auschwitz, a volunteer for the corpse-carriers, who cannot understand his own actions in the death camps and is ashamed of them. Arpad Kovacs is a Hungarian who forged his papers and joined the Hungarian S.S. during the war, serving as a double agent, enthusiastically Nazi even while he betrays the Nazi's secrets to the underground. He is the first character in the novel to demonstrate what Campbell will call "that boon to modern man—schizophrenia." Bernard Mengel, the final guard, describes how he helped to hang Rudolph Franz Hoess, the notorious commandant of Auschwitz. Mengel placed the straps around Hoess's ankles, then, a few hours later, strapped a leather belt around his broken suitcase. "Twice within an hour, I did the very same job—once to Hoess, and once to my suitcase. Both jobs felt about the same" (25).

The four guards personify four different responses to history and the Holocaust—it's ancient history, thus dead; it's a shameful past that should be forgotten; it can only be dealt with by compartmentalizing the mind and being "schizophrenic"; it results in the deadening of feeling, the flattening of affective response. Each of these positions will be adopted, then rejected by Campbell during the course of the novel that follows—a textbook example of how Von-negut explores multiple possible responses to a morally ambiguous and com-plex scenario.

By comparison, Gordon's treatment of these characters in his film serves as a warning, in miniature, of how his film goes wrong. On the surface, it's an acceptable, even familiar directorial maneuver to conflate and combine several minor characters from a novel into one film character, Gordon's "Bernard Marx," who is basically the "Bernard Mengel" character from the novel. This sort of liberty is traditional, even necessary, in filming a novel, because of the differing demands of the media in question. But subtle changes (such as the loss of the resonance of the name "Mengel," with its reminiscences of the infamous "Dr. Mengele" of Nazi medical experiment fame) can go undetected under cover of such license. In the novel, Mengel tells Campbell that he has heard Campbell calling out names during his troubled sleep: Helga and Resi (29). In the film, "Bernard Marx" tells Campbell that he called out two names, "Helga—and Hoess." This apparently minor change speaks volumes about the different projects involved in the two works. In the novel, Campbell is concerned with his personal past, reconciling his private self with his public deeds. In the novel, he met Hoess once, at a party; in the film, Campbell is supposedly so obsessed, so wracked with guilt for his complicity with Nazi crimes that he calls out Hoess's name in his sleep, fifteen years later. Vonnegut's Campbell is presented with several options for his personal ethical evaluation, in the persons of his four guards. Gordon's audience is presented with a single perspective, imposed from the outside, on Campbell's moral culpability.

To drive the point home in the film, a character found nowhere in the novel is introduced outside the radio studio in Berlin, just after one of Campbell's virulently anti-Semitic broadcasts. This character, a stock German Jew from Central Casting, castigates Campbell for his lies: "You are all cowards. You are murdering children." The small shabby man, yellow star prominently displayed, is taken off-camera by jack-booted thugs and beaten. The scene is completely gratuitous; it plays as if Gordon doesn't trust his audience to remember Nazi brutality and draw the appropriate conclusions from memory. In a similarly manipulative fashion, the "Bernard Marx" character will be given the final "word" of judgment, visually, in the film—a point to which we will return later. The issue is not whether the film should be a comic farce or a tragedy, but whether the author or director should enforce a single perspective for judgment on the viewers. Vonnegut avoids closure (Howard's offstage "suicide") and begins the novel by problematizing single simple interpretations (the three morals to the story), rejecting the idea of control implicit in traditional literary author/reader or author/character relationships (cf. his freeing of his characters in Breakfast of Champions). In contrast, the movie's heavy-handed symbolism in depicting Howard's suicide provides an example of the type of closure of meaning, authorial control over intent, and monoperspectival interpretation that the novel explicitly examines and rejects as being complicit with totalitarian modes of thought.

Still allowing for the differences between the media, what Gordon omits is as revealing as what he adds. The novel is an exploration of different responses to the ethical crisis of private beliefs in conflict with public action, with each response being ultimately untenable. Vonnegut explores the options, of which two are most prominent. One, he labels "schizophrenia" (what Frank Wirtanen, the American spymaster who runs Campbell, calls the ability "to be many things at once, all sincerely. . . . It's a gift"[144]), while the other is what Campbell will call "the totalitarian mind"—the fervent adherence to a single explanatory system of belief, which distinguishes the Nazis (American and German) and other "true believers" from the common run of humankind. This is:

> a mind which can be likened unto a system of gears whose teeth
> have been filed off at random. Such a snaggle-toothed thought

machine, driven by a standard or even a substandard libido, whirls
with the jerky, noisy, gaudy pointlessness of a cuckoo clock in
Hell. . . . The missing teeth, of course, are simple, obvious truths,
truths available and comprehensible even to ten-year-olds, in most
cases. . . . That is the closest I can come to explaining the legions,
the nations of lunatics I've seen in my time. (162–63)

Campbell moves, in the novel, toward the realization that he himself has been
among the "true believers," because of his underlying romanticism, a romanticism
exemplified by Resi Noth in her choosing to die for love. He has always seen himself as one of the compartmentalized "schizophrenics," like his friend George
Kraft—brilliant modernist artist, alcoholic, and haplessly incompetent Soviet spy,
all at once, but Campbell's ability to keep his "real me, the me deep inside, a me
made in heaven" separate from his public self—and its guilt—collapses by novel's
end. Early in the novel, Frank Wirtanen, the American spymaster, suggests that he
has learned a great deal about Campbell by reading his plays: "'That you admire
pure hearts and heroes,' he said. 'That you love good and hate evil,' he said, 'and
that you believe in romance'" (41). Traditionally, such values would be unprob-
lematic for a novel's protagonist, but in Vonnegut's *Mother Night*, such absolute
beliefs are a recipe for disaster. Absolute beliefs are a prerequisite for totalitarian
actions, and Campbell realizes too late that his early romantic idealism—his belief
in romance that lured Resi Noth to him in New York—offers other true believers the support for their own absolutism that made his radio broadcasts such an
inspiration to Nazis in Germany and America. His romanticism, like Resi's, is a
form of the "totalitarian mind," and he used his romantic escapism during the war
to avoid the reality of what he was doing, as he escaped into his "Nation of Two"
with his beloved Helga. Vonnegut again and again attacks such absolutism in the
novel, suggesting that it is a necessary, if not a sufficient, prerequisite for atrocity.

These assaults on absolutism are not (cannot) be reproduced in a movie
that offers a single, monolithic perspective from which judgment can be passed,
as they work against the presuppositions of such a project. In a scene Gordon
omits, Campbell and Resi Noth are bar-hopping in New York. Campbell meets
a barfly, who begins drunkenly to preach the virtues of his "answer to Communism. . . . Moral Rearmament."

> "What the hell is that?" I said.
> "It's a movement," he said.
> "In what direction?" I said.
> "That Moral Rearmament movement," he said, "believes in
> absolute honesty, absolute purity, absolute unselfishness, and
> absolute love."
> "I certainly wish them all the luck in the world," I said.
> In another bar, Resi and I met a man who claimed he could
> satisfy, thoroughly satisfy, seven women in a night, provided they
> were all different.

"I mean, really different," he said.
Oh, God—the lives people try to lead.
Oh, God—what a world they try to lead them in! (108)

Admittedly, a minor scene in the novel, an obvious candidate for omission, yet Vonnegut's equation of moral absolutism with sexual braggadocio is but one example of the instances where Gordon has compromised Vonnegut's contribution to the complex issue of moral responsibility, closing off possibilities in the interest of a single, unambiguous moral judgment. Vonnegut's problem, of course, is not with honesty, purity, unselfishness, and love, as such; it's the modifying "absolute" that earns Campbell's derision.

Three far more important scenes are reworked by Gordon in such a manner as to reduce Vonnegut's highly nuanced presentation of Campbell's moral crisis to a straightforward assignment and acceptance of unequivocal guilt. First, when Howard Campbell Jr. delivers the eulogy of August Krapptauer (former *Vice-Bundesfuhrer* of the German-American *Bund,* a WWII Nazi front organization) to the Iron Guard of the White Sons of the American Constitution (Doctor Lionel Jason David Jones's absurd little group of present-day teenage neo-Nazis), Vonnegut presents the speech as a double-coded piece of ironic denunciation of their beliefs. "I delivered my eulogy of August Krapptauer, saying, incidentally, what I pretty much believe, that Krapptauer's sort of truth would probably be with mankind forever, as long as there were men and women around who listened with their hearts instead of their minds" (133). This self-aware plea for reason on Campbell's part—his awareness that the Nazi *was* a "crap tower," a pile of crap—follows a special treat that Doctor Jones has prepared for Campbell: the playing of a tape of one of Howard's rabidly anti-Semitic wartime propaganda broadcasts. Campbell's reaction is typical.

> The experience of sitting there in the dark, hearing the things I'd said, didn't shock me. It might be helpful in my defense to say that I broke into a cold sweat, or some such nonsense. But I've always known what I did. I've always been able to live with what I did. How? Through that simple and widespread boon to modern mankind—schizophrenia. (133)

By way of contrast, in Gordon's filmed version of this scene, Nick Nolte as Campbell views a film of himself spouting hateful racist epithets; as he sits in a darkened room, the filmed image of his younger self is superimposed over his world-weary features. The visual symbolism is inescapable, as inescapable as the ascription of guilt to Campbell. Nolte's character appears "shocked" and may be in a cold sweat. He lacks Campbell's schizophrenia, and the compartmentalized, anaesthetized reactions that come with it. Gordon must visually connect Campbell with the full realization of his complicity with the horrors of the Nazi regime, but does so in a way that completely fails to differentiate the character from the monomaniacal Nazis he served.

After the G-men raid the basement in which the Iron Guard was meeting, Campbell, bereft of friends, lover, and volition, returns to his apartment. Gordon's Campbell returns to a trashed apartment, where he sits down and recovers from the floor a significant item: a single pawn from the chess set he had carved. Gordon's Campbell *is* a pawn, and not a particularly well-played one at that. In the chapter "St. George and the Dragon . . . ,"Vonnegut's Campbell discovers, in *his* trashed apartment, the man who, as an American GI, had captured him at the end of the war, Bernard V. O'Hare. O'Hare has been a total failure since the war, and, fortified by alcohol, has convinced himself that Campbell's continued existence in the world has given him a chance to redeem himself and provide a meaning for his existence: "'This thing's been a-building over the years. . . . Just when you think there isn't any point to life—' he said, 'then all of a sudden you realize you're being aimed right straight at something'" (178). After recounting his years of frustration in marriage, family, and career, O'Hare continues, "'And I asked myself. . . . What does it all mean? Where do I fit in? What's the point of any of it?,'" Campbell replies "'Good questions,' I said softly, and put myself close to a pair of fire-tongs" (178). In the presence of a true believer, addressing cosmic questions about the meaning of life, the appropriate response is to arm oneself. Campbell, O'Hare declares, is "pure evil," and O'Hare is there to punish him. When O'Hare threatens to attack him, Campbell breaks his arm with the fire tongs, then delivers Vonnegut's ringing denunciation of the real "pure evil" of fanaticism:

> "I'm not your destiny, or the Devil either!" I said. "Look at you! Came to kill evil with your bare hands, and now away you go with no more glory than a man sideswiped by a Greyhound bus! And that's all the glory you deserve!" I said. "That's all that any man at war with pure evil deserves."
>
> "There are plenty of good reasons for fighting," I said, "but no good reason ever to hate without reservation, to imagine that God Almighty Himself hates with you, too. Where's evil? It's that large part of man that wants to hate without limit, to hate with God on its side. It's that part of every man that finds all kinds of ugliness so attractive."
>
> "It's that part of an imbecile," I said, "that punishes and vilifies and makes war gladly." (181)

Vonnegut the satirist here lets his satiric persona slip, in order to deliver a condemnation of totalitarian plenitude—the condition of a mode of thought that offers to explain all phenomena by one overarching theory. Vonnegut decries "absolute" *anything*. Campbell's scene with O'Hare is the moral high point for his character in the novel, and Gordon omits it completely, in favor of a scene in which Campbell ruefully regards a chess pawn.

The final scene of the film encapsulates the ways in which this film fails to match the complexity, seriousness, and experimental nerve of Vonnegut's novel. Both the novel and film both end in Campbell's Israeli jail cell, where Campbell receives a letter from his one-time American spymaster, offering to testify on Campbell's behalf in his upcoming trial for crimes against humanity. Gordon has Nolte begin reading the letter, then lets the voice of John Goodman (who portrays Frank Wirtanen in the film) take over: "If there must be a trial of Howard W. Campbell Jr., let it be one hell of a contest. And may justice be served," Goodman declares. "May justice be served. I like the sound of that," Nolte repeats, then retrieves the typewriter ribbons from his desk drawer and weaves a rope with which to hang himself. As he does so, the cigarette smoke from the ever-burning cigarette of Bernard Marx, his guard, blows in through the door of his jail cell, in a transparently symbolic reference to the Zyklon-B wafting through the ventilators at Auschwitz, a ham-fisted reenactment of the murders for which Campbell is supposedly punishing himself. The totalizing, "hating with God on its side" logic that created the Holocaust is reproduced, in the name of a single, monoperspectival "justice" to be served.

Contrast this with the wording of Wirtanen's letter in the novel: "If there is to be a trial of Howard W. Campbell, Jr., *by the forces of self-righteous nationalism*, let it be one hell of a contest!" (emphasis added). Campbell then declares his intention to commit suicide, concluding with "Goodbye, cruel world! *Auf wiedersehen?*" The novel's ending is humorous, ironic, ambiguous, morally unsettling—completely lacking in the self-congratulatory retributive vindictiveness of the film.

Gordon *must* omit the reference to "self-righteous nationalism," because his single-minded condemnation of his protagonist relies on just such an underpinning. This is seen in the film's repeated reliance on stock representations of Nazis and their paraphernalia to evoke, in the most conventional of fashions, the repertoire of associations that film audiences have with such images. Vonnegut, on the other hand, goes to great lengths to mock the ideological connotations of visual icons. A pair of examples (not in the film) must suffice here. Campbell demonstrates his current political beliefs to George Kraft, his neighbor in New York, by drawing, in the dust on three windows, a swastika, a hammer and sickle, and the Stars and Stripes. "I had given a hearty cheer for each symbol, demonstrating for Kraft the meaning of patriotism to, respectively, a Nazi, a Communist, and an American. 'Hooray, Hooray, Hooray,' I'd said" (69). Later, Campbell is knocked unconscious outside of his apartment. When he awakes, he is in the basement headquarters of the ludicrous American neo-Nazi household that consists of the anti-Semitic, anti-Catholic, and anti-black Lionel Jason David Jones and his two best friends (after the death of Krapptauer): the Black Fuhrer of Harlem and Father Keeley, a defrocked Catholic priest. The first thing Campbell sees on awakening is a "bedspread of simulated leopard skin," covering him as a blanket. "'Don't tell me,' I said . . . 'I've joined the Hottentots'" (112). In the corresponding scene in the film, Campbell fades into consciousness (using the cinematic cliché for regaining consciousness) and an enormous red swastika banner is the first thing he sees, treated unequivocally as the emblem of absolute evil.

The ultimate acceptance by Howard Campbell of his responsibility for this absolute evil is the message hammered home by the film's ending; Campbell is treated throughout as an existentially culpable being, not as a contradictory construct of conflicting motivations or as a discursive construct. Throughout the novel, various characters are offered as foils for Campbell's moral situation. Arpad Kovacs, the Hungarian Jew who guards him in his cell, served in the Hungarian S.S. enthusiastically in the war and remembers his S.S. days with pride: "What an Aryan I made!" At the same time, he betrayed the S.S.'s plans to the Jewish underground. Like George Kraft and Frank Wirtanen, he is a practitioner of what Vonnegut's Campbell calls "schizophrenia"—Wirtanen describes Kraft to Campbell as follows:"He's like you . . . he can be many things at once, all sincerely. . . . It's a gift" (144). This "gift" is one trait that distinguishes Campbell from Dr. Jones, Adolph Eichmann, Werner Noth (his father-in-law, who can abuse slave women while showing aesthetic pleasure in artworks), and the other "totalitarians," but all comparisons between Campbell and other characters are elided in the film, which centers relentlessly on the character of Campbell. In the novel, denied the solace of the totalitarian mindset, Campbell is finally unable to maintain the willing separation of selves necessary for successfully schizophrenic coping. This complex moral balancing act is totally missing from the film, which assumes a tragic linearity as Gordon's Campbell gradually assumes total responsibility and is labeled as ultimately evil.

Even the centrally important comparison of Campbell, the one-time romantic, with Resi Noth, the totalitarian for love, is avoided in the film, which ends up playing out the conventions of a tragic love story, while avoiding the ways in which Resi's absolute love is, in the end, in the service of death, rather than life, because it is absolute.

Absolutists are notoriously humorless. When Resi dies, she complains to the American G-man who has led the raid on Jones's basement:"You say very funny things . . . I'm sorry I can't say funny things back. This is not a funny time for me. . . . I am sorry I have nothing to live for. All I have is love for one man, but that man does not love me. . . . I can't say anything funny, but I can show you something interesting" (165–66). She then takes cyanide and dies in Howard's arms. When Campbell differentiates between himself and Adolf Eichman (in prison with him in Israel), he defines the one advantage of the awareness of ethical distinctions that he has and Eichmann lacks: Campbell can occasionally see humor in situations where Eichmann sees nothing funny. This is a capsule description of the difference between Vonnegut's novel and Gordon's film. The novel takes place in the boundary area between comedy and tragedy, between black humor and seriousness, between different ideologies, and uses its iconoclastic humor to dissolve and transgress these boundaries, while Gordon's film colors strictly within the lines. Incidents like the recasting of Lincoln's Gettysburg Address as a Nazi funeral oration (with concern from the highest-level Nazis about whether Lincoln was Jewish, with a first name like "Abraham") are riotously funny in the novel, opening dizzyingly multiple perspectives on everyday reality, while the film grimly and relentlessly adheres to its monologic precepts. It is, perhaps, illustrative of the relationship between multiple perspectives—different takes on reality revealed by the examination of the construction of that reality—and humor itself to see that the greatest omission in Keith Gordon's version of *Mother Night* is the omission of laughter.

Just as Gordon's adaptation of *Mother Night* bypasses Vonnegut's humor, Steven Paul's *Slapstick of Another Kind* circumvents everything that is intelligent about Vonnegut's fiction. Vonnegut's humor rests as heavily on the serious issues it critiques as his seriousness relies on humor. To excise either from his text is to gut the very qualities that make Vonnegut's writing uniquely his, and Paul's oversights are blatant and numerous. He completely excludes Vonnegut's notion of extended families—groups, as Lawrence Broer notes, "whose spiritual core is common decency" (116)—and the importance of courtesy, kindness, and dignity are of critical importance to the body of Vonnegut's work. Even the warm, human relationship between Wilbur and Eliza is reduced to a bizarre alien predilection. *Slapstick of Another Kind* fails to capture any of the wonder of Vonnegut's novel. The direction and editing are pedestrian, the humor is clumsy and garish, and the script is fatally flawed. Like *Harrison Bergeron*, the film employs the talents of great comedic actors, casting Jerry Lewis and Madeline Kahn in the title roles of Wilbur and Eliza Swain, but even comedians of their caliber can't breathe life into a script that misses every thematic element of the novel. The film was written, produced, and directed by Paul, the actor who played Paul Ryan in the stage production of Vonnegut's *Happy Birthday Wanda June* and reprised the role in Mark Robson's film of the play. Unfortunately, that bit of trivia is the only interesting thing about *Slapstick of Another Kind*. Vonnegut describes his novel as "situational poetry" (1), but there is nothing poetic about the movie, which is of critical interest only as a demonstration of how far off target a filmmaker can be and ranks as the worst attempt at a film adaptation of Vonnegut's work to date.

Arthur Crimm fares a bit better with his 1995 adaptation of Vonnegut's "Harrison Bergeron" into a full-length feature for Showtime. Crimm is working with a shorter, less significant work of Vonnegut's, and sets his bar much lower than Gordon does with *Mother Night*. Although brief and primitive, "Harrison Bergeron" is one of Vonnegut's better short stories, and it does relay a Vonnegutesque message about the value of human expression in a world that has become dehumanized by the machinery of institutionalized thinking. In a typically Vonnegut gesture, the parents of fourteen-year-old Harrison are not shaken into awareness by the execution of their son on television. Neither is anyone else. Harrison's attempt to shake free from the bonds of conformity fails, and Vonnegut makes no attempt to imply that the system has been affected, although it is clearly a system he scorns. Thus, a sense of futility threads the human hope for change. Glimmers of this futility make it into Crimm's film. For example, Harrison learns after his broadcast of great music, films, and literature to the entire American population that he has managed to reach only

1.3 percent of the population, and that nothing of any consequence was gained by his rebellious actions against the National Administration Center. Unfortunately, this point is undermined at the end of the film where we learn that compact discs of the broadcast are being traded secretly among the country's young people, suggesting that this intellectual contraband will eventually provoke awareness in the next generation and that Harrison has managed to infect the hegemony of the intellectual ruling class at a grass-roots level.

Harrison Bergeron is not a brilliant or particularly innovative piece of cinema, and it does not capture what we might call, for want of a better term, the "spirit" of Vonnegut's novels. But neither is it a complete failure. Unlike most of the film adaptations of Vonnegut's work, *Harrison Bergeron* does manage to infuse some humor into a primarily tragic tale of equal rights gone horribly askew. Several jokes are written into the script, which, for the most part, deliver a chuckle to a receptive audience: When we learn, for instance, that Macaulay Culkin became a great Shakespearean actor in his later years and played King Lear, or when a TV producer, whose function it is to edit anything of value out of television shows, implies that television wasn't much different before the second American revolution. But the film's scant humor benefits more from casting than from Crimm's screenplay. The producers wisely cast several major comedic actors in secondary roles: Eugene Levy as the president of the United States, Andrea Martin as an administrator responsible for "leveling the playing field" in sports, Buck Henry as a TV producer, and Howie Mandel as a television talk-show host. Each of these four comedians brings vibrancy to scenes that would fall flat with dramatic actors.

There are a few poignant lines in the film as well, such as when Administrator Klaxon says, "The system is perfect, Harrison, just sometimes the people who run it aren't," or when Harrison tells his audience at the end of his rebellious broadcast that "when they took away envy, they took away love, too." But these are offset by the film's tendency to romanticize Harrison's innocence and the nobility of his efforts. The last great film he shows during his broadcast, for example, is Frank Capra's *It's a Wonderful Life*, implying that what America has lost is the sense of small-town community, and the innate decency of George Bailey. This gesture exposes a clumsy flaw in the film's design, for it is precisely the middle-class, middle-American life valorized in *It's a Wonderful Life* that the National Administration Center was formed to create. They even fashioned their middling world after life in the 1950s, very close to the time period *It's a Wonderful Life* portrays. George Bailey learns that it is the simple pleasures of family and community and not individual accomplishment that make for a wonderful life, precisely what the system of rule in Harrison Bergeron's world valorizes.

Other flaws mar the film as well. For instance, Harrison's world is reportedly designed to eliminate competition, yet it abounds with competitive sports. There are golf tournaments and boxing matches on television. Harrison's father roots for his favorite football team. In a population supposedly programmed to prefer sameness, there is plentiful evidence that they desire determinations of difference, hierarchies of superiority (as implied by the continued existence of the Super Bowl). We might claim that this continued love for competition hints at some essential human need that the ruling class is working to extinguish, if it weren't for the fact that it is the authoritative body of the ruling class, the National Administration Center, which broadcasts, and thereby sanctions, those competitive events.

The most glaring contradiction in the film is that the ruling class of superintelligent citizens operates to eliminate superintelligent people. They are not allowed to reproduce, and they work to limit the possibility that other intelligent people will be born. Nevertheless their leader, Administrator Klaxon, admits that the world would fall into anarchy if "average" people ran it. So Klaxon claims to be saving the world from the brutality of war and anarchy by eliminating the very people he argues are essential to the mission of preventing anarchy. Thus, the National Administration Center is committing national suicide: It can only succeed in achieving its objectives by failing to achieve its objectives. The film asks us to believe that the most intelligent people in the country have failed to notice this all-too-obvious paradox.

Despite its shiny surface, *Harrison Bergeron* does not live up to the promise of Vonnegut's story. In Vonnegut's story, the handicaps that weigh people down function as a metaphor for ideological systems, such as religion. Harrison's mother, for example, says that if she were Handicapper General, she would have the handicapper radios in people's ears play "chimes on Sunday—just chimes. Kind of in honor of religion." When her husband tell her that he "could think, if it was just chimes," she says, "Well—maybe make 'em real loud" (8). The critique is obvious: if religion is chimed in our ears loud enough, we will lose the ability to think, and we will all become the same. The film possesses no such parallel, and maintains only the surface of Vonnegut's story—the handicaps as a means for assuring equality. *Harrison Bergeron*, like its predecessors, loses the tenor of Vonnegut's metaphor. But the film does successfully, albeit unintentionally, pull off one bit of irony: when all its plusses and minuses are tallied, it is, at best, average.

Unlike *Harrison Bergeron*, Alan Rudolph's *Breakfast of Champions* does not even rise to the level of mediocrity. Although the film is marked with moments of brilliance (such as several dramatically ironic scenes between Dwayne Hoover and Harry Le Sabre) and a visionary job of casting that puts Nick Nolte in the role of Le Sabre, Albert Finney in the role of Kilgore Trout, and Barbara Hershey as the ideal Celia Hoover, the film too frequently favors the burlesque elements of Vonnegut's novel at the expense of poignancy. As a further disservice to the novel, Rudolph (who wrote the screenplay) sidesteps Vonnegut's ending, thus missing the central theme of the story. Instead of having Vonnegut free the character of Kilgore Trout from the mechanistic prison of authorial control, Rudolph has Trout enter Alice-like through a mirror into the wonderland of his own imagination. Thus the clever reflexivity of the novel is lost, and we are left with mere sentimentality.

If not for George Roy Hill's version of *Slaughterhouse Five*, a film Vonnegut himself calls "flawless" (*Between Time and Timbuktu* xv), we might have questioned whether Vonnegut's work could be successfully adapted to film. In his 1972 adaptation of Vonnegut's most famous novel, Hill proves that Vonnegut's aversion to mawkish sentimentality, his resistance to closure, his tendency toward nonlinearity, and his coupling of humor with poignancy can be captured on film. Credit is also due Stephen Geller for the screenplay on which Hill's film is based. Geller manages to cull and cleverly organize key visual elements from Vonnegut's novel and to reproduce, in a primarily visual medium, the tone and timbre of Vonnegut's work.

Key to the success of the film is the way that time is handled. The structure of the film reproduces the effect of time-tripping. To watch the film is to become like Billy Pilgrim—unstuck in time. We, like Pilgrim, are torn from scene to scene, leaping from one moment in Pilgrim's life to another with no *seeming* rationale. In a lesser filmmaker's hands, such a nontraditional structure could have been disastrous, but Hill pulls it off—twenty-two years before Quentin Tarantino receives praise for accomplishing the same feat in *Pulp Fiction*.

One of the major difficulties Hill had to overcome in filming *Slaughterhouse-Five* was to come up with a way to present moments of Pilgrim's life in a seemingly random manner, while still maintaining a sense of continuity. He solves this problem through the extensive use of form cuts, crosscutting, and by suspending the soundtrack from one scene to the next, or by having the soundtrack anticipate[10] the next scene. These techniques are continuity devices that smooth the transition from one scene to the next.

Almost every transition from one scene to the next in the entire film involves a form cut. A shot of Pilgrim showering in a prison camp during the war cuts to a shot of Pilgrim showering as a child just moments before his father throws him into the pool. When Pilgrim, Lazarro, and Weary are captured by the Germans, the Germans mention Weary's boots. Hill cuts from a close up of Weary's boots to a pair of Valencia's shoes next to the bed on her and Pilgrim's wedding night. When Pilgrim is on the train on his way to prison, Hill shoots a point-of-view shot of him pulling a blanket over his head, leaving the screen black. When the blanket is pulled back, we discover that Hill has cut to the hospital room where Pilgrim is put after his nervous breakdown, and Pilgrim's mother is saying, "The war's over, you can come out now." The high whine of Pilgrim's electric shock treatments becomes the scream of a train whistle during the war. Sometimes the continuity device that connects two otherwise discordant scenes is subtle, but it is almost always there. For example, after Pilgrim and the others come out of the shelter to a Dresden in ruins, the young German soldier—whom our attention has been drawn to throughout the film—throws down his rifle and runs home to his house, which is aflame. As he runs toward the building he cries out "Mama" several times, but as he enters, and is dragged back out again, he calls out "Papa." Hill cuts from this scene to Pilgrim's bedroom years later shortly after Valencia's accident, and after Pilgrim has returned from the hospital. Pilgrim's own son, Robert, is standing over the bed, shaking Pilgrim, and calling out, "Dad? Dad?" In bitter irony faithful to Vonnegut's novel, Robert is dressed in his uniform, and he tells his father that he made the right decision by joining the military. Robert salutes his father from the doorway as he leaves (recalling Valencia's comment on her wedding night when she says, after making love for the first time, "We've begun the life of a new hero").

Crosscutting, although normally not considered a continuity device, is used skillfully by Hill several times in *Slaughterhouse-Five* to achieve that effect. Several times in the film, Hill crosscuts rapidly back and forth between two parallel scenes. When German soldiers take Pilgrim's picture in Germany, Hill uses rapid crosscuts between that scene and a ribbon-cutting ceremony for the opening of the Pilgrim Building. When Pilgrim nominates Edgar Derby to represent the American prisoners, Hill uses rapid crosscuts between that scene and Pilgrim's acceptance speech when he is elected president of the Lion's Club. When Pilgrim and the others walk up the stairs leading out of the shelter after the bombing of Dresden, Hill uses rapid crosscuts between that scene and Pilgrim walking up the stairs to his room (with Spot in his arms)[11] after returning from the hospital. In Dresden, he walks through darkness. At home, he walks through light. In Dresden, he exits a door onto the ruins of war. At home, he closes himself off in his room (where the Tralfamadorians will soon pick him up).

The most significant places where Hill uses suspension in the film, is when the Tralfamadorians are explaining to Pilgrim that the end of the universe is inevitable, and that nothing can stop it. As they explain, the film cuts to Dresden after the bombing. Pilgrim, Derby, Lazzaro and the others are stacking and burning bodies. All three men's faces are covered, recalling the masked skiers Pilgrim saw standing in the crowd on the runway as his fated plane was about to take off. Just as the Tralfamadorians are explaining that nothing can be done about the end of the universe because "the moment is structured that way," the soldiers torch a stack of human corpses. Without being dogmatic or sentimental, Hill makes the point that Vonnegut stresses in his novel, that there will "always be wars" (3), that they are as inevitable as glaciers—a point stressed by Pilgrim's inability to prevent the plane from crashing even though he has foreseen the disaster. Significantly, Hill avoids making this point with dialogue or with action; instead, he uses the medium of film and makes the point by overlapping two seemingly unrelated scenes.

Hill's critique of war is not heavy handed, which is one of the primary reasons it works, and one of the reasons it matches the tone of Vonnegut's novel so well. Vonnegut is also subtle, and reluctant to force idealistic conclusions onto his readers. It is Hill's subtlety that allows the power of Vonnegut's voice to resonate. For example, if we look exclusively at the scenes taking place after Pilgrim arrives in Dresden, we discover that the German soldiers become younger with the progressing scenes. Scenes just prior to the bombing—particularly the scenes shown as Rumfoord (in voice-over) rationalizes the bombing of Dresden—are filled with children, in uniform, in streets, in windows, and in carriages. Skillfully, Hill forces us into the determination that war is never valorous, that war results in the death of people who are, regardless of the nationality, human beings. The film, like Vonnegut's novel, presents the deaths of Germans with the same force with which it presents the death of Americans. Edgar Derby's death is no more tragic than the death of the young German soldier's mother and father. Roland Weary's death is no less tragic than Wild Bill's. Even Paul Lazzaro, for all his psychotic tendencies, is envious of the love Derby feels for his son.

Hill, despite the poignancy he manages to capture in his film, does not abandon Vonnegut's humor. *Slaughterhouse-Five* is full of jokes, puns, and physical gags: Valencia repeatedly promising to lose weight out of gratitude to Pilgrim; Pilgrim catching his son masturbating in the bathroom; Pilgrim telling Montana Wildhack that the Tralfamadorians furnished their dome from Sears and Roebuck; Pilgrim passing out in his soup from hunger because the British soldier won't shut up long enough for him to eat. The first time we see Pilgrim trying to teach Spot tricks, Pilgrim commands him to "stay," but Spot ignores him and runs right alongside Pilgrim. The next shot is Pilgrim teaching Spot to run alongside him. And between each lesson, Valencia steps out of the house with offers of food: the first time, holding a pie, the next time, a cake. Right before Pilgrim's plane crashes, the barber shop quartet sings the line, "They'll be some changes made today." And near the end of the film, Pilgrim gets trapped beneath a grandfather clock, thus trapped by time.

Hill's skill as a filmmaker and his understanding of Vonnegut's work enabled him to retain much of what is engaging about Vonnegut's novel. We are invited into the moments of Billy Pilgrim's life, as fragmented as they are, and by intelligently linking these moments, Hill gives the film a sense of cohesiveness without abandoning the force of Vonnegut's message or his humor. By the end, our point of view parallels Pilgrim's. We understand what the Tralfamadorians mean when they say, "A pleasant way to spend eternity is to ignore the bad times and concentrate on the good," because we, like Pilgrim, have just been exposed to a series of good and bad times "strung together in beautiful random order." Thus, we can, if so inclined, choose to join Pilgrim at the end of the film in a celebration of life, complete with applause and fireworks.

Slaughterhouse-Five and the other film adaptations discussed here re-present Vonnegut's writing, thus inviting comparative critique. As with all translated or adapted works, they are linked inextricably to their sources, and their inevitable lack of fidelity to those sources reveals characteristics of Vonnegut's writing that are often difficult to articulate. Vonnegut's prose is not Proustian; his characters do not achieve the psychological complexity of a Stephen Deadalus, a Clarissa Dalloway, or a Humbert Humbert; and his plots are usually outré fabulations that resist classification. His fiction is performative, but not in the manner of other experimental writers such as Donald Bartheme and Gilbert Sorrentino. Nevertheless, his voice is one of the most representative voices of the late twentieth century, despite the tendency of his works to flail at literary convention. Although some perceive his work as merely playful, a strong ethical imperative underscores it. But the work never becomes dogmatic or didactic. It offers no solutions for the chaos of the twentieth century, no path back to order, and often condemns social attempts at order while illuminating the inhumanity of anarchy.

The implied narrator of Vonnegut's work is a hopeful nihilist, an anti-intellectual philosopher, a spiritual existentialist, a serious humorist, who is devoutly noncommittal or clearly ambiguous on all issues except for the importance of human courtesy—the "pinpoint of hope" (Boon, *Chaos* 169) to which all his fiction points. This implied narrator, this "Vonnegut," with his gift for synchronizing seemingly contradictory issues, for making unresolved paradoxes palatable, and for locating the humane in the inhuman machinations of the technological age, is indispensable to Vonnegut's work. Vonnegut's writing is embraced, not by a generalized readership, but by individual sparks of human life that recognize in the works their own uncertainty and confusion, both of which are, in Vonnegut's universe and the late twentieth century, inevitable. Most of these film adaptations fail because of a slavish adherence to conflict resolution. Their filmmakers take sides on the irresolvable issues Vonnegut's work critiques, thus engaging the very ideological mechanisms against which Vonnegut so consistently warns. The films fail their source materials because, in privileging plot and character, they overlook the question that backbones Vonnegut's canon: how does one behave humanely in a world balanced irreconcilably between rigid totalitarianism and chaotic anarchy?

NOTES

1. Directed by Mark Robson in 1971, and starring several of the cast members from the original stage production, including William Hickey in the role of Col. Looseleaf Harper and Steven Paul as the young Paul Ryan. In this version, Rod Steiger takes the role of Harold Ryan (played by Kevin McCarthy in the stage production), and Susannah York takes the role of Penelope Ryan (played by Marsha Mason in the stage production).

2. Vonnegut appears in the uncredited role as a sad old man on the street.

3. *Breakfast of Champions*—which was directed by Alan Rudolph and produced by Bruce Willis, who plays the role of Dwayne Hoover—reportedly debuted in London, raising the ire of Hollywood, on October 29, 1998, but did not make it to American screens until 1999. Even then, the film only appeared during short runs in small, art-house theaters.

4. When John Huston, heeding Howard Hawks's advice, decided on *The Maltese Falcon* as his first directorial project, he gave the novel to his secretary to type into

screenplay format, asking her to "set up the book in basic shots" (Nolan 179). Somehow Jack Warner got hold of a copy, called it a "great script," and gave the project a green light. The novel adapted so easily to film format that it made a great script with no creative input from a screenwriter, a director, or a producer. (For a more in-depth discussion of Huston's adaptation of Hammett's novel, see my article, "In Debt to Dashiell.")

5. See the two essays in this collection: Jerome Klinkowitz's "Vonnegut the Essayist" and Jeff Karon's "Science and Sensibility in the Short Fiction of Kurt Vonnegut."

6. For example, the handicapping of human beings to create a truly equalitarian world that we find in *The Sirens of Titan* makes its first appearance in "Harrison Bergeron."

7. Also known as *Welcome to the Monkey House*.

8. An earlier version of "Next Door" was produced in 1975; it was directed and written by Andrew Silver.

9. At the end of the twentieth century, the attempt to question this aesthetic of realism (or illusionism, as it has polemically been relabeled by the British cultural materialists) in a wide variety of media has been identified, for better or worse, with the oft-maligned name of "postmodernism." Jean-François Lyotard's definition of postmodernism is one among many for this maddeningly indefinite term: maddening because, although the term itself has been so overused as to become almost meaningless, still it seems to refer to something distinctive about certain contemporary artists (such as Vonnegut) that differentiates their work from the high literary modernism of the early twentieth century. Without wishing to disinter the great postmodernism debates of the 1980s (R.I.P.), we might still usefully cite Lyotard's exposition of the responsibilities of (and necessity for) postmodernism, in "An Answer to the Question: What is Postmodernism?" (a brief essay appended to Lyotard's seminal *The Postmodern Condition: A Report on Knowledge*). Lyotard suggests that

> photographic and cinematographic processes can accomplish better, faster, and with a circulation a hundred thousand times larger than narrative or pictorial realism, the task which academicism had assigned to realism: to preserve consciousness from doubt. Industrial photography and cinema will be superior to painting and the novel whenever the objective is to stabilize the referent, to arrange it according to a point of view which endows it with a recognizable meaning, to reproduce the syntax and vocabulary which enable the addressee to decipher images and sequences quickly, and so to arrive easily at the consciousness of his own identity as well as the approval which he thereby receives from others—since such structures of images and sequences constitute a communication code among all of them. This is the way the effects of reality, or if one prefers, the fantasies of realism, multiply.
>
> If they too do not wish to become supporters (of minor importance at that) of what exists, the painter and novelist must refuse to lend themselves to such therapeutic uses. They must question the rules of the art of painting or of narrative as they have learned and received them from their predecessors. Soon those rules

must appear to them as a means to deceive, to seduce, and to reassure, which makes it impossible for them to be "true." Under the common name of painting and literature, an unprecedented split is taking place. Those who refuse to reexamine the rules of art pursue successful careers in mass conformism by communicating, by means of the "correct rules," the endemic desire for reality with objects and situations capable of gratifying it. Pornography is the use of photography and film to such an end. It is becoming a general model for the visual or narrative arts which have not met the challenge of the mass media. (74–75)

10. Suspension and anticipation are both musical terms that I am relating here to the relationship between the soundtrack and the film. In music, a suspension is a note from one chord that continues to resonate into the next chord before resolving into a new chord tone. An anticipation is a chord tone that is played before the chord changes, thus it anticipates the next chord in a progression. For our purposes here, I use suspension for any instance in the film where the soundtrack (music, dialogue, or sound effects) for one scene continues after a cut in the film to the next scene. I use anticipation for any instance when the film has not yet cut to a new scene, but the soundtrack (again, music, dialogue, or sound effects) for the next scene has already begun to play.

11. Spot, like Odysseus's old dog, is loyally waiting on the porch for Pilgrim when he returns.

WORKS CITED

Boon, Kevin. *Chaos Theory and the Interpretation of Literary Texts: The Case of Kurt Vonnegut.* Lewiston: Edwin Mellen, 1997.

———. "In Debt to Dashiell. *Creative Screenwriting* 4.2 (Summer 1997): 99–115.

Broer, Lawrence R. *Sanity Plea: Schizophrenia in the Novels of Kurt Vonnegut.* Rev. ed. Tuscaloosa: U of Alabama P, 1994.

D. P. Produced by Barry Levinson. Dir. Alan Bridges. Screenplay by Fred Barron. Perf. Stan Shaw, Rosemary Leach, and Julius Gordon. Hemisphere Productions, 1985.

Harrison Bergeron. Screenplay by Arthur Crimm. Dir. Bruce Pittman. Perf. Sean Astin, Miranda DePencier, Christopher Plummer, Eugene Levy, and Buck Henry. Atlantis Films and Showtime, 1995.

Kurt Vonnegut's Monkey House. Produced by Jonathan Goodwill and Gordan Mark. "All the King's Horses": Screenplay by Stan Daniels. Dir. Allan King; "Next Door": Screenplay by Jeremy Hole. Dir. Paul Shapiro; "The Euphio Question": Screenplay by Jeffrey Cohen. Dir. Gilbert Shilton; "Fortitude": Screenplay by Stan Daniels. Dir. Wayne Tourell. Showtime, 1991.

Lyotard, Jean-François. *The Postmodern Condition: A Report on Knowledge.* U of Minnesota P, 1985.

Nolan, William F. *Hammett: A Life at the Edge.* New York: Congdon & Weed, 1983.

Slapstick of Another Kind. Screenplay by Steven Paul. Prod. and Dir. Steven Paul. Perf. Jerry Lewis, Madeline Kahn, and Marty Feldman. The S. Paul Company, 1983.

Slaughterhouse-Five. Screenplay by Stephen Geller. Dir. George Roy Hill. Perf. Michael Sacks, Ron Liebman, and Valerie Perrine. Universal, 1972.

Vonnegut, Kurt. *Between Time and Timbuktu, or Prometheus-5.* New York: Delta/Dell, 1972.

———. *Mother Night.* New York: Dell, 1961.

———. *Wampeters, Foma, and Granfaloons.* New York: Delta, 1965.

———. *Welcome to the Monkey House.* New York: Dell, 1950.

———. *Slapstick.* New York: Dell, 1976.

———. *Slaughterhouse-Five.* New York: Dell, 1988.

Who Am I This Time? Produced and Written by Neal Miller. Dir. Jonathan Demme. Perf. Susan Sarandon and Christopher Walken. Rubicon Productions, 1981.

CONTRIBUTORS

DAVID ANDREWS is the author of *Aestheticism, Nabokov, and* Lolita. Kurt Vonnegut says of Andrews's analysis of his work: "Most striking to me, simply as a reader is the clarity of his language in the service of his scholarship and acute reasoning . . . he [Andrews] lay bare what I could not state didactically, did not know: The core of my beliefs about the purposes and effects of modern paintings."

KEVIN ALEXANDER BOON is an assistant professor at Penn State. He is the author of *Chaos Theory and the Interpretation of Literary Text: The Case of Kurt Vonnegut, An Interpretive Reading of Virginia Woolf's* The Waves, and *Absolute Zero*, and the editor of *Reading the Sea: New Essays on Sea Literature*. He is on the executive board of the New York College English Association and is currently writing a book on the Human Genome Project.

LAWRENCE R. BROER is a professor at University of South Florida and a well-known specialist in Vonnegut studies. His book on Vonnegut (*Sanity Plea*, University of Alabama Press, 1994) critiques psychological factors influencing Vonnegut's novels.

TODD F. DAVIS is associate professor at Goshen College where he is currently chair of the English department. Davis is an alumni of Northern Illinois University where he wrote his dissertation on Vonnegut: *Comforting Lies: Postmodern Morality in the Works of Kurt Vonnegut*. He has written reviews on Vonnegut for Leonard Mustazza's *The Critical Response to Kurt Vonnegut*, Marc Leeds' *The Vonnegut Encyclopedia: An Authorized Compendium*, and *The Vonnegut Chronicles: Interviews and Essays*, edited by Peter J. Reed and Marc Leeds. He is co-editor of *Mapping the Ethical Turn: Ethics and Literature in New Theoretical Contexts* and co-author of *Formalism and Reader-Response Theory*.

BILL GHOLSON is assistant professor of writing and coordinator of writing at Southern Oregon State College. He specializes in modern American literature and rhetoric. His 1994 dissertation, *Rhetoric and Morality in the Later Novels of Kurt Vonnegut*, examines issues central to Vonnegut's canon.

JEFF KARON's background is in philosophy, rhetoric, and literature. He is an assistant professor at the University of Tampa where he teaches rhetoric, composition, and literature. He is currently at work on *Ethics of Reading*, which explores the ethical traditions in contemporary American and British literature.

JEROME KLINKOWITZ is a University Distinguished Scholar at the University of Northern Iowa and a scholar of international reputation. He is the author/editor of thirty-four books, including seven dealing with Vonnegut. Jerry edited *The Vonnegut Statement* (Delacorte, 1973) and *Vonnegut in America* (Dell, 1977), the most authoritative biographical accounts of the author currently in print. Jerry is the general editor of *Crosscurrents / Modern Critiques* (third series), which includes books by Ihab Hassan, Naomi Jacobs, Regina Weinreich, and others.

DONALD E. MORSE is currently Professor of English and Rhetoric at Oakland University and a professor at Kossuth University in Hungary. He is the author/editor of eight books including several that deal with Vonnegut's work (e.g. *Kurt Vonnegut*, Peter Lang, 1995). He has translated plays by Csaba Lászlóffy and Andras Sütö from the Hungarian, and he has published extensively on the fantastic in American and Irish literature. He is currently at work on "'Conscience of the Creator': The Thought and Art of Kurt Vonnegut" and *Imagine Being an American: The Novels of Kurt Vonnegut,* a major long-term research project under contract to Borgo Press.

DAVID PRINGLE is currently on the faculty at the University of South Florida where he teaches courses in literature and writing. He has written a book-length work on hypertext, and specializes in contemporary critical approaches.

LOREE RACKSTRAW is well known in Vonnegut Studies. She is an Emeritus Professor of English at the University of Northern Iowa where she specializes in mythology, cultural studies, writing, and the contemporary novel. She is a former student of Kurt Vonnegut and has published and spoken extensively on his work.

HARTLEY S. SPATT is Professor of English at SUNY Maritime College and is a long-time student of utopian and dystopian studies. He is Secretary-Treasurer of the William Morris Society in the United States, and has published extensively on Tennyson, Morris, Rossetti, and their circle. He has also published numerous articles on intersections between technology and the arts, from *Frankenstein* to the International Style, and he is a conributing editor of *The Encyclopedia of Modern Science and Technology.*

INDEX

Hudson, Thomas, 74, 85

humanism, xi, 10, 18, 26, 78, 80–81, 88, 150–151, 159–163

Hume, Kathyrn, 18, 42, 87, 89, 98, 103, 124, 126, 133

Huston, John, 193

Hutcheon, Linda, 150, 163–165

Hutton, James, 91

Huxley, Aldous, 154

Iowa Writers Workshop, 3

James, Henry, 46, 83

Jantsch, Eric, 60, 62

Jesus Christ, xii, 35, 69, 81, 124, 162; " Sermon on the Mount," 81, 98

Jones, James: *From Here to Eternity*, 86

Kafka, Franz, 10, 106

Kandinsky, Wassily, 43, 45

Kant, Immanuel, 31

Karabekian, Rabo, x, 20, 27, 30, 59, 71, 74, 77, 81–84, 87, 128–129, 138–139, 140, 172

Karon, Jeff, xi, 105, 194

Kelly, Colonel, 174–176

Kemp, Marilee, 22, 31, 36–37, 40, 45

Kitchen, Terry, 20, 22–24, 32–33

Klee, Paul, 20, 26

Klinkowitz, Jerome, xi, 1, 17, 43–45, 55, 63, 106, 109, 114, 116, 125, 126, 133, 137, 139, 159–160, 162, 164, 194

Kopper, Edward, 30, 43, 46

Korean War, 4, 67

Kosinski, Jerzy, 79

Kraft, George, 182, 185, 186

Kubrick, Stanley, 97, 167

Kuhn, Thomas S., 52, 63

Ladies Home Journal, 4

Langer, Lawrence, 85

Lazzaro, Paul, 124, 191–192

Le Sabre, Harry, 189

Levy, Eugene, 188, 195

Lincoln, Abraham, 67, 83, 90, 143, 186

Little, Dr., 177

Livingston, Robert B., 62–63

Luddite, xi, 119–120, 122, 124

Lundquist, James, 42, 46, 162, 164

Lyotard, Jean-François, 151, 164, 194–195

MacIntyre, Alasdair, 136, 146

Madison, Polly. *See* Berman, Circe

Maharishi, 10–11

Mailer, Norman, 2

Maltese Falcon, The, 170, 193

Manson, Charles, 161, 163

Martin, Andrea, 188

Martin, Linda Wagner, 85–86

Mason, Marsha, 193

Massachusetts Institute of Technology, 1

Mata Hari, 178–179

Matisse, Henri, 20, 23, 26

McConnel, Frank, 68, 70–71, 86, 89

McHale, Brian, 162, 164

Mellard, James M., 162, 164

Merrill, Robert, 24–25, 43, 45–46, 105, 114, 117, 124, 133, 164–165

Metzger, Eloise, 95, 143

Midland City, 95–96, 143, 159

Miller, Linda, 85

Mondrian, Piet, 43

Morse, Donald, xi

Museum of Modern Art, 26, 74, 81–82, 87

Mustazza, Leonard, 42, 46, 62–63, 96, 103–104, 114, 117, 162, 165

Nabokov, Vladimir, x, 42, 169

narrative, xi, 89, 135, 137, 143

Nash, Harry, 171, 177

Nazi, 68, 126, 155, 179–181, 183, 185–186

New York Times Book Review, 5, 9, 15–16, 103

Newman, Barnett 22–23, 31, 42–43

Newton, Isaac, 51

Night Gallery, 176

Nolan, William F., 194, 196

Nolte, Nick, 183, 185, 189

Noth, Helga, 143, 177, 179, 180 –182

Noth, Resi, 71, 179–180, 182, 186

Nuwer, Hank, 131, 133

O'Hare, Bernard., 157–158, 184

O'Hare, Mary, 157–158

Vonnegut, Kurt: book-length works
   .(continued)
   3; "More Stately Mansions," 4, 15,
   106; "Next Door," 176, 194–195;
   "Report on the Barnhouse Effect,"
   3–4, 16, 113–114; "Thanasphere," 3,
   16; "The Big Space Fuck," 4, 15, 117;
   "The Euphio Question," 3, 15, 174,
   176, 195; "The Foster Portfolio," 4, 15;
   "There's a Maniac Loose Out There,"
   10, 16; "Torture and Blubber," 10, 16;
   "Welcome to the Monkey House,"
   4–5, 7, 15–16, 117, 171, 174, 194, 196;
   "Where I Live," 5, 7, 16; "Yes, We
   Have No Nirvanas," 10, 16
Vonnegut, Mark: *The Eden Express*, 3, 16

Wakefield, Dan, 5, 10, 16; *Going All the
   Way*, 10, 16
Walken, Christopher, 196
Waltz, Rudy, x, 35, 71, 74, 77, 81, 82, 84,
   87, 95, 119, 135, 140, 143, 169
Warner, Jack, 194

Waugh, Patricia, 88, 90
Wayne, John, 10, 158
Weary, Roland, 192
Wesleyan University, 156
Who Am I This Time?, 171
William Smith College, 144, 161
Wilson, Robert, 72
Wirtanen, Frank, 72, 177, 181, 182, 185,
   186
Wolf, Fred Alan, 49
Wölfflin, Heinrich, 47
Woodly, Norbert, 67, 74, 76
World War I, vii
World War II, 1, 20, 22, 45, 53, 56, 68,
   70, 75, 83, 86, 157, 172
Wymer, Thomas L., 122, 134

Xanadu, 78, 81, 84

Yeats, William Butler, 170
Ying, 174, 175
York, Susannah, 193
Young, Philip, 86